Legal Writing
and
Research Manual

Legal Writing
and
Research Manual

Sixth Edition

by

Michael J. Iosipescu

B.A., B.Sc., M.A., LL.B. (Dal.)
Former Lecturer in Law, Dalhousie University

and

Philip W. Whitehead

B.Sc., LL.B. (Dal.)
Director of Research, Legal Research Council

Founding Authors

John A. Yogis, Q.C.

Professor of Law, Dalhousie University

and

Innis M. Christie, Q.C.

Former Dean and Professor of Law, Dalhousie University

Previous Edition Contributing Author

Michael E. Deturbide

Associate Professor of Law, Dalhousie University

LexisNexis™
™ Butterworths

Legal Writing and Research Manual, Sixth Edition
© LexisNexis Canada Inc. 2004
May 2004

Members of the LexisNexis Group worldwide

Canada	LexisNexis Canada Inc, 75 Clegg Road, MARKHAM, Ontario
Argentina	Abeledo Perrot, Jurisprudencia Argentina and Depalma, BUENOS AIRES
Australia	Butterworths, a Division of Reed International Books Australia Pty Ltd, CHATSWOOD, New South Wales
Austria	ARD Betriebsdienst and Verlag Orac, VIENNA
Chile	Publitecsa and Conosur Ltda, SANTIAGO DE CHILE
Czech Republic	Orac sro, PRAGUE
France	Éditions du Juris-Classeur SA, PARIS
Hong Kong	Butterworths Asia (Hong Kong), HONG KONG
Hungary	Hvg Orac, BUDAPEST
India	Butterworths India, NEW DELHI
Ireland	Butterworths (Ireland) Ltd, DUBLIN
Italy	Giuffré, MILAN
Malaysia	Malayan Law Journal Sdn Bhd, KUALA LUMPUR
New Zealand	Butterworths of New Zealand, WELLINGTON
Poland	Wydawnictwa Prawnicze PWN, WARSAW
Singapore	Butterworths Asia, SINGAPORE
South Africa	Butterworth Publishers (Pty) Ltd, DURBAN
Switzerland	Stämpfli Verlag AG, BERNE
United Kingdom	Butterworths Tolley, a Division of Reed Elsevier (UK), LONDON, WC2A
USA	LexisNexis, DAYTON, Ohio

National Cataloguing in Publication Data

Yogis, John A., 1940-
    Legal writing and research manual / John A. Yogis and Innis M. Christie. — 6th ed. / prepared by Michael J. Iosipescu and Phillip W. Whitehead

Includes index.
ISBN 0-433-44278-6 (bound)   ISBN 0-433-44279-4 (pbk.)

    1. Legal composition. 2. Legal research — Canada. 3. Citation of legal authorities — Canada. I. Christie, Innis, 1937- . II. Iosipescu, Michael J. III. Whitehead, Phillip W. IV Title.

KE265.Y64 2004   808'.06634   C2004-902052-8
KF240.Y64 2004

Printed and bound in Canada.

About the Authors

Michael Iosipescu, B.A., B.Sc., M.A., LL.B. (Dal.), began working as a researcher for Legal Research Council in 1978 and took over as Director of Research in 1982. He lectured at Dalhousie Law School between 1983 and 1997 while maintaining his position as Director of Research of Legal Research Council. Mr. Iosipescu is involved with large government research projects and speaks at international conferences, and has been a practicing member of the Nova Scotia Bar since 1979.

Philip Whitehead, B.Sc., LL.B. (Dal.), began working for Legal Research Council as a full-time researcher in 2000 and became Director of Research in January of 2003. While continuing in the role of Director of Research at Legal Research Council, Mr. Whitehead is also a practicing member of the Nova Scotia Bar.

Preface to the Sixth Edition

The sixth edition of this manual continues to preserve the basic goal of the first edition, written by Professor Innes Christie in 1970, which was to assist first-year law students in becoming familiar with the research tools available to lawyers and to provide them with assistance in drafting documents. The sixth edition is the culmination of each of the successive editions and includes the contributions of Professors John Yogis and Michael Deturbide. Throughout the last 30 years the manual has had several updates and two major revisions.

Some of the material in the fifth edition has been updated, while other material has been substantially modified to reflect the realities of research and writing in 2004. Additional writing chapters have been added to assist students in drafting their first legal documents. The text is organized to simplify the students' entry into all major Canadian abridgments, encyclopedias and digest services. The chapter on "Introduction to Legal Research" includes a step-by-step guide to basic legal research while the chapters on legal writing provide suggestions and samples of: a Memorandum of law, a Chamber's Brief, and a Factum. The chapter on "Computerized Legal Research" has been revised to update programs, online research services and to include references to the useful Internet sites.

We wish to express special appreciation to Lyndsay Jardine, Nick Robichaud and James Giacomintonio for many hours of hard work on the sixth edition during the past months.

Legal Research Council
Halifax, Nova Scotia
January 2004

Michael J. Iosipescu
Philip W. Whitehead

Table of Contents

CHAPTER 3
SECONDARY LEGAL MATERIALS

CHAPTER 7
WRITING A FACTUM

CHAPTER 8
GENERAL RULES OF CITATION

Fact Scenario

In order to provide feedback and test the methods suggested in this book, we intend to use a sample fact scenario (based on a real case) throughout this book. For our purposes, imagine that the fact scenario below is information that a senior partner in your firm learned from a new client, Mrs. Lisa Smith. The partner has now provided you with the facts and asked you to prepare a memorandum. We will apply the research and writing methods suggested in the coming chapters to the fact scenario and provide samples of our work, so that you can compare your results.

FACTS: Mr. Smith was 35 years-old at the time of his death. He was a successful accountant, and his wife was pregnant with their first child. Mrs. Smith stated that her husband had many friends. She was happy with their marriage, and thought that he was happy as well. He seemed excited for the birth of their first child.

In his spare time, Mr. Smith enjoyed participating in "extreme" activities, such as bungee jumping and skydiving. Mrs. Smith described her husband as "fearless" when it came to trying new things.

According to Mrs. Smith, her husband rarely drank alcohol. On those occasions when he did, however, she stated that he had a tendency to "overdo it", and would get extremely intoxicated. She also recalled a few occasions when her husband had been drinking that he would attempt foolish activities, such as walking along balcony ledges, or even on one occasion jumping off the roof of a friend's house into a swimming pool. She said she wouldn't characterize her husband as having a drinking problem.

Around the time that Mrs. Smith became pregnant, Mr. Smith bought a handgun. He stated that he bought the gun for protection for his family. Mrs. Smith stated that she had reservations about having a gun in the house, especially with the baby on the way, but she reluctantly agreed when Mr. Smith promised that it would be kept in a locked safe, and never loaded. In the months preceding his death, Mrs. Smith saw her husband cleaning his gun several times at the kitchen table, and she also knew that he had taken it to a shooting range several times for target practice.

Mrs. Smith stated that on the night of Thursday, August 14, 2003, she and her husband had a fight. She could not recall exactly how the fight had started, but it soon developed into an argument over money. Mr. Smith seemed to be upset over her spending habits, and told her that from now she would have to "tighten the purse strings". Mrs. Smith was aware that they had some debt, but did not know the exact amount since Mr. Smith handled the family's finances. He went on to tell her that their financial situation was worse than he had previously let on to her.

Mrs. Smith did not feel that this fight was a very serious one. She attributed it mainly to her husband feeling stressed about money, especially with the baby on the way. In fact, once they had both calmed down, they were able to talk rationally about how they could save money in the future.

The next night, Mrs. Smith went to her parents' house for an overnight visit. She usually made these visits about three times a year, and Mr. Smith seldom accompanied her. She thought that he enjoyed having the time alone, relaxing at home and watching television, and she had no reservations about leaving him alone on this or any other occasion.

When Mrs. Smith returned home on the morning of Saturday, August 15, 2003, she found her husband's body slumped over the kitchen table. She was able to recall a large amount of blood around the head of the deceased and on the floor around him, and saw his gun on the floor beside him. On the table, she saw an open bottle of liquor, some broken glass, and her husband's gun cleaning supplies.

Mr. Smith's body was cremated two days later. The following week, Mrs. Smith was notified by ABC Insurance Company, her husband's life insurer, that they would not be paying on his Accidental Death Benefit Policy, because they did not consider Mr. Smith's death an accident. Mrs. Smith would now like to know what possible action she can take to obtain the benefit of the policy.

CHAPTER 1

Introduction to Legal Research

In many Canadian law schools the beginning student is asked to cast himself or herself in the role of an articling student in a law firm and to prepare a memorandum setting out the state of the law relevant to a given factual situation. Our goal is to provide you with a basic resource for research, drafting, citation and general writing.

We will guide you through the process from the initial research and issue spotting based on the initial facts from an imaginary client, to preparation of a memorandum, to preparation of a trial brief, to including additional information from the Discovery process, and finally to preparation of an appeal Factum.

This chapter will:

- Help you to identify the legal issues;
- Outline a procedure for researching a problem;
- Apply our research suggestions to the "Fact Scenario" and provide results.

Chapters 2 through 4 provide information and advice on using a variety of research sources.

Chapter 5 will continue the process by:

- Suggesting a method of preparing a memorandum;
- Providing a sample memorandum prepared based on our "Fact Scenario" and research results from Chapter 1.

Chapter 6 takes it to the court level by:

- Suggesting a method of trial brief preparation;
- Provide a sample trial brief based on our "Fact Scenario" additional facts, and our memorandum from Chapter 5.

Chapter 7 takes it to the appellate level by;

- Providing a number of points for appeal;
- Suggesting a method of Factum preparation;
- Providing a sample Factum, based on our "Fact Scenario" and our trial brief from Chapter 6.

Chapter 8 provides information on the proper citation of case and statutory authorities.

A. RESEARCH

Methods of research vary considerably according to the area of the law. For example, a problem in contract law is usually researched in a different manner than a problem in constitutional or criminal law. As well, the type and number of services consulted depends on the complexity of the problem, the extent of the information known to the researcher, and the instructions given by the person requesting the research and a memorandum. The procedure outlined below may be followed to research a broad range of legal problems. It assumes little prior knowledge of legal issues and particular case names or statutes.

1. Identifying the Legal Issues

The process of identifying the legal issues raised by a given set of facts often is not clear-cut. Sometimes it is only as research proceeds that the issues become clearly defined, and facts which at first appeared insignificant assume more importance. Early on, it may be helpful to recognize that the purpose of the process is, first, to formulate a set of questions and, second, to decide which questions are important and which questions should not be pursued any further.

The first step in the process is to review the facts several times, decide which are relevant, and make a list of them. Consider the following legal problem:

> During a two-day corporate conference at a Holiday Inn near the Toronto airport, a senior male office supervisor of a Canadian subsidiary of a well-known U.S. food giant asked his personal secretary if she was "in the mood for a late dinner with champagne in his executive suite". The "invitation" followed a series of remarks that he had made about her work habits, after-hour interests, previous marital status, and personal dress and grooming habits.

"Office supervisor", remarks about her "previous marital status" and the statement "Are you in the mood for a late dinner with champagne in my executive suite" are relevant facts. "U.S. food giant", "Holiday Inn", and "a two-day corporate conference" would normally be viewed as irrelevant facts.

As the second step in the process, the student should consult a legal index. Refer to the "General Index" to *The Canadian Abridgment,* or consult the online subject catalogue in your library and find a textbook or a specialized looseleaf service, which deals with human rights. Scan *all* the major headings (in the "General Index"), select the appropriate one and carefully read *all* the subheadings to find the words which most closely relate to the issues raised by the legal problem.

NOTE: A legal index is, in essence, a listing of the legal topics of a book, or set of books, arranged alphabetically according to the major areas of the law. As a result, before looking at an index, it may be helpful to make a list of the concepts, *e.g.*, human rights, employer, employee and sexual harassment, which best describe the given factual situation. Further, take a few moments to clarify and describe: (1) the nature of the activity or event (*i.e.*, a proposition or advance by a member of the opposite sex); (2) the relationship between the parties (*i.e.*, employer-employee); (3) the place where the event or activity took place (*i.e.*, hotel conference room); and (4) the general subject area (*i.e.*, human rights).

This exercise may make it easier for you to match the facts of your legal problem with the legal topics in an index so that it will help you better define the legal issues.

The third step, then, is to read the relevant passages of the text, look for any facts and ideas which seem to describe or relate to your problem and note any references to cases and statutes. Table V, below, reproduces portions of the index from W.S. Tarnopolsky and W.F. Pentney, *Discrimination and The Law* (Don Mills, Ontario: Richard De Boo, 1985), which is now a looseleaf service.

TABLE V

Discrimination and The Law

Employment
> advertising, 12-1-12-4
> affirmative action defined with reference to, 4-80-4-81
> age discrimination, 7-5-7-11
> > occupational qualifications, 7-20
> > in U.S., 7-5-7-11
> harassment
> statutory reform, 8-40-8-41
> . . .

Sex discrimination
> ability to perform, 8-58-8-63
> . . .
> dictionary definitions of "sex", 8-1-8-2
> . . .
> personality reasons, 8-44-8-47
> pregnancy, see **Pregnancy**
> protective motive, 8-43
> retirement policy, 4-33
> sexual harassment, 8-18-8-42
> sexual orientation, 8-2-8-4
> . . .

Sexual harassment
amounted to disparate treatment, female victim won, 8-21
Canadian cases, 8-23-8-40
course of conduct, 8-32-8-33
Courts unsympathetic at first, 8-19-8-20
covered by prohibition of discrimination based on sex, 8-23-8-24
     distinction between "free speech" and, 8-24-8-25
employer's liability, 8-21, 8-25, 8-35-8-40
equal application of principles, 8-24
objective standard test, 8-31-8-32
poisoned environment, 8-26, 8-27-8-30, 8-33
preventive measures for employers, 8-21-8-22
prior complaint, 8-30-8-31
problems of proof, 8-33-8-35
quid pro quo, 8-25-8-27, 8-33
"reasonable" social interaction, evaluating limits of, 8-32
responsibility of employer for actions of supervisory personnel, 8-21, 8-25
statutory reform, 8-40-8-42
U.S. cases, 8-19-8-21
U.S. guidelines, 8-22-8-23

[Emphasis added]

Table V lists the most common issues within each major division and directs the user to the appropriate paragraph of the text.

Another useful source of ideas is *The Canadian Encyclopedic Digest (Ontario), Third Edition*. If you are uncertain of the subject title, refer first to the "Index Key" in the *Research Guide and Key*. The entries in this key will help direct you to the appropriate volume and title. Turn to the "Table of Contents" or "Index" for that title. Scan all the major headings, select the appropriate one, and scan the subheadings for the appropriate word or words which relate to the problem. Consult the paragraph numbers as directed for a general statement of law. Make a note of references to cases and statutes, and check the supplement in the yellow pages preceding the main text for more recent entries. A companion volume to *The Canadian Abridgment* entitled *Key and Research Guide* may be used for the same purposes.

While the procedure outlined above may help the genesis of a statement of issues, it is important to remember that the process is an ongoing one. Often, the issues will not be fully understood until the late stages of the research. This means that as the research proceeds the researcher will often need to expand the number of topics, key words or even titles investigated. For this reason, the student researcher should use work sheets to identify each library source and make notes of titles, topic headings, key words and/or numbers contained in each source. In addition, the researcher should record promising case citations throughout the research process and give a brief description of the facts and legal principle(s).

For certain areas of the law a more useful first step may be to consult an annotator or a topical law looseleaf service. To research criminal law problems, refer to one or more of the following criminal code annotators:

1. G.P. Rodrigues, ed., *Crankshaw's Criminal Code of Canada* (Toronto: Thomson Canada (Carswell), 1993-) (Supplemented by regular inserts).
2. E.L. Greenspan, ed., *Martin's Criminal Code of Canada* (Toronto: Canada Law Book, 1993-) (Supplemented by regular inserts).
3. R. Heather, ed., *Snow's Annotated Criminal Code* (Toronto: Carswell, 1989-) (Supplemented by regular inserts).
4. D. Watt & M. Fuerst, eds., *Tremeear's Annotated Criminal Code* (Toronto: Thomson Canada (Carswell), 1994-) (Supplemented by regular inserts).

To research problems involving the *Charter of Rights*, students may refer to the following:

1. J.B. Laskin *et al.*, eds., *The Canadian Charter of Rights Annotated* (Aurora, Ontario: Canada Law Book, 1993-) (Supplemented by regular inserts).
2. R.M. McLeod *et al.*, *Canadian Charter of Rights* (Toronto: Carswell, 1983-) (Supplemented by regular inserts).
3. D. Stratas, *The Charter of Rights in Litigation* (Aurora, Ontario: Canada Law Book, 1990-) (Supplemented by regular inserts).
4. G.A. Beaudoin, *The Canadian Charter of Rights and Freedoms* 3rd ed. (Toronto: Thomson Canada (Carswell), 1996).

To find material relating to the various Canadian constitutional documents, refer to P. Hogg, *Constitutional Law of Canada*, 3rd ed. (Toronto: Thomson Canada (Carswell), 1992-) (Supplemented by regular inserts).

To research specialized areas such as employment, tax, labour, health, or insurance law, consult the relevant looseleaf service offered by Commerce Clearing House (CCH) called *Topical Law Reports*. These include:

1. Employment Benefits and Pension Guide;
2. Employment Safety and Health Guide;
3. Industrial Relations and Personnel Developments;
4. Insurance Law Reporter; and
5. Municipal Assessment and Taxation.

2. Consulting the Primary Sources of Law

Once you have collected the first few citations from your readings, it is advisable to refer to the primary source materials. A reference to a provincial statute should be checked against the text of the statute. Electronic versions of most Canadian legislation is easily accessible and made electronically available by provincial and federal governments across Canada. These electronic versions represent up-to-date versions of the legislation, (the Ontario site, <http://www.e-laws.gov.on.ca/> purports to be no more than two days out of date) however, they are not official versions of the text.

It is always a good idea to check the official text of the legislation especially when your case turns on the wording of a particular section. To search Ontario statutes, as an example, look in the 1990 *Revised Statutes of Ontario*, or in an annual volume of the *Statutes of Ontario* after 1990. If a federal statute is indicated, confirm its accuracy in the *Revised Statutes of Canada*, or in an annual volume published since the latest revision. Every statement of law of interest in the C.E.D. (Ont. 3d) should be checked against the original case report for accuracy and to make sure that you understand the context from which the statement was taken.

3. Checking for Amendments to Statutes and Finding Judicial Interpretations of Statutes

In order to bring the statute research forward from the latest supplement insert for the desired title in the C.E.D. (Ont. 3d), refer to the third column of the "Table of Public Statutes" in the most recent volume of the *Statutes of Ontario*. Consult the *Ontario Statute Citator* and annotations for the text of amendments, as well as for the most recent legislative activity. Changes subsequent to the stated cut-off of the supplement are easily tracked by reference to *Canadian Current Law — Legislation*.

NOTE: The cover page of the "Supplement" states: "This supplement contains ...statutory material drawn from...statutes up to and including [year] *C.C.L. Legislation* No. [n.]". With this information the student need only check those parts of *Canadian Current Law — Legislation* which were published after the date indicated in the supplement.

Once you have discerned whether the desired statute or section of the statute has been changed, refer again to the *Ontario Statute Citator* and a companion volume, *Ontario Statute Annotations*, to determine if it has been judicially interpreted. It may be wise, as well, to refer to *Canadian Statutes Citations* and check for the desired section of the statute in relevant bound and looseleaf volumes of the set. If the research uncovers a federal statute in the C.E.D. (Ont. 3d) (white or yellow pages), confirm the entry in the "Table of Public Statutes" in the latest annual volume of the *Statutes of Canada*, or in the most recent cumulative table in the *Canada Gazette, Part III*. Check for amendments and read the relevant statute in the appropriate statute volume. Next, examine the *Canada Statute Citator* (for the text of amendments) and a companion volume, *Canada Statute Annotations* (to determine how the amendments have been judicially treated). Consult, as well, the relevant volumes of *Canadian Statutes Citations* under the applicable statute.

4. Expanding the Research to All Canadian Jurisdictions and Finding Judicial Consideration of Cases

Once you have collected and read the relevant case authorities from the sources noted above, consult the Can. Abr. for digests of cases from other Canadian jurisdictions. Scan the spines of the jackets for the equivalent title in the Can. Abr. (2nd), or refer to the "Subject Titles Table" in *The Canadian Abridgment Key and Research Guide*. Next, turn to the "Table of Classification" in the main volume for the selected subject title, scan the classification headings, locate the relevant topics, and record the key classification entry.

After this is completed, refer to the appropriate pages for the digests relating to the selected topic. Bring the research forward (using the key classification entry) by referring to a supplement, if one is available, and *Canadian Current Law — Case Law Digests*. Every promising case culled from these sources should be checked against the original case report.

At the completion of this stage of the research, it is advisable to determine whether any case that you plan to rely on has been considered in a later case or if it is under appeal. Consult the soft-cover supplement and/or the bound volumes of *The Canadian Abridgment — Canadian Case Citations* beginning with the volume which includes the year (if it is known to you) of the desired case. Complete this part of the research by referring to the cumulative supplement and the monthly paper parts of *Canadian Case Citations*.

NOTE: If the problem under investigation involves one of the four Western provinces or the Territories, begin the search in the *Canadian Encyclopedic Digest (Western), Third Edition*, and check any statement or textual reference against an official source. If a statute is noted, consult the appropriate services for amendments and judicial consideration, and then expand the research as outlined directly above. If the problem involves one of the Atlantic provinces (and the encyclopedic research indicates that the given legal issue is governed by Ontario statute law), consult the "Table of Public Statutes" in the most recent statute volume to determine if there is equivalent legislation for the selected jurisdiction.

If there is equivalent legislation, refer to the appropriate statute volume and decide whether or not the language of the relevant provision is similar to that of the corresponding provision in the Ontario statute. If it is relevant, check a statute citator (*e.g.*, *Nova Scotia Reports* (2d), *Digest and Indexes — Statutes Noticed*, or *Canadian Statutes Citations*) for a relevant case authority.

5. Computer Research

The completion of the basic encyclopedic research is an opportune time to conduct a computer search. There are a number of electronic services available to students of most Canadian law schools, in addition to some public access services, most notably CanLII and <http://www.legis.ca>.

Complete a search planner by using the key legal concepts or words (*e.g.*, sexual harassment) found in the cases retrieved during the manual search. The computer will search for case or statute law containing the word or word combinations entered by the operator. For example, in either Quicklaw or Westlaw-*e*Carswell, the query "sex! /1 harassment" will retrieve cases (full text or headnote only), in the selected database, in which the word "sex" or its natural derivatives ("sexual" or "sexually") appears within one word of the term "harassment".

Computer research for a major assignment will usually be conducted in several steps. A good starting point is to search a topical database on Quicklaw since cases will be restricted to the area of law in which you are interested, thereby allowing you to do a more general search of certain terms. This process will be more forgiving of a novice's inexperience with formulating efficient search queries. Once the issues are better defined and the student has gathered leading or other applicable cases, it may be useful to modify your search to include other desired terms or restrict it to a particular court (*i.e.*, Supreme Court of Canada (SCC)), or a jurisdiction (*i.e.*, Ontario).

A student should take care to note the treatment given to any case on which they intend to rely. Westlaw and Quicklaw have symbols located in front of the case reference that show if there has been any negative treatment.

Quickciting in Quicklaw, or clicking on the KC Citing Tab in Westlaw-*e*Carswell often provides links to other cases which have examined the same issue.

6. Supplementary Manual Research

Computer searching may not always be a useful first, or even second, step in the research process. Faced with a complex legal problem, the beginning student may be unable to sufficiently develop the issues early on in the research process to justify a computer search. When this happens, a student is advised to do additional background research. The "Table of Subject Authorities" or "Subject Index" to the *Index to Canadian Legal Literature* (part of *The Abridgment*) will permit the student to access journal articles and case commentary. These may give a perspective, or overview, of a particular legal issue, together with citations to case and statute law not uncovered from the preliminary research.

Once the basic manual and computer research is completed it may be wise to examine other sources of law for the elusive case on point or to make sure that no important cases may have been omitted. Students may wish to check digests such as the *All-Canada Weekly Summaries* (civil), *Weekly Criminal Bulletin* (criminal), *Canadian Weekly Law Sheet, Canadian Current Law — Case Law Digests* and *The Lawyer's Weekly*.

In addition, the student may research an appropriate provincial publication: (1) *Alberta Weekly Law Digest*; (2) *Alberta Decisions*; (3) *British Columbia Weekly Law Digest*; (4) *British Columbia Decisions*; (5) *Manitoba Decisions*; (6) *Nova Scotia Law News*; (7) *Ontario Decisions* (criminal); and (8) *Saskatchewan Decisions*.

NOTE: Some students may wish to begin their research with *The Abridgment* rather than with the C.E.D. (Ont. 3d). If so, it is important to know that generally *The Abridgment* does not note the legislative provisions relevant to the legal issues under consideration. For this reason, before undertaking a search in *The Abridgment*, consult the appropriate "Table of Public Statutes" to see if the legal issue is covered by legislation.

7. Expanding the Research to Other Jurisdictions Case Authorities

When the law in a Canadian jurisdiction is unclear on any point, English law, Australian law, or American Law may become important. In some instances, particularly having regard to Charter rights, insurance law (personal injury) and aviation law, to mention only a few areas, American material may be useful. Australian law is now often cited in Canadian business cases, whereas English law remains the foundation of Canadian contract and property law.

All of these jurisdictions are available through Quicklaw and Westlaw-*e*Carswell (depending on your subscription) and through the LII network.

B. FACT SCENARIO RESEARCH RESULTS

Based on the Fact Scenario, located at the beginning of this book, the following is a list of cases which we have located, and which we feel provide useful statements of applicable law. This list is by no means exhaustive. There are many additional cases on point. This list simply represents a number of cases which we have noted. (For research purposes, we have decided to proceed as if the incident occurred in Nova Scotia).

Martin v. American International Assurance Life Co., [2003] 1 S.C.R. 158, [2003] S.C.J. No. 14.

Shertsone v. Westroc Inc., [2001] A.J. No. 640, 2001 ABQB 414 (Q.B.).

Bertalan Estate v. American Home Assurance Co. 2001 BCCA 131, 86 B.C.L.R. (3d) 1, 196 D.L.R. (4th) 445, 25 C.C.L.I. (3d) 16, [2001] 4 W.W.R. 401, 149 B.C.A.C. 244, 244 W.A.C. 244, [2001] I.L.R. I-3958 (C.A.).

C.J.A. v. American Home Assurance Co., [1998] B.C.J. No. 2634 (S.C.).

Kucher v. Seaboard Life Assurance Co., [1997] A.J. No. 466 (Q.B.).

Beischel v. Mutual of Omaha Insurance Co., [1991] A.J. No. 757, 122 A.R. 32 (Q.B.).

Greening v. Commercial Union Assurance Co., [1988] I.L.R. 1-2300 (Nfld. C.A.).

Fairley v. Mutual Life Assurance Co. of Canada, [1980] N.J. No. 177, 26 Nfld. & P.E.I.R. 133, 72 A.P.R. 133 (S.C. (T.D.)).

Stein v. Crown Life Insurance Co., [1979] M.J. No. 43, [1979] 2 W.W.R. 649, [1979] I.L.R. para. 1-1081 at 116 (C.A.).

MacInnes v. London Life Insurance Co., [1979] N.S.J. No. 602, 33 N.S.R. (2d) 326, 57 A.P.R. 326, S.H. No. 11274 (S.C. (T.D.)).

Caban v. Sun Life Assurance Co. of Canada, [1978] O.J. No. 399, [1978] I.L.R. para. 1-965 at 996 (H.C.).

Brown v. Maritime Life Assurance Co. (1971), 2 N.S.R. (2d) 790, [1972] I.L.R. 1-474 (S.C. (A.D.)).

Hanes v. Wawanesa Mutual Insurance Co., [1963] S.C.R. 154.

Candler v. London & Lancashire Guarantee & Accident Co. of Canada (1963), 40 D.L.R. (2d) 408 (Ont. H.C.).

Bjorkman and Toronto Flying Club Ltd. v. British Aviation Insurance Co. Ltd., [1953] 2 D.L.R. 249 (Ont. H.C.), aff'd [1954] 3 D.L.R. 224 (Ont. C.A.) aff'd (1956) 2 D.L.R. (2d) 81 (S.C.C.).

Turner v. Northern Life Ass'ce Co., [1953] 1 D.L.R. 427 (N.S.S.C.).

Smith v. Smith, [1952] 2 S.C.R. 312.

Barnard v. Prudential Insurance Co. of America, [1949] 4 D.L.R. 235 (Ont. H.C.).

New York Life Insurance Co. v. Ross Estate, [1945] S.C.R. 289.

MacPhadyen v. Employers' Liability Ass'ce Co., [1933] 3 D.L.R. 505 (Ont. C.A.).

London Life Insurance Co. v. Lang Shirt Co. (Trustee of), [1929] S.C.R. 117.

Mader v. Sun Life Ass'ce Co., [1934] 4 D.L.R. 59 (N.S.S.C.).

CHAPTER 2

Primary Legal Materials

A. STATUTES

Primary materials are the records of rules laid down by those bodies vested with the authority to declare law. Generally, the most important primary materials are legislation and case reports. Legislation includes statutes and subordinate legislation. Subordinate legislation is made under powers conferred by a statute. It includes regulations, orders, rules, bylaws and ordinances. Case reports are the records of court decisions. This chapter discusses statutes, regulations, and case reports from Canada and the United Kingdom.

A statute, or "act", has been defined in English law as "a pronouncement by the Sovereign in Parliament, that is to say, made by the Queen by and with the advice and consent of both Houses of Parliament, or, in certain circumstances, the House of Commons alone, the effect of which is either to declare the law, or to change the law (normally for the future only, but sometimes with retrospective effect), or to do both".[1]

Statutes may be classified in various ways based on the scope of their operation. A public general act (or public statute) applies to the whole community (for example, the *Ontario Human Rights Code*); a local act is generally restricted in terms of area (for example, the *London-Middlesex Act, 1992* of Ontario); a private act may be restricted to specific individuals or groups (for example, the *Women in Crisis (Northumberland County) Act, 1992*). The distinction between public general acts and local acts is often difficult to determine. Many jurisdictions have abolished the distinction and classify statutes as public general or private acts. In the sessional or annual volumes of statutes, public general acts are found in the first section and private and local acts are found in the second section. Only public general acts are included in revised editions of statutes.

Because of their broader application, public general statutes are of primary interest to lawyers and will be the exclusive subject of the discussion that follows.

The main functions of public general statutes are:

(i) to codify an area of law which has become excessively convoluted through the accretion of case law (for example, the *Sale of Goods* legislation in the common law provinces and territories);

---

[1] *Halsbury* (4th), Vol. 44, at 484.

(ii)   to change or reform the case law (for example, the Ontario *Occupiers' Liability Act* removed a confusing common law distinction between an "invitee" and a "licensee"); and

(iii) to deal with areas previously untouched by case law (for example, the federal *Atomic Energy Control Act*).

The following discussion is designed to familiarize the student with the publication and organization of Canadian and United Kingdom statutes and to detail the basic steps to statute research.

The discussion is in three parts:

(a)   publication and organization;
(b)   research techniques; and
(c)   citation.

1. Canadian Statutes

(A) PUBLICATION AND ORGANIZATION

Preceding official publication, a federal public statute begins as a legislative proposal called a bill and is introduced during a legislative session. When a bill is introduced into a legislature, it is given a number. For example, Bill C-5 respecting the *Protection of Wildlife Species at Risk in Canada* was the fifth bill introduced in 2001 during the first session of the thirty-seventh Parliament. Before it can become law, a bill must pass through three readings in the House of Commons and the Senate. A bill is published in pamphlet form one or more times during its passage through the legislature. If approved, after the third reading, federal bills are sent to the Governor-General to receive Royal Assent. At this stage a bill officially becomes law. Upon receiving Royal Assent the new statutes are given consecutive chapter numbers and published again in pamphlet form (for instance, the *Species at Risk Act* became chapter 29 of the 2003 *Statutes of Canada*). New acts are also published in *The Canada Gazette, Part III*. At the close of the calendar year, all the acts are bound in an annual volume, referred to as the *Statutes of Canada*. The acts appear in the order that they received Royal Assent.

The *Statutes of Canada* annual bound volumes include amendments to previously existing acts, new acts and subsequent amendments to new acts up to the end of the most recent calendar year (allowing some lag time for publication). The annual volume also includes a "Table of Contents", a "Table of Public Statutes", a table of the "Proclamations of Canada", and an "Index" detailing the contents of each act.

The procedure for provincial bills is similar, taking into account the absence of an upper house. Royal Assent is accorded by the provincial Lieutenant-Governor. Ontario, Québec, Northwest Territories and Manitoba follow the federal practice and publish their statutes in annual volumes. This means that statutes are collected and bound at the end of each year. The acts are assigned a series of consecutive chapter numbers within each calendar year and the publication in bound form may be available within a few months of the end of the year. Alberta, British Columbia, New Brunswick, Newfoundland, Nova Scotia, Prince Edward Island, Saskatchewan and the Yukon publish their statutes in sessional volumes. A session of a legislature may be only a few months long or may span more than one year. The acts are given a series of consecutive chapter numbers for the session and are published in bound form at the end of the session.

Sessional or annual volumes include an invaluable cumulative "Table of Public Statutes"[2] which lists in alphabetical order, by short title, all public general acts from the current sessional or annual volume and all previous sessional or annual volumes as far back as the last revision of statutes for the jurisdiction. The table includes the revised statutes, subsequent amendments, new acts, amendments to those acts, and a few acts that are still in force which may not have been included in a revision.

From time to time[3] both federal and provincial governments establish commissions to revise and consolidate their respective public general acts in order to eliminate errors, consolidate amendments, and, in particular, to reorganize and renumber statutes, combine or eliminate sections or subsections, and add, delete, or replace certain words. When a revision is completed, the revised statutes are proclaimed in force and the former versions are repealed.[4]

Two points should be noted concerning revised statutes. First, no new material is added to the law by a revision. Secondly, a few acts remain unconsolidated and unrepealed. An illustration of this is *An Act to provide for the recognition of the Beaver (Castor Canadensis) as a symbol of the sovereignty of Canada.*

---

[2] Manitoba's *Table of Public Statutes* lists (i) all statutes in the C.C.S.M.; (ii) public acts not in the C.C.S.M.; (iii) municipal acts not in the C.C.S.M.; (iv) private acts; and (v) acts and parts of acts coming into force on proclamation.

Saskatchewan publishes two bound volumes: *Table of Public Statutes* and *Table of Regulations*. The Law Society of Saskatchewan Libraries has published an *Index to the Statutes of Saskatchewan, Second Edition*, which is updated regularly.

The "Table of Public Statutes" in the *Statutes of Canada* is found at the back of the annual volumes and from time to time is also published separately in a softcover edition.

[3] The last federal revision was in 1985. The last provincial or territorial revisions are as follows: Alberta in 2000; British Columbia, 1996: New Brunswick, 1973; Newfoundland, 1990; Northwest Territories, 1988; Nova Scotia, 1989: Ontario, 1990; Prince Edward Island, 1988; Québec, 1977; Saskatchewan, 1978; Yukon Territory, 1986. In 1990, Manitoba published what are referred to as *Re-enacted Statutes*.

[4] Most provinces have looseleaf versions of the latest revised statutes. These publications are called "continuing consolidations" because they incorporate new acts and amendments since the last revision. Their value is in keeping the statute law current under one cover. In addition, the publication of looseleaf versions lessens the need for periodic revisions. Ontario and Newfoundland do not have looseleaf statutes. All but Manitoba's and Québec's are unofficial; nonetheless, in several provinces, it is becoming increasingly common to include a reference to the consolidation in a citation.

The most recent revision of the federal statutes is the *Revised Statutes of Canada, 1985*. This set consists of 17 volumes, which includes eight volumes of federal statute law, five supplements, two indices, a table of concordance and a volume of appendices. The eight volumes of the set consolidate federal statute law to December 31, 1984. The supplements contain new acts and amendments to the *Revised Statutes of Canada* made between December 31, 1984 and November 30, 1991. The supplements also contain acts not included in the main revision, such as the *Divorce Act* and the *Income Tax Act*. The appendices include a schedule of acts repealed, constitutional documents, and the *Bill of Rights, 1960*.

Statutes are published in both English and French versions in the *Revised Statutes of Canada*. The acts are arranged alphabetically by the short title[5] and each act is given an alphanumeric designation. For example, the *Copyright Act* in the *Revised Statutes of Canada, 1985*, is chapter C-42. In the example, the alpha designation refers to the first letter of the first word of the act and the numeric designation is the number of the act in its alphabetical order within that letter. The *Revised Statutes of Canada* is also published in a looseleaf format and is kept up to date with regular releases.

The revised statutes of most provinces are also arranged alphabetically by the short title of the act,[6] but not all have adopted an alphanumeric system of numbering chapters. The *Revised Statutes of Nova Scotia* and the *Revised Statutes of British Columbia*, for example, still use a simple numeric system.

The alphanumeric systems adopted by some provinces have unique features designed to complement the publication of their revised statutes in a looseleaf format. The looseleaf edition of the Manitoba statutes is entitled the *Continuing Consolidation of the Statutes of Manitoba* and contains re-enacted (and revised) acts. Chapters are designated to allow acts passed since the completion of the re-enactment to be easily incorporated into the binder. For example, *The Ecological Reserves Act*, *The Education Administration Act*, and *The Elderly and Infirm Persons' Housing Act*, all re-enacted statutes, appear as chapters E5, E10, and E20, respectively. *The Economic Innovation and Technology Council Act* which has been passed since the re-enactment appears as chapter E7. The looseleaf service is current to the date noted by the publisher. Acts passed by the legislature after that date are not included in the service. For these, the student should consult the appropriate red-bound annual volume or the separate chapters of acts available from the Queen's Printer.

The bound edition of the *Revised Statutes of Prince Edward Island* uses the same basic alphanumeric system as the *Revised Statutes of Canada*. However, the system has been modified by incorporating a decimal notation which permits infinite expansion for use in the looseleaf edition. For example, the *Cooperation*

---

[5] When they are enacted all statutes have a long title found at the head of the text and most also have a short title located in the first or last section. When a statute appears in a revision the long title is usually omitted and the short title is placed at the head of the text.

[6] The *Revised Statutes of Newfoundland* have a long title and usually a shorter title.

Act, passed after the 1988 *Revised Statutes of Prince Edward Island*, was numbered chapter M-1.1 following the *Maintenance Enforcement Act* which is chapter M-1. A similar system is used for the *Revised Statutes of New Brunswick*, the *Revised Statutes of Saskatchewan*, the *Revised Statutes of Québec* and the *Revised Statutes of Alberta*. In Prince Edward Island, however, the decimal notation appears only in the "Table of Public Statutes", and not in the body of the statute volume itself (as in Saskatchewan, for instance).

(B) RESEARCH TECHNIQUES

(1) Finding a Statute

As mentioned earlier, federal statutes are published in bound form in the *Revised Statutes of Canada* or in the annual volumes of the *Statutes of Canada*. To locate a statute a student need only refer to the "Table of Public Statutes" in the latest annual volume of the *Statutes of Canada*. It lists[7] all acts in force as of December 31 of that year.

The student may also refer to the "Table of Public Statutes" when only the subject-matter is known, since most titles of acts suggest the subject-matter with which the act is concerned.

It is not always necessary to consult the table. If the short title and date are known, the student may simply refer to the "Table of Contents" for that annual volume. Also, if the name of the act and its alphanumeric designation for the *Revised Statutes of Canada* is known, refer directly to the volume that includes that chapter. (The chapter numbers of the statutes contained in each volume are printed on the spine.)

The procedure for finding provincial statutes is similar to that for finding federal statutes. To locate a particular provincial statute the student should refer to the "Table of Public Statutes"[8] in the latest annual or sessional volume for the selected jurisdiction. The "Table of Public Statutes" may also be of assistance in determining whether there has been any legislation on a selected topic. Alternatively, the student may refer to a separately bound subject index, if one is available for the selected jurisdiction.[9]

---

[7] The acts in the table are listed alphabetically by the short title. Thus, if only the long title is known, guess at the short title before reading the table.

[8] The name of the table differs slightly from province to province: "Table of Public Statutes" (New Brunswick, Nova Scotia, Ontario, Yukon, Alberta and Saskatchewan), "Table of Public Acts" (Prince Edward Island), "Table of Ammendments" (Quebec), "Table of Legislative Changes" (British Columbia), "Table of General Public Statutes" (Newfoundland-Labrador), "Acts in the Continuing Consolidation of the Statutes of Manitoba" (Manitoba), "Public Acts of the Northwest Territories" (Northwest Territories).

[9] Maritime Law Book Co., for example, has prepared an index for New Brunswick.

(2) Checking for Amendments

To find all the amendments to a federal statute, refer to the text of amendments, if any, under the title of the statute in the "Table of Public Statutes" in the latest annual or volumes of the *Statutes of Canada*. It lists all the amendments enacted as of December 31 of that year. The amendments will usually be found in statutes bearing the name of the revised statute; however, in some instances the amendments will be included in an umbrella statute, commonly referred to as an "omnibus act". For example, amendments to the *Access to Information Act* and the *Broadcasting Act*, in 1987, were included in the *Miscellaneous Statute Law Amendment Act, 1987*, which is found in chapter 1 of the *Revised Statutes of Canada, 1985* (4th Supplement).

Some of the amendments to the *Transfer of Offenders Act* which appear in the "Table of Public Statutes" in the 1998 *Statutes of Canada* are reproduced in Table 1 below.

On the left of the table, the section numbers (in bold-face type) refer to the sections of the *Transfer of Offenders Act* which have been amended. The dates refer to the bound volumes of statutes (or the supplement to the revision) in which the amending statutes are found. The chapter and section numbers (in light-face type) refer to the amending acts.

TABLE I

Transfer of Offenders Act — R.S., 1985, c. T-15
(Transfèrement des délinquants, Loi sur le)

s. 2, 1992, c. 20, s. 216(1)(f); 1993, c. 34, s. 121
s. 6, R.S., c. 31 (1st Supp.), s. 104
s. 8, 1992, c. 20, s. 208; 1995, c. 42, s. 83
s. 10, 1992, c. 20, s. 209; 1995, c. 42, ss. 71(d)(F) and 72(d)(F)
s. 11, 1992, c. 20, s. 210; 1995, c. 42, s. 84
s. 11.1, added, 1995, c. 42, s. 84
s. 12, 1992, c. 20, s. 211; 1995, c. 42, s. 84
s. 16, R.S., c. 27 (1st Supp.), s. 203; 1995, c. 22, s. 17 (Sch. III, items 6 to 9)
s. 17, 1993, c. 34, s. 122
s. 23, c. 34, s. 123
s. 24, R.S., c. 31 (1st Supp.), s. 105
s. 25, repealed, 1993, c. 34, s. 124
Sch., SOR/86-49, SOR/86-297; SOR/87-583; SOR/89-156; SOR/91-91; SOR/95-293; SOR/97-83; SOR/98-441
General, 1992, c. 20, s. 216(2)
General, 1995, c. 22, s. 26
CIF, R.S. c. 27 (1st Supp.), s. 203 proclaimed in force 04.12.85 *see* SI/85-211

CIF, R.S., c. 31 (1st Supp.), ss. 104 and 105 proclaimed in force 15.10.85 *see* SI/85-188
CIF, 1992, c. 20, ss. 208 to 211 and 216 in force 01.11.92 *see* SI/92-197
CIF, 1993, c. 34, ss. 121 to 124 in force on assent 23.06.93
CIF, 1995, c. 22, s. 17 (Sch. III, items 6 to 9) and s. 26 in force 03.09.96 *see* SI/96-79
CIF, 1995, c. 42, ss. 71(F), 72(F), 83 and 84 in force 24.01.96 *see* SI/96-10
CIF, 2002, c.1, s. 198 in force 01.04.2003 *see* SI/2002-91

The student may also find amendments to a federal statute in the *Canada Statute Citator*. The *Citator* lists the names of the acts of Canada with a reference to their location in the *Revised Statutes of Canada* or in a bound volume of statutes. The *Citator* includes the text of all amendments (except for amendments to the *Criminal Code* and the *Income Tax Act*) to the acts, arranging them according to the section numbers of the original act.

The procedure for finding amendments to provincial statutes is similar to that used for finding amendments to a federal statute. The student should refer to the "Table of Public Statutes"[10] in the latest bound volume of statutes for all jurisdictions, except for Saskatchewan where the statute volumes include a separate part for "Public Acts" and "Amending and Repealing and Temporary Public Acts".[11] The tables list the amendments (new sections and repealed sections are also included) in force as of December 31 of the year of the volume. The tables are not, however, uniformly prepared. For example, the "Table of Public Statutes" in the *Statutes of Ontario*, by and large, does not list the specific sections of statutes which have been amended.

A statute citator is an efficient tool for locating amendments to provincial acts. Currently there are publications known as "Statute Citators" for: Ontario, British Columbia and Nova Scotia. For example, the *Ontario Statute Citator* provides the full text of amendments to acts; whereas the *British Columbia Statute Citator* merely lists the amendments.

Canadian Statutes Citations is a research tool that provides references to reported cases that have considered statutes. *Canadian Statutes Citations* includes a section for federal law and one for each province.

(3) Canadian Statutes on the Internet

The easiest way to search for statutes online is through one of the central Canadian portals: <http://www.canlii.org> and <http://www.legis.ca>. Both sites have links to the individual provincial and federal government sites that publish the statutes. Links to P.E.I. and Newfoundland-Labrador statutes are

---

[10] *Supra*, note 8.
[11] There is a companion volume entitled "Saskatchewan Tables" or *Table of Public Statutes* and *Table of Regulations*.

only available on <http://www.legis.ca>. Canlii.org also maintains its own searchable library for statutes and regulations for: Canada (federal), Alberta, Saskatchewan, Manitoba, Ontario, Quebec, New Brunswick, and Nova Scotia. The <http://www.canlii.org> searchable database is a more efficient tool than the provincial or federal websites alphabetical indexes.

Individual sites	
Canada	<http://laws.justice.gc.ca/>
British Columbia	<http://www.qp.gov.bc.ca/statreg/>
Alberta	<http://www.qp.gov.ab.ca/>
Saskatchewan	<http://www.qp.gov.sk.ca/>
Manitoba	<http://www.gov.mb.ca/chc/statpub/>
Ontario	<http://www.e-laws.gov.on.ca/>
Quebec	<http://publicationsduquebec.gouv.qc.ca/home.php>
New Brunswick	<http://www.gnb.ca/0062/acts/acts-e.asp>
Nova Scotia	<http://www.gov.ns.ca/legi/legc/>
Prince Edward Island	<http://www.gov.pe.ca/law/statutes/>
Newfoundland	<http://www.gov.nf.ca/hoa/sr/>
Yukon	<http://www.canlii.org/yk/sta/>
Northwest Territories	<http://www.canlii.ca/nt/sta/>
Nunavut	<http://www.nunavutcourtofjustice.ca/library/index.htm >

(4) Checking for New Acts or Recent Amendments for the Current Year

New acts, amendments, or repealed acts passed after the publication of the latest annual volume of the *Statutes of Canada* may be found in *The Canada Gazette, Part III*, or, failing that, in the collection of third reading of bills which is kept in most libraries.

The student may also refer to a separate paper bound volume entitled "Table of Public Statutes and Responsible Ministers" published with the looseleaf up-dates of *The Canada Gazette, Part III*, or to the "Table of Contents" for individual volumes of *The Canada Gazette, Part III*, not yet included in the "Table of Public Statutes and Responsible Ministers". As a final check, the student may refer to the *Canada Statute Citator* which lists acts not yet included in the last published "Table of Public Statutes".

Proposed changes to federal statutes which are still in the form of a bill may be discovered by means of secondary tools, including the following:

(i)   "Progress of Bills Through Parliament", found in the *Newsletter of the Ottawa Letter*;

(ii)   "Canada Statute Citator Monthly Bulletin Service";

(iii) "Progress of Bills", found in *Canadian Current Law — Legislation*;
(iv) *Status of Bills and Motions Reported*, published under authority of the Speaker of the House of Commons;
(v) Votes and proceedings of the House of Commons and Senate; and
(vi) Quicklaw's Canada Status of Bills database (CSB).

New acts, amendments, or repealed acts which are not included in the "Table of Public Statutes" in the bound volume of provincial statutes often may be found in the looseleaf edition of the revised statutes for selected jurisdictions.[12] Alternatively, the student may contact the librarian of the provincial legislature or the provincial government bookstore for the selected jurisdiction. The latter may have selected acts reprinted in pamphlet form.

Proposed changes to provincial statutes which are still in the form of a bill may be discovered by means of secondary tools, including the following:

(i) "Ontario Statute Citator Weekly Bulletin Service", found in the *Ontario Statute Citator* (or as a companion volume);
(ii) *The Provincial Legislative Record*;
(iii) *Ontario Legislative Digest Service*.

In addition to these sources, a number of tables and indices relating to the status of bills are published by the Legislative Counsel of most provinces and by law libraries.

Perhaps the quickest way to determine the status of bills before the legislatures is to consult the particular jurisdiction's Web page. These pages usually provide up-to-date information on new bills, including changes that have been made between readings, and a history of recently proclaimed laws. It is vital to check the date of the last updating of the Web page, especially during a period when the legislature or parliament is sitting.

The status of bills is available through the national parliament website and through the provincial legislative websites. They can be accessed centrally through legis.ca or by accessing each site individually.

Canada's Parliament	<http://www.parl.gc.ca/common/index.asp>
Legislative Assembly of British Columbia	<http://www.legis.gov.bc.ca/>
Legislative Assembly of Alberta	<http://www.assembly.ab.ca/>
Legislative Assembly of Saskatchewan	<http://www.legassembly.sk.ca/

---

[12] Always check acts in a consolidation against the original legislation, if possible, in those jurisdictions for which the consolidation is not authoritative. The consolidations of Alberta and Saskatchewan, for example, are not authoritative. The student should refer to the title page to determine the status of the consolidation for the selected jurisdiction.

Legislative Assembly of Manitoba	<http://www.gov.mb.ca/leg-asmb/>
Legislative Assembly of Ontario	<http://www.ontla.on.ca/>
National Assembly of Quebec	<http://www.assnat.qc.ca/>
Legislative Assembly of New Brunswick	<http://www.gnb.ca/legis/index.asp>
Nova Scotia Legislature	<http://www.gov.ns.ca/legislature/>
Legislative Assembly of Prince Edward Island	<http://www.assembly.pe.ca/>
House of Assembly, Newfoundland and Labrador	<http://www.gov.nf.ca/hoa/>
Yukon Legislative Assembly	<http://www.gov.yk.ca/leg-assembly/>
Legislative Assembly of the Northwest Territories	<http://www.assembly.gov.nt.ca/>
Legislative Assembly of Nunavut	<http://www.assembly.nu.ca/>

(5) Determining the Date of Coming into Force

Following the third reading in the appropriate legislative body, a bill receives Royal Assent and becomes law; however, the date of Royal Assent, usually noted below the title of an act in a statute book, is not usually the same date as the date of coming into force (the effective date).

There are three ways that a federal law may be brought into force:

(i) The act may provide for its own coming into force. Reference should be made to the last section of the statute;

(ii) The act may state that it will come into force on a date to be set by proclamation. If so,

    (a) refer to the "Table of Public Statutes" or to the table of "Proclamations of Canada" in the latest annual volume of the *Statutes of Canada*, or

    (b) refer to the table of proclamations in *The Canada Gazette, Part III*, or

    (c) refer to the table of proclamations in the quarterly index of *The Canada Gazette, Part I*, or

    (d) refer to the heading "Proclamations" in the index to individual volumes of *The Canada Gazette, Part I*; or

(iii) The act may be silent as to the date of coming into force. Reference should be made to the *Interpretation Act*, R.S.C. 1985, c. I-21, s. 6(2).

NOTE: Other secondary sources for finding proclamation dates include the "Statutes Amended, Repealed, or Proclaimed in Force" section of *Canadian Current Law — Legislation*, the *Canada Statute Citator* and the *Ottawa Letter*.

Provincial acts, like federal acts, may be brought into force in three ways:

(i)   The act may provide for its own coming into force. Refer to the last section of the statute; or

(ii)   The act may state that it will come into force on a date to be set by proclamation. If so, check one or more of the following sources for the selected province:

  (a)   a table of proclamations or the "Table of Public Statutes" in the latest bound volume of statutes;

  (b)   "Acts Proclaimed" (Saskatchewan); "Acts in Force" (British Columbia); "Proclamation" (Ontario, Québec, Alberta, Manitoba); "Proclamations" (New Brunswick, Nova Scotia, Prince Edward Island, Northwest Territories); "A Proclamation" (Newfoundland); "Statutory Instruments" (Yukon) in the appropriate provincial or territorial Gazette;

  (c)   the "Statutes Amended, Repealed, or Proclaimed in Force" section in *Canadian Current Law — Legislation*;

  (d)   a statute citator (for example, *Ontario Statute Citator*); or

(iii) The act may be silent as to the date of coming into force.

In the latter case, the dates of coming into force are governed by the following general provisions for each province:

Alta.   —   *Interpretation Act*, R.S.A. 1980, c. I-7, s. 4(1).

B.C.   —   *Interpretation Act*, R.S.B.C. 1996, c. 238, s. 3(2).

Man.   —   *The Interpretation Act*, R.S.M. 1987, c. I80, s. 5(4) (C.C.S.M. I80).

N.B.   —   *Interpretation Act*, R.S.N.B. 1973, c. I-13, s. 3(2).

Nfld.   —   *The Statutes Act*, R.S.N. 1990, c. S-26, s. 4.

N.W.T.   —   *Interpretation Act*, R.S.N.W.T. 1988, c. I-8, s. 4(1).

N.S.   —   *Interpretation Act*, R.S.N.S. 1989, c. 235, s. 3.

Ont.   —   *Statutes Act*, R.S.O. 1990, c. S.21, s. 5(1).

P.E.I.   —   *Interpretation Act*, R.S.P.E.I. 1988, c. I-8, s. 3(1).

Qué.   —   *Interpretation Act*, R.S.Q. 1977, c. I-16, s. 5, as am. by S.Q. 1982, c. 62.

Sask.   —   *Interpretation Act*, S.S. 1995, c. I-11.2, s. 4(2).

Yukon   —   *Interpretation Act*, R.S.Y.T. 1986, c. 93, s. 3.

(C) CITATION

One of the more difficult tasks for the first-year law student is to master the proper citation of statutes which have been published in the official statute volumes. The introduction, in recent years, of looseleaf editions of statutes has added to the difficulty. The outline below will assist the student in mastering the basic "rules" of citation. Appendix I lists the recommended method of citation for federal acts and for provincial acts.

Rule 1: Title

Refer to the short title, if there is one. The correct form of the short title is that which appears in the provision for the short title in the bound volume of statutes or in the revised statutes. Note in particular that if the year or the word "the" appear in the title, they are reproduced in a citation. The titles of statutes in all Canadian jurisdictions should be italicized.

Rule 2: Statutory Reference and Jurisdiction

(i)   Refer to a statute as "S." and to a revised or re-enacted statute as "R.S.".

(ii)   Combine "S." or "R.S." with the following abbreviations for Canada and for each province and territory: C., B.C., A., S., M., O., Q., N.B., P.E.I., N.L.,[13] N.S., Nu., Y. and N.W.T.

Rule 3: Year or Session

(i)   Include the year in any citation of a statute found in a revision or an annual volume.

Examples:
R.S.C. 1985, c. A-2.
S.O. 1985, c. 20.

(ii)   Include the year or years in any citation of a statute found in a sessional volume.

Examples:
S.N.S. 1984, c. 1.
S.C. 1980-81-82-83, c. 5.

(iii)   Include a reference to the number of the session where there is more than one session in a year, each of which are numbered separately.

Example:
S.O. 1971 (2nd Sess.), c. 2.

---

[13]   Newfoundland is referred to as N. before December 6, 2001 for statutes, December 13, 2001 for regulations and December 21, 2001 in the Gazette. After these dates it is referred to as N.L.

(iv)   Supplements to the *Revised Statutes of Canada* contain statutes that were passed after the cut-off date and before the release date for the set. Such statutes should be cited to the supplement and it is necessary to include the number of the supplement.

Example:
R.S.C. 1985, c. 8 (2nd Supp.), s. 2.

Rule 4: Chapter and Schedule

(i)   When citing a chapter use the designation "c.", and "cc." for more than one chapter, notwithstanding any other abbreviation which might be used in the statute volume in the jurisdiction.[14] Refer to Schedule as "Sch.", and Schedules as "Schs.".

Rule 5: Section, Subsection and Paragraph

Refer to a section with the designation "s.". Refer to more than one section as "ss.".[15] Otherwise, include the number of the subsection in brackets, *e.g.*, s. 91(1). Refer to paragraph as "para.", and paragraphs as "paras.".

Rule 6: Citation of New Acts

Acts which have not been included in a revision or re-enactment are cited to the appropriate bound volume published after the revision or re-enactment.

Example:
Environmental Bill of Rights, S.O. 1993, c. 28.

Rule 7: Citation of Amending and Repealing Acts

(i)   Refer to an amendment as "as am. by", to a repealed act as "as rep. by", and if repealed and re-enacted as "re-en. as".

(ii)   Refer to amending acts by, first, citing the revised statute, if there is one, and, second, citing the bound volumes of statutes.

Examples:
Management Board of Cabinet Act, R.S.O. 1990, c. M-1, as am. by S.O. 1991, vol. 2, c. 14, s. 11; 1993, c. 38, s. 69 (1) and (2).

---

[14]   Prior to 1977, statutes in Newfoundland sessional volumes were referred to by number and not chapter and the abbreviation "No." was used in the citation of a statute.

[15]   Provisions of the *Québec Code* are referred to as articles rather than sections; therefore, use the abbreviations "art." and "arts.".

Regional Transit Authority Act, R.S.N.S. 1989, c. 389, as am. by S.N.S. 1990, c. 19, ss. 83, 84; 1994-1995, c. 7; as rep. by *Municipal Government Act,* S.N.S. 1998, c. 18 s. 576

Plant Diseases Act, R.S.N.B. 1973, c. P-9, re-en. as *Plant Health Act,* S.N.B. 1998, c. P-9.01.

NOTE: In citing amendments, the title of the amending act is always omitted unless it has a different title than the original act. If the difference is found only in the words "An Act to amend", it is not necessary to repeat the title. The jurisdiction may also be omitted.

(iii)   Include a reference to the amended and amending sections if the point under consideration involves only a particular section or subsection of a statute.

Example:

An amendment to section 41 of the *Historical Resource Act* is cited R.S.A. 2000, c. H-9, s. 41, as am. by S.A. 2001, c. 28, s. 11.

(iv)   Include the amending section if the amendment is included in a general purpose act (commonly referred to as an "omnibus act").

Example:

A 2002 amendment to the *Expropriation Act* located in the *Miscellaneous Statutes Amendment Act* is cited: *Expropriation Act,* R.S.A 2000, c. E-13, s. 15(2) as am. by the *Miscellaneous Statutes Amendment Act,* S.A. 2002, c. 30, s. 6.

(v)   Refer to a new or additional section with the designation "added" or "add".

Example:

Criminal Records Act, R.S.C. 1985, c. C-47, s. 2.2(1) added, S.C. 1992, c. 22, s. 2(1) and 2(2)(E).

Rule 8: Punctuation

Include periods after every abbreviation, commas after the title, a chapter or section designation, if required (see example above), and year, as well as before modifications, *e.g.,* "as am. by".

Rule 9: Pinpoint Reference of Acts

A pinpoint reference to a specific section of an act follows the chapter designation.

Example:
Mental Health Act, R.S.O 1990, c. M-7, s. 20.

Rule 10: Looseleaf Statute Services

There are looseleaf consolidations for Canada and most provinces,[16] but these various jurisdictions have not adopted a standard form of designation for the consolidations, as is the case for revised or bound volumes of the statutes. The practice generally appears to be to refer not to the name of the consolidation but only to chapter references of the consolidation in a citation, if it is different than the revision or the bound volume.

Canada

When referring to acts in the bound edition of the *Revised Statutes of Canada, 1985*, cite the revision. When referring to subsequent acts, cite to the *Statutes of Canada*. Do not cite to the looseleaf.

Alberta

The consolidation does not have official status. Thus, cite to the revision and subsequent bound volumes.

Examples:
Land Titles Act, R.S.A. 2000, c. L-7.
Student Financial Assistance Act, S.A. 2002, c. S-20.5.

NOTE: The same chapter designations for the same acts are used in the consolidation and in the bound volumes.

British Columbia

Statutes are cited to the revision. Acts which were passed after the last revision are cited to the bound volume of statutes.

Examples:
Fish Protection Act, S.B.C. 1997, c. 21.

Manitoba

The consolidation of the statutes of Manitoba is now generally referred to as C.C.S.M. (*i.e.*, *Continuing Consolidation of the Statutes of Manitoba*) and the designation has been adopted by several Canadian texts on legal citation.

---

[16] Except for Ontario and Newfoundland. None of the Territories have a looseleaf edition.

Examples:
The Emergency Measures Act, S.M. 1987-88, c. 11, C.C.S.M. c. E80.
The Business Practices Act, S.M. 1990-91, c. 6, C.C.S.M. c. B120.

Re-enacted Statutes of Manitoba in bilingual format are contained in the consolidation and appear with the same chapter numbers as are found in the bound re-enactment volumes.

Example:
The Employment Standards Code, S.M. 1998, c. 29, C.C.S.M. E 110.

New Brunswick

Statutes contained in the *Revised Statutes of New Brunswick, 1973*, and which were incorporated in the looseleaf service, use the same alphanumeric numbering system. Cite to the revision.

Example:
Companies Act, R.S.N.B. 1973, c. C-13.

Acts which are included in the supplement to the revision and new acts passed after the revision are assigned an alphanumeric designation (with a decimal notation). It is used in the bound volumes and in the consolidation. Thus, the citation below applies to both.

Example:
Canadian Judgements Act, S.N.B. 2000, c. C-0.1.

Amending acts are numbered in the traditional alphanumeric manner in the sessional volume and incorporated into the appropriate act in the consolidation. A reference to an amendment to the revised statute appears as follows:

Notaries Public Act, R.S.N.B. 1973, c. N-9, as am. by S.N.B. 1979, c. 50, s. 6; 1981, c. 55, s. 6; 1983, c. 60, ss. 1, 6 ; 1987, c. 6, ss. 1, 6.

Similarly, amendments to a new act will be cited as follows:

Advanced Life Support Services Act, S.N.B. 1976, c. A-3.01, as am. by S.N.B. 1985, c. 4, s. 1; 1986, c. 8, s. 1; 1990, c. 61, s. 3; 1992, c. 52, s. 1; 1994, c. 78, s. 1; 2000, c. 26, s. 1; as rep. by S.N.B. 2001, c. 6, s. 1.

Newfoundland

A new revision and a new consolidation were published in 1990. Both have the same chapter designations and are cited in the traditional manner to the bound revision and sessional volume.

Examples:
Adult Corrections Act, R.S.N. 1990, c. A-3.
Petroleum Products Act, S.N. 2001, c. P-11.
Access to Information and Protection of Privacy Act, S.N.L. 2002, c. A-1.1.[17]

Amendments are cited:
Notaries Public Act, R.S.N. 1990, c. N-5 as am. by S.N. 1996, c. R-10.1, s. 52; 2001, c. N-3.1, s. 2.
Prepaid Funeral Services Act, S.N. 2000, c. P-18, as am. by S.N. 2000, c. 30, s. 1; 2001, c. 3, s. 1.

Northwest Territories

A new revision and a new consolidation were published in 1988. Both have the same chapter designations and are cited in the traditional manner to the bound revision and sessional volume.

Examples:
Defamation Act, R.S.N.W.T. 1988, c. D-1.
Personal Property Security Act, S.N.W.T. 1994, c. 8.

Amendments are cited:
Consolidation of Fine Option Act, R.S.N.W.T. 1988, c. F-5, as am. by S.N.W.T. 1997, c. 3.
Consolidation of Adoption Act, S.N.W.T. 1998, c. 9, as am. by S.N.W.T. 2000, c. 13; 2002, c. 6.

Nova Scotia

A new revision and a new consolidation were published in 1989. Both have the same chapter designations and are cited in the traditional manner to the bound revision and sessional volume.

Examples:
Architects Act, R.S.N.S. 1989, c. 21.
Public Sector Compensation Restraint Act, S.N.S. 1991, c. 5.
Forest Enhancement Act, R.S.N.S. 1989, c. 178, as am. by S.N.S. 1993, c. 9, s. 6.

Prince Edward Island

The revised statutes of 1988 were published in bound and looseleaf formats. Acts passed after the *Revised Statutes of Prince Edward Island, 1988*, are given

---

[17] Newfoundland statutes published after December 6, 2001 are cited N.L.

a different chapter number in the continuing consolidation than in the bound volume. The looseleaf reference is indicated in brackets at the end of the citation to the bound volume of the *Statutes of Prince Edward Island*.

Example:
Credit Union Act, S.P.E.I. 1990, c. 14 (c. C-29.1); as am. by S.P.E.I. 1997, s. 90 (1)(a); s. 90 (3) added; s. 173 (2.1) added; s. 169 re-en. by s. 2.

Québec

Québec statutes may be cited to either the bound revision or to the looseleaf revision. The citation, *Charter of Human Rights and Freedoms*, R.S.Q. 1977, c. C-12, is a reference to the bound 1977 revision. Statutes passed after the revision are cited to the looseleaf service or to the *Statutes of Québec*.

Examples:
An Act Respecting Trust Companies and Savings Companies, R.S.Q. c. S-29.01.
An Act Respecting the Composition of the Office of the National Assembly, S.Q. 1990, c. 2.

NOTE: The omissions of the year in the citation refers to the looseleaf service; no comma appears before "c".

Saskatchewan

The *Revised Statutes of Saskatchewan, 1978*, are published in bound and looseleaf formats. The looseleaf consolidation is not officially sanctioned for use in a court of law. Cite to the bound volume of statutes.

Examples:
The Police Act, 1990, S.S. 1990-91, c. P-15.01.
The Crown Employment Contracts Act, S.S. 1991, c. C-50.11.
The Absconding Debtors Act, R.S.S. 1978, c. A-2.

NOTE: An alphanumeric system with decimal notation has been adopted for acts assented to after the revision for ease of use with a looseleaf format, presumably at some later date.

Nunavut

Nunavut began publishing statutes when it became Canada's newest territory on April 1, 1999. Nunavut borrowed from the statutes of the Northwest Territories to form the basis of its consolidated statutes. From April 1, 1999 Nunavut has been publishing statutes to add on to that base. Currently statute information is only published online. Each new statute is given a chapter number based on the order that the statute is published. No revision has been done in Nunavut.

Example:
Technical Standards and Safety Act, S. Nu. 2002, c. 1.

2. United Kingdom Statutes

(A) PUBLICATION AND ORGANIZATION

Two basic distinctions should be drawn between English and Canadian statutes. First, English statute law does not undergo the periodic and systematic consolidations that Canadian statute law enjoys. Nevertheless, there is a continuing process of updating which involves consolidation of individual statutes and their amendments into new acts and the repeal of spent and undesired statutes. The second distinction is that while only one or two series of statute volumes serves each Canadian jurisdiction, there are a number of series containing United Kingdom statutes:

(1) Modern Sources of United Kingdom Statutes

(i) Public General Acts and Measures (1932 to date)

The most comprehensive official source of statutes of the United Kingdom is a series of red bound volumes called the *Public General Acts and Measures*. The series began in 1832 and, until 1939 the volumes of the statutes contained all the acts passed in a particular session of the British Parliament. After that date, the volumes contained all the acts passed in a calendar year. At the beginning of each volume are alphabetical and chronological tables of short titles, a subject index, a table showing their effect on existing legislation, and a table showing the derivations of consolidating acts.

(ii) Halsbury's Statutes of England and Wales, Fourth Edition

This set, like its predecessor, *Halsbury's Statutes of England, Third Edition*, is intended to provide a complete record of all acts of the English Parliament grouped according to subject-matter.

The following publications are included in the set:

(a)   *Main Fourth Edition Volumes 1 to 50*. These replace the 39 main and continuation volumes of the third edition. The complete set contains all acts under 127 subject titles. The cut-off date for materials in individual volumes is noted following the title page.

(b)   *Reissue Volumes*. These are intended to replace main volumes which have undergone numerous changes. They include all relevant acts, and exclude any repealed statutory provisions. They have been published regularly since 1987.

(c)   *Cumulative Supplement.* This work records the amendments, additions, and other changes to the main, reissue and *Current Statutes Service* volumes. It is updated and published annually.

(d)   *Noter-Up Service.* This is a looseleaf service binder. It records amendments, additions and other changes made during the current year to the material in the main volumes and the *Current Statutes Service.* The "Noter-Up" also contains material relating to "Unannotated Acts" and updates the annual volumes of *Halsbury's Is it in Force?.* Each issue of the "Noter-Up" supersedes the last, and three issues are published each year. The "Noter-Up" is used in conjunction with the current *Cumulative Supplement.*

(e)   *Current Statutes Service.* This is a multi-volume looseleaf publication which contains the text of all acts which post-date the main and reissue volumes. The *Current Statutes Service* is classified by subject-matter and divided by guide cards bearing the number of the parent volume to which the new material relates. It includes an "Alphabetical List of Statutes" and a "Chronological List of Statutes", along with a subject index, all of which are supplementary to the annual *Table of Statutes and General Index* volume. It is updated six times a year. When a bound volume is reissued, the material that is contained in the *Current Statute Service* binder for that title is incorporated into the reissue volume.

(f)   *Table of Statutes and Consolidated Index.* This service contains the annual index to the fourth edition of *Halsbury's Statutes of England.* It lists the acts which are contained in the main and reissue volumes, as well as in the service binders. Each volume also includes chronological and alphabetical lists of statutes, as well as volume and service indexes. It was first published in 1989 and has been updated since then.

(g)   *Is it in Force?* This work lists the commencement dates and other information for every act of general application in England and Wales and General Synod Measures passed since January 1, 1963. The text is arranged according to calendar year beginning with the most recent year. The work is updated and published annually. It lists (a) the dates on which the acts received Royal Assent; (b) the date or dates which have been appointed for the provision of the acts to come into force; and (c) provisions which are not in force. The cut-off date for material contained in the volume is noted in the Preface. Commencement dates and other changes for the current year are listed following the guide "Is it in Force?" in the *Noter-Up Service* binder.

(B) Research Techniques

(1) Finding United Kingdom Statutes

(i) Public General Acts and Measures

If both the title and date are known, consult the alphabetical list of statutes in the official *Public General Acts and Measures* for that year.

(ii) Halsbury's Statutes

If the name of the act is known (and if the act is likely to appear in a particular title), consult the spines of the volumes or the list of titles (at the front of each volume) to find the appropriate act. For example, volume 8 contains the title "Companies", where the *Companies Act, 1985*, appears.

Alternatively, refer to the alphabetical or chronological lists of acts in the selected volume for what appears to be the appropriate title. For example, the "Table of Statutes" at the front of the "Companies" title in volume 8 (2003 Reissue) shows that the *Companies Act, 1985*, begins on page 88.

If the name of the act is not known, but you have a general idea of the particular area of law, *i.e.*, the title, consult the spines of individual volumes, or the list of titles published at the front of each volume or at the front of the *Table of Statutes and Consolidated Index*. The *Table of Statutes and Consolidated Index* is also a useful source of information where the name of the particular act relating to a certain area is known and one wishes to check for additional legislation on that subject. Simply by looking up the relevant subject area in the *Consolidated Index* any other acts dealing with that subject will be identified. For example, to find the *Review of Justices Decisions Act, 1872* use the "Alphabetical List of Statutes" at the front of the *Table of Statutes and Consolidated Index* and it should lead you to volume 27, page 13.

To update a search or to find a very recent act, refer to the "Alphabetical List of Statutes" at the front of the first binder of the *Current Statutes Service*.

(2) Checking for Amendments

The amended text of statutes is reprinted in *Halsbury's Statutes*. For more recent amendments, consult:

(i) the latest annual *Cumulative Supplement*. This *Supplement* directs the user to the main volumes, reissue volumes and the *Current Statutes Service*, updating the act, section and schedule found in those sources; and

(ii) the *Noter-Up Service*. The "Noter-Up" directs the user to the main volumes, reissue volumes and to the *Current Statutes Service*. The "Noter-Up" is a preview of what will appear in the next *Cumulative Supplement*.

It is the final check on the state of a given act and should always be used in conjunction with the *Cumulative Supplement.*

(3) Determining the Date of Coming into Force

Unless another date is specified, a statute of the United Kingdom comes into force on the date of Royal Assent: *Acts of Parliament (Commencement) Act, 1793* (U.K.), 33 Geo. III, c. 13. The date of Royal Assent will be found under the long title. If the date of commencement is to be fixed by proclamation, consult "Is it in Force?" of *Halsbury's Statutes, Fourth Edition,* or the "Dates of Commencement" in the monthly issues or year books of *Current Law.*

(C) CITATION

United Kingdom statutes are cited in the same way as Canadian statutes with the following exceptions:

(1)   Date: The regnal year must be used for the date when you cite a statute passed before 1963. The calendar year may be used when you cite a statute passed during or after 1963.

(2)   Jurisdiction: Although it would not appear in an English work, an indication of the jurisdiction should be included when you are writing for Canadian lawyers. The abbreviation in parenthesis, either "(Imp.)" or "(U.K.)", should be inserted after the date.

Examples:
Punishment of Offences Act, 1837 (Imp.), 7 Will 4 & 1 Vict., c. 91.
Military Lands Act, 1892 (Imp.), 55 & 56 Vict., c. 43.
Fur Farming (Prohibition) Act, 2000 (U.K.), 2000, c. 33.
Police Reform Act, 2002 (U.K.), 2002, c. 30.

NOTE: Many statutes of the United Kingdom include a date in the short title. In such cases, the date must be included again in its proper place.

B. SUBORDINATE LEGISLATION

Subordinate legislation has been defined as "legislation enacted by a person, body or tribunal, subordinate to a sovereign legislative body".[18]

Subordinate legislation includes regulations, orders, rules, bylaws, and municipal ordinances. The most important of these, for purposes of general research,

---

[18]   G.L. Gall, *The Canadian Legal System,* 3rd ed. (Toronto: Carswell, 1990), at 37. For example, s. 39 of the *Public Libraries Act,* c. P.44 of the 1990 *Revised Statutes of Ontario,* states, in part, that "the Lieutenant Governor in Council may make regulations".

are regulations and orders. The term "regulation" is generally taken to comprise subordinate legislation of general and substantive effect. The term "order" is generally understood as comprising subordinate legislation issued for a particular situation. These definitions are loose and often difficult to apply to a particular instrument. In any case, most jurisdictions provide functional definitions of these terms in statutes which govern subordinate legislation. Owing to the limited scope of this book, the following outline confines itself to those pieces of subordinate legislation which are defined as "regulations" in Canadian jurisdictions and as "statutory instruments" in the United Kingdom.

In all jurisdictions in Canada, there is a statute of general effect which systematizes the central filing and publication of regulations. For example, the *Regulations Act* of Ontario (R.S.O. 1990, c. R.21, s. 5) provides that "[e]very regulation shall be published in *The Ontario Gazette* within one month of its filing". Subsection 2(1) provides, in part, that "[e]very regulation shall be filed in duplicate with the Registrar together with a certificate in duplicate of its making signed by the authority making it or a responsible officer thereof...".

These statutes also provide important information relating to the following:

(i)   definition of "regulation" or "statutory instrument";
(ii)   commencement date of regulations;
(iii) regulations exempt from publication; and
(iv)   indexing, revision, and consolidation of regulations.

The following outline offers a method for researching regulations from the federal and provincial jurisdictions of Canada. For each jurisdiction, there is, first, a summary of the publication procedure and, second, a suggested method of researching regulations. This method involves the following four steps:

(1)   finding a regulation;
(2)   updating the regulation;
(3)   determining the date of coming into force; and
(4)   citation.

1. Regulations in Canada

(A) FEDERAL REGULATIONS

The *Statutory Instruments Act*, R.S.C. 1985, c. S-22, governs the publication of federal regulations. Section 5 of the Act provides that "every regulation-making authority shall, within seven days after making a regulation, transmit copies...to the Clerk of the Privy Council for registration". Section 11 of the Act requires all regulations to be published in *The Canada Gazette* within 23 days of registration, unless exempted.

The main body of federal regulations is published in a 19-volume set, the *Consolidated Regulations of Canada, 1978*, which brings together regulations in force on December 31, 1977. The consolidation has a "Table of Contents" listing all the regulations (except those exempt from publication) made under each federal statute. The consolidation has a supplement referred to as *The Canada Gazette, Part II, Special Issue*. The *Special Issue* contains amending regulations made between December 31, 1977, and December 31, 1978. The "Schedule", volume 19, is a list of regulations which have been revoked.

(1) Finding Federal Regulations

The indispensable tool for finding federal regulations is the *Consolidated Index of Statutory Instruments*.

NOTE: This is not a subject index to the regulations. As such, the student must know the name of the regulation or statute under which the regulation was made.

This cumulative index is published quarterly in conjunction with *The Canada Gazette, Part II*. It consists of two tables.

Table I lists, alphabetically, *inter alia*, by title, regulations showing the statutes under which regulations were made and, below each statute, lists the regulations and amendments to regulations which the statute has authorized.

Table II lists, *inter alia*, in alphabetical order and by short title, the statutes under which regulations were made and, below each statute, lists the regulations and amendments to regulations that the statute has authorized.

Hence, the first step in finding a federal regulation is to consult the third table in the *Consolidated Index of Statutory Instruments* in order to determine whether the regulation was exempt from publication. The second step, if the title of the regulation is known, is to consult the first table in the *Consolidated Index* in order to discover the short title of the statute under which the regulation was made. The third step, once the short title of the enabling statute is known, is to consult the second table of the *Consolidated Index* under the short title of the enabling statute. It contains a list of regulations with references to their location in the *Consolidated Regulations of Canada, 1978. The Canada Gazette, Part II*, or the Consolidation of 1955.

(2) Updating the Regulations of Canada

A search is brought up to date by consulting the bi-weekly issues of *The Canada Gazette, Part II*, published since the last *Consolidated Index of Statutory Instruments*. Each issue includes an index of regulations contained in that issue.

(3) Coming Into Force

If a federal regulation does not itself specify the date, it comes into force on the day it was registered which is indicated at the top of the text. If the regulation is exempt from registration, it comes into force on the day it was made (*Statutory Instruments Act*, R.S.C. 1985, c. S-22, s. 9(1)).

(4) Citation

Regulations published in *The Canada Gazette, Part II*, are cited as follows:

Access to Information Regulations, SOR/83-507.

"SOR" abbreviates "Statutory Order and Regulations"; "83" indicates the year; "507" indicates the number of the order or regulation.

Regulations published in the 1978 Consolidation are cited as shown below:

Arctic Waters Pollution Prevention Regulation, C.R.C., c. 354.

"C.R.C." abbreviates *Consolidated Regulations of Canada.*[19]
Amendments to the consolidation are cited, first, to the consolidation and, second, to a regulation number appearing in *The Canada Gazette, Part II*, as shown below:

Children of Deceased Veterans Education Assistance Regulations, C.R.C., c. 399 as am. by SOR/91-310, ss. 2-3; SOR/86-807, s. 1.

Amendments to regulations passed after the consolidation are cited:

Steering Appliances and Equipment Regulations, SOR/83-810, as am. by 86-1027 s. 1; 2002-426, s. 1; 2003-86, s. 1.

NOTE: Alternative sources for finding federal regulations include: (a) Quicklaw's federal regulations database (SOR); (b) Carswell's *Canada Regulations Index*; (c) The "Regulations" table in *Canadian Current Law — Legislation Annual* and the supplement to the *Legislation Annual (Canadian Abridgment (3rd))*.

(B) ALBERTA REGULATIONS

Regulations are published in *The Alberta Gazette, Part II*, issued every two weeks. A cumulative index is published every month in conjunction with *The Alberta Gazette, Part II*.

---

[19] Note that it is not necessary to include either the volume or the page number of the consolidation. The inclusion of the year is optional.

The Alberta regulations are consolidated annually in a bound volume called "Alberta Regulations" which contains a cumulative index of regulations arranged in alphabetical order by the short title of the enabling statute.

(1) Finding Alberta Regulations

The index in each bound volume of Alberta regulations lists all regulations filed under the *Regulations Act* that are still in force as of December 31 of the given year. Thus, to find Alberta regulations (as well as amendments thereto), consult the index in the most recent annual volume of the regulations.

(2) Updating Alberta Regulations

To find regulations and amendments published after the latest annual volume, refer to a "Cumulative Index" issued in conjunction with *The Alberta Gazette, Part II*. Then refer to individual issues of *The Alberta Gazette, Part II*, which were published after the latest "Cumulative Index". As a final check, consult *Canadian Current Law — Legislation*.

NOTE: In the early part of the year you may find the "Cumulative Index" for the last calendar year, as well as for the current year.

(3) Coming Into Force

An Alberta regulation comes into force on the day it is filed, unless a later date is provided. The filing date appears under the title (*Regulations Act*, R.S.A. 2000, c. R-14, s. 2(2)).

(4) Citation

Alberta regulations are cited to a regulation number printed in The *Alberta Gazette*. For example, the Adoption Regulation, which was filed in 2002, is cited:

Alta. Reg. 37/2002.

(C) BRITISH COLUMBIA REGULATIONS

Regulations are published in *The British Columbia Gazette, Part II*, which is issued every two weeks. The regulations are consolidated in a multi-volume looseleaf set. The regulations are listed under the enabling statutes in the "Table of Contents". New regulations and amendments to regulations are incorporated in the consolidation up to the date noted at the bottom of the pages containing the text of the regulations. Any amendments subsequent to that date may be found in *The British Columbia Gazette, Part II*.

(1) Finding British Columbia Regulations

To find a British Columbia regulation (or an amendment to a regulation), consult the "Index of Current B.C. Regulations" in volume 1 of the consolidation or in the paperback bi-annual publication of the Ministry of the Attorney General. The notation at the bottom left corner of each page indicates the currency of the index.

(2) Updating British Columbia Regulations

To find new regulations or amendments to regulations which may have been published after the cut-off date for the consolidation, refer to the "Index to Published Regulations", found at the back of the latest bound annual volume of the collected parts of *The British Columbia Gazette, Part II*. Since 1985, these bound volumes have been titled "British Columbia Regulations". If this is not as current as the paperback index or the index in the consolidation, consult the indices to the individual paper parts of *The British Columbia Gazette, Part II*, after the cut-off date noted in the "Index to Current B.C. Regulations". As a final check refer to *Canadian Current Law — Legislation*.

(3) Coming Into Force

A British Columbia regulation comes into force on the day it is deposited with the Registrar, unless a day is specifically prescribed, or a later date is presented in the regulations or an earlier date is authorized by the enabling statute (*Regulations Act*, R.S.B.C. 1996, c. 402, s. 4(1)).

(4) Citation

British Columbia regulations are cited to a regulation number printed in *The British Columbia Gazette, Part II*. For example, the *Adoption Reunion Regulation*, which was deposited with the Registrar of Regulations in 1991, is cited:

B.C. Reg. 257/91.

(D) MANITOBA REGULATIONS

Regulations are published in *The Manitoba Gazette, Part II*, which is issued every week. Regulations are collected in annual volumes, which also contain an "Index to Regulations Registered under the Regulations Act in Force as of December 31, [year]" (yellow pages). This is a cumulative index of all regulations to the end of the given year. It is arranged according to enabling statute. A quarterly index of regulations is published in *The Manitoba Gazette, Part II*. Generally, no regulations are published in the *Continuing Consolidation of the Statutes of Manitoba* (C.C.S.M.). An index of regulations is provided in the "Information Tables". The index is current to the date specified at the bottom of each page of the index.

(1) Finding Manitoba Regulations

To find Manitoba regulations, consult the "Index of Regulations Registered under the *Regulations Act* in force as of December 31, [year of volume]" (yellow pages) published in the latest bound annual volume of *The Manitoba Gazette, Part II*, or as a separate insert in an issue of *The Manitoba Gazette, Part II*, for the current year. This index indicates any amendments.

(2) Updating Manitoba Regulations

To check for new regulations and recent amendments for the current year, consult the "Table of Contents" in *The Manitoba Gazette, Part II*. Alternatively, refer to *Canadian Current Law — Legislation*.

(3) Coming Into Force

Unless a later day is provided, Manitoba regulations come into force on the day of filing with the Registrar. This date is indicated under the title of the regulation (*The Regulations Act*, S.M. 1988-89, c. 7, C.C.S.M. R60, s. 3).

(4) Citation

Regulations are cited with reference to a regulation number in *The Manitoba Gazette, Part II*. For example, *The Documentation for Verifying Age Regulation-Non-Smokers/Health Protection Act*, which was filed in 2002 is cited:

Man. Reg. 170/2002.

In 1987 and 1988, most of Manitoba's regulations were re-enacted in French and English. When citing a regulation that was re-enacted, an "R" is added to the number. For example, *The Tobacco Tax Regulation* is cited as follows:

Man. Reg. 77/88 R.

Amendments to *The Tobacco Tax Regulation* are cited:

Man. Reg. 77/88 R, as am. by 345/88; 476/88; 156/89; 236/90; 99/91; 211/93; 20/95; 133/95; 44/2001; 104/2002.

NOTE: Each of the amended regulations is published in English and in French.

(E) NEW BRUNSWICK REGULATIONS

New Brunswick regulations are published in *The Royal Gazette* under the heading "Statutory Orders and Regulations, Part II". The regulations are collected in annual volumes. Each volume contains a "Cumulative Index of New Brunswick Regulations" and a "Table of New Brunswick Regulations Subject Matter".[20] There is also a multi-volume consolidated looseleaf edition for these regulations.

---

[20] If more than one volume is published for the year, the first volume includes the "Subject Matter" index and, the second volume, the "Cumulative Index".

The consolidation was effective as of November 1, 1984. New regulations and amendments are incorporated into the looseleaf set on a regular basis. The cut-off date for the most recent releases for the consolidation is indicated at the beginning of volume 1. Regulations are filed under the name of the enabling statute. The consolidation includes a "Table of Contents" which lists in order of appearance all regulations contained in the consolidation, a "Cumulative Index of New Brunswick Regulations" which lists all regulations recorded as filed with the Registrar of Regulations from 1963 to the date of consolidation and an index of "Not Consolidated Not Repealed Regulations".

(1) Finding New Brunswick Regulations

To find New Brunswick regulations, refer to the "Cumulative Index" in the last volume of the consolidated looseleaf edition of the *Regulations of New Brunswick*. It contains a list of the regulations in force as of the date of publication, with amendments.[21]

(2) Updating New Brunswick Regulations

To find the most recent regulations or amendments to regulations, check the paperbound "Index" of *The Royal Gazette* published after the cut-off date noted in the "Cumulative Index" to the consolidation, if available. As well, refer to the heading "Statutory Orders and Regulations" in individual issues of *The Royal Gazette* after the cut-off dates noted in the indices and to *Canadian Current Law — Legislation*.

(3) Coming Into Force

Unless a later date is specified, New Brunswick regulations come into force on the date of filing. The date of filing is indicated beneath the title of the regulation (*Regulations Act*, S.N.B. 1991, c. R-7.1, s. 3).

(4) Citation

New Brunswick regulations are cited to a regulation number printed in *The Royal Gazette*. For example, the *District Education Council Election Regulation — Regulation Act*, which was filed in New Brunswick in 2001, is cited:

N.B. Reg. 2001-23.[22]

---

[21] If the volume is not available, refer to the "Cumulative Index" in the latest annual volume of the *Regulations of New Brunswick*; although this will not usually be as current as the index in the consolidation.

[22] In citing New Brunswick regulations, the year appears first and the number of the regulation appears second.

(F) NEWFOUNDLAND REGULATIONS

The Newfoundland regulations are published in *The Newfoundland Gazette, Part II*, issued every week. The Office of the Legislative Counsel publishes an *Index of Subordinate Legislation* for *The Newfoundland Gazette*. The *Index* is arranged alphabetically with respect to the acts that provide for the making of the subordinate legislation. The *Index* is updated and printed on a regular basis. The title page indicates the cut-off date for entries to the *Index*.

(1) Finding Newfoundland Regulations

To find a Newfoundland regulation or an amendment, refer to the *Index of Subordinate Legislation*. The regulations appear under the name of the enabling statute. There are separate entries for the number of the regulation, amendments to the regulation and its location in *The Newfoundland Gazette*.

(2) Updating Newfoundland Regulations

To find regulations published after the cut-off date for the *Index of Subordinate Legislation* (noted on the second page of the *Index*), refer to the "Continuing Index of Subordinate Legislation" in the issues of *The Newfoundland Gazette, Part II*, published after the cut-off date. Also check *Canadian Current Law — Legislation*.

(3) Coming Into Force

Unless another day is provided, subordinate legislation comes into force on the day it is published (*Statutes and Subordinate Legislation Act*, R.S.N. 1990, c. S-27, s. 10(2), as am. by S.N. 1996, c. R-10.1, s. 69(1)).

(4) Citation

Newfoundland regulations are cited to a regulation number printed in *The Newfoundland Gazette, Part II*. For example, the *Archives Public Records Management Regulations, 1991* and the *Endangered Species Regulations — Endangered Species Act*, which were assented to in 2002, are cited:

Nfld. Reg. 93/91.
N.L. Reg. 57/02.

(G) NORTHWEST TERRITORIES REGULATIONS

Northwest Territories regulations are published in the *Northwest Territories Gazette, Part II*, under the heading "Regulations". These are collected in annual binders, and each binder contains a cumulative index of regulations to the cut-off date, with amendments. Table A and Table B of the index list repealed and spent regulations, respectively, and Table C (pink and yellow-page inserts) lists regulations currently in force, under their enabling statutes. A complete revision of the regulations was published in five volumes in 1990.

(1) Finding Northwest Territories Regulations

To find Northwest Territories regulations, refer to Table C (pink-page sections) following the tab "Part 2" in a recent *Northwest Territories Gazette* binder. It contains a list of the regulations in force as of the date of publication, with amendments.

(2) Updating Northwest Territories Regulations

To find new regulations or amendments subsequent to the cut-off date for Table C, refer to the heading "Regulations" in individual issues of the *Northwest Territories Gazette, Part II*. Also check *Canadian Current Law — Legislation*.

(3) Coming Into Force

Unless a different date is specified, Northwest Territories regulations come into force on the day of registration. This date is indicated in the *Northwest Territories Gazette* (*Statutory Instruments Act*, R.S.N.W.T. 1988, c. S-13, s. 8).

(4) Citation

Regulations published in the revision are cited to the *Revised Regulations of the Northwest Territories, 1990*. For example, the Fort Good Hope Snowmobile Regulations, are cited:

R.R.N.W.T. 1990, c. A-3.

Amendments to the revision are cited, first, to the revision and, second, to a regulation number printed in the *Northwest Territories Gazette, Part II*. For example, the *Petroleum Products Tax Regulations*, which were amended by regulation number 081 in 1992, number 96 in 1994 and so on are cited:

R.R.N.W.T. 1990, c. P-3, as am. by N.W.T. Reg. R-081-92; R-096-94; R-064-95; R-073-95; R-023-97.

New regulations passed since the revision are cited by reference to a regulation number in the *Northwest Territories Gazette, Part II*. For example, the *Elections Forms Regulations — Elections Act*, which were filed in 2003, are cited:

N.W.T. Reg. R-051-2003.[23]

(H) NOVA SCOTIA REGULATIONS

Nova Scotia regulations have been published in the *Royal Gazette, Part II*, since 1977. There is no current official consolidation or revision of the regulations of Nova Scotia. A bi-weekly and an annual index are published in conjunction with the *Royal Gazette, Part II*.[24]

NOTE: A five-volume set, *Regulations of Nova Scotia*, was issued for the years 1973 to 1977. Prior to this, selected regulations were published in the sessional volumes of the *Statutes of Nova Scotia* (1943 to 1973) under the heading "Rules and Regulations".

(1) Finding Nova Scotia Regulations

To find Nova Scotia regulations, refer to the "cumulative index" in the annual issue of the *Royal Gazette, Part II* commencing with 1977.[25]

NOTE: For 1973 to 1977, refer to *Regulations of Nova Scotia*. Finding regulations prior to 1973 requires perseverance. Assistance may be obtained by referring to the "Index to the Regulations" for 1942 to 1970, contained in the 1970-71 volume of the *Statutes of Nova Scotia*, or to a single-volume consolidation of selected regulations published in 1942.

(2) Updating Nova Scotia Regulations

To check for new regulations and amendments since the last annual index, refer to the bi-weekly index which is published in conjunction with the *Royal Gazette, Part II*. Also check *Canadian Current Law — Legislation*.

(3) Coming Into Force

Unless a later date is provided, a regulation comes into force on the day it is filed with the Registrar of Regulations (*Regulations Act*, R.S.N.S. 1989, c. 393, s. 3(6) (s. 3(6) not yet proclaimed)).

---

[23] The prescribed method of determining regulation numbers is derived from the *Revised Regulations*, R.R.N.W.T. 1980, Reg. 239, s. 4(6).

[24] The Registrar of Regulations publishes an unofficial *Sectional Index to Nova Scotia Regulations*. This looseleaf index lists all post-1977 regulations currently in force, up to the cut-off date at the front of the binder. Part A of the *Index* has the name of each regulation listed under its enabling statute, and cross-indexes each statute to a more detailed index in Part B. Part B also lists regulations by their respective statutes, lists amendments by section, and provides a history of repealed regulations. Part C is a consolidated list of proclamations.

[25] Alternatively, simply refer to the listing of the regulation under its enabling statute in Part B of the *Sectional Index*.

(4) Citation

Current Nova Scotia regulations are cited to a regulation number printed in the *Royal Gazette, Part II*. For example, the *Psychologists Regulations — Psychologists Act* which were filed in 2002 are cited:

N.S. Reg. 70/2002.

(I) ONTARIO REGULATIONS

Regulations are published in *The Ontario Gazette*, which is issued every week. They are consolidated in annual volumes with a cumulative "Table of Regulations". A complete revision of the regulations was published in 1990. This nine-volume set brings together all regulations in force on December 31, 1990. A three-volume supplement to the revision contains regulations after the cut-off date of December 31, 1990 and before November 16, 1992, the day the revision was proclaimed in force.

(1) Finding Ontario Regulations

To find Ontario regulations, refer to the "Table of Regulations" in the latest bound annual volume of the *Statutes of Ontario* or the *Ontario Regulations*. This shows, *inter alia*, the regulations contained in the revision and subsequent regulations and amendments to regulations to December 31 of the last calendar year of publication. The table has three columns: the first gives the number of the regulation, if it is located in the revision; the second gives the number of the regulation, if it was made after December 31, 1990; and the third shows amendments to the regulations. Alternatively, refer to Carswell's *Ontario Regulations Service* (check the annual consolidated index and the monthly cumulative index) and Quicklaw's Regulations of Ontario (RO) database.

(2) Updating Ontario Regulations

To check for new regulations and amendments to regulations after the cut-off date noted above, refer to the most recent "Table of Regulations" which is issued with a weekly edition of *The Ontario Gazette*. As well, consult the semi-annual index of *The Ontario Gazette* (if available) and the index on the overleaf of the back cover of each subsequent issue of the *Gazette* (not included in the "Table of Regulations" or the semi-annual index) under the heading "Publications under the Regulations Act". Refer as well to *Canadian Current Law — Legislation*.

(3) Coming Into Force

Unless otherwise stated, an Ontario regulation comes into effect on the day it is filed. The filing date is indicated immediately beneath the title of the regulation (*Regulations Act*, R.S.O. 1990, c. R.21, s. 3).

(4) Citation

Regulations published in the revision are cited to the *Revised Regulations of Ontario*. For example, the *Bailiffs Act Regulation*, which is the 53rd regulation in the revision, is cited:

R.R.O. 1990, Reg. 53.

Amendments to the revision are cited, first, to the revision and, second, to a regulation number printed in *The Ontario Gazette*. For example, the *Bailiffs Act Regulation*, which appeared as number 53 in the revision and was amended by regulation number 689 in 1991, and regulation number 513 in 1997 is cited:

R.R.O. 1990, Reg. 53, as am. by O. Reg. 689/91; 513/97.

New regulations passed since the revision are cited by reference to a regulation number in *The Ontario Gazette*. For example. the *Identification Regulation*, made under the *Regulation Act, 1994*, is cited:

O. Reg. 574/94.

(J) PRINCE EDWARD ISLAND REGULATIONS

Regulations are published in the *Royal Gazette, Part II*, and issued every week. The regulations are consolidated in looseleaf binders, *The Revised Regulations of Prince Edward Island*.

New regulations and amendments to regulations found in the revision are incorporated on a continuing basis. The cut-off date for the revision is noted on the pages of the regulations. The revision contains a "Table of Contents" which lists the regulations under the name of the enabling statute. It also includes a "Table of Regulations" (blue pages) which provides a history of regulating provisions, including their derivations and modifications.

(1) Finding Prince Edward Island Regulations

To find a Prince Edward Island regulation, refer to the "Table of Contents" in the revision under the name of the enabling statute. To check for amendments, consult the "Table of Regulations".

(2) Updating Prince Edward Island Regulations

To find new regulations and amendments to regulations, refer to the "Continuing Index to the Regulations of Prince Edward Island" and to the "Regulations

Index" in all issues of the *Royal Gazette, Part II*,[26] after the cut-off date for the latest "Table of Regulations". Refer as well to *Canadian Current Law — Legislation*.

(3) Coming Into Force

Every regulation not expressed to come into force on a particular day comes into force on the day the regulation is published in the *Royal Gazette* (*Interpretation Act*, R.S.P.E.I. 1988, c. I-8, s. 3(4)).

(4) Citation

Prince Edward Island regulations published in the revision are cited to the *Revised Regulations of Prince Edward Island*. The "EC number (Executive Council)" of revised regulations is found in the *"Table of Regulations"* at the back of the binder. For example, the *Animal Protection Regulations*, are cited:

R.R.P.E.I. EC1990-71.

Regulations not yet included in the revision are cited to a regulation number printed in the *Royal Gazette, Part II*. For example, the *Education Negotiating Agency Regulations Amendment*, which were issued in 1999, are cited:

P.E.I. Reg. EC1999-86.

(K) QUÉBEC REGULATIONS

Regulations are published in the *Québec Official Gazette, Part II*, which is issued every week. The regulations are consolidated in a 12-volume set, the *Revised Regulations of Québec, 1981*. A companion work, the *Tableau des modifications et index sommaire*[27] permits access to the revision and indicates amendments to regulations. This volume is updated and replaced once or twice annually. An earlier work, the *Index cumulatif des textes reglementaires de 1867 au 1er juillet 1981* covers regulations and amendments before the revision.

(1) Finding Québec Regulations

To find Québec regulations, consult the "Tableau des modifications" in the *Tableau des modifications et index sommaire*. The cut-off date for the table is indicated on the title page.

---

[26] This will usually entail a search through the individual issues of the *Royal Gazette, Part II*, for the current year.

[27] Prior to 1985, this work was referred to as the *Index cumulatif des actes reglementaires*.

(2) Updating Québec Regulations

To check for new regulations and amendments to regulations after the cut-off date in the *Tableau des modifications et index sommaire*, refer to the latest paper part "Index Statutory Instruments" issued as part of the *Québec Official Gazette, Part II*. Alternatively, it may be easier to check under the heading "Regulations", in the "Table of Contents" in the back pages of the "Index". Also check *Canadian Current Law — Legislation*.

(3) Coming Into Force

Unless another date is specified, a regulation comes into force 15 days after the date of publication in the *Québec Official Gazette* (*Regulations Act*, R.S.Q. c. R-18.1, s. 17).

(4) Citation

Regulations published in the revision are cited to the Revised Regulations of Québec. For example, the *Regulation Respecting the Quality of the Work Environment* is cited:

R.R.Q. 1981, c. S-2.1, r. 15.

Amendments to the revision are cited, first, to the revision and, second, to a regulation number printed in the *Québec Official Gazette*. For example, an amendment to the *Regulation Respecting Waterworks and Sewer Services* is cited:

R.R.Q. 1981, c. Q-2, r. 7; as am. by O.C. 1160-1984 G.O.Q. 1984.II.1820; O.C. 647-2001, G.O.Q. 2001.II.2641.

A textual reference will appear in the following form:

The *Regulation Respecting the Sale of Livestock by Auction*, R.R.Q. 1981, c. P-42, r. 4, made under the *Animal Health Protection Act*, R.S.Q. c. P-42, s. 45, as amended by O.C. 1262-1986, 20 August 1986, G.O.Q. 1986.II.3749; O.C. 1135-1987, 22 July 1987, G.O.Q. 1987.II.5297; O.C. 1766-1990, 19 December 1990, G.O.Q. 1990.II.1776; O.C. 337-1993, 17 March 1993, G.O.Q. 1993.II.1954; O.C. 1830-1993, 29 December 1993, G.O.Q. 1993.II.7013. O.C. 362-2000, April 12 2002, G.O.Q. 2000.II.1930.

New regulations passed after the revision are cited by referring to a regulation number in the *Québec Official Gazette*. For example, the *Capitalization Loan Program* is cited:

O.C. 1911-85, G.O.Q. 1985.II.3963; as am. by O.C. 782-86, G.O.Q. 1986.II.1040.

NOTE: In the examples, the citations include a reference to the *Québec Official Gazette.*

(L) SASKATCHEWAN REGULATIONS

There are two official sources of Saskatchewan regulations: *The Saskatchewan Gazette, Part II,* and *The Saskatchewan Gazette, Part III. Part II* contains revised regulations and amendments to revised regulations. The regulations printed in *Part III* are new regulations and amendments to existing regulations which have not been revised.[28]

Saskatchewan regulations have been consolidated in a multi-volume looseleaf set entitled *The Regulations of Saskatchewan.* This looseleaf publication consists of consolidations of *The Revised Regulations of Saskatchewan* and the amendments to those regulations printed in *The Saskatchewan Gazette, Part II.* The cut-off date for the consolidation is indicated on the first page. The looseleaf publication is supplemented semi-annually. Saskatchewan regulations printed in *Part III* are not included in the consolidation.

(1) Finding Saskatchewan Regulations

To find Saskatchewan regulations and amendments to the regulations, refer to the "Table of Regulations" printed in the *Tables to the Statutes of Saskatchewan and Saskatchewan Regulations.* As well, refer to the "Table of Repealed Revised Regulations" in the same publication.

(2) Updating Saskatchewan Regulations

To find regulations and amendments which are not included in the "Table of Regulations" and the "Table of Repealed Revised Regulations", refer to *Canadian Current Law — Legislation* or to the *Saskatchewan Decisions Citator.* There is also an "Index of Revised Regulations" and an "Index of Unrevised Regulations" published in the current paper part of *The Saskatchewan Gazette.*

(3) Coming Into Force

A Saskatchewan regulation comes into force on the day it is published, if no other date is specified, or on the day it is filed, if it has been exempted from publication and no other date is specified (*The Regulations Act,* S.S. 1995, R.16.2, s. 5).

---

[28] The regulations printed in *Part II* are a component of the *Revised Regulations of Saskatchewan* which are being compiled over a period of years.

(4) Citation

The *Revised Regulations of Saskatchewan* are cited to their short titles, which appear in section 1 of the regulations, together with their location in *The Revised Regulations of Saskatchewan*. For example, *The Ethanol Fuel Act*, passed in 2003 is cited:

R.R.S. 2002, c. E-11.1, Reg. 1, O.C. 750/2002.

An amendment to a revised regulation is given a Saskatchewan regulation number in *The Saskatchewan Gazette*. For example, the amendment to The *Municipal Police Equipment Regulations, 1991*, made under the authority of The *Police Act*, are cited:

R.R.S. 1991, c. P-15.01, Reg. 3, O.C. 920/1991, as am. by S. Reg. 66/93; 19/94; 81/95; 77/97; 44/2000; 101/2002.

Regulations which have not been revised are given a Saskatchewan regulation number. For example, The *Dangerous Goods Transportation Amendment Regulations*, which was issued in 2002, are cited:

S. Reg. 110/2002.

The *Day Care Amendment Regulations, 1986*, amending *The Day Care Regulations* of 1975 (which have not been revised to date), are cited:

S. Reg. 213/75, as am. by 63/86.

(M) YUKON REGULATIONS

Regulations of the Yukon Territory are published in a continuing looseleaf consolidation; they do not always appear in *The Yukon Gazette*, as only the titles of the regulations are required to be published there. The first volume of the consolidation contains a cumulative "Index of Regulations in Force", listing all regulations under their respective enabling statutes and amendments.

(1) Finding Yukon Regulations

To find Yukon regulations, refer to the "Index of Regulations in Force" in the first binder of the consolidation, under the regulation's enabling statute. Besides indicating the regulation number, the index also cross-indexes each statute with a corresponding tab number in the consolidation; each tab marks the location of all regulations enacted pursuant to that statute. Unpublished regulations can be obtained from the Yukon government.

(2) Updating Yukon Regulations

To find the titles of new regulations, or amendments subsequent to the latest update of the consolidation, refer to the heading "Regulations" in *The Yukon Gazette, Part II*, or to *Canadian Current Law — Legislation*.

(3) Coming Into Force

Unless a later date is specified, Yukon regulations come into force on the date of filing. This date is printed above the regulation's title in *The Yukon Gazette* (*Regulations Act*, R.S.Y.T. 1986, c. 151, s. 2(2)).

(4) Citation

Yukon regulations are cited to the numbers of the Orders-in-Council registering them and the years of registration. For example, the *Activities Requiring Environmental Assessment Regulation*, which were registered by the 67th Order-in-Council of 2003, are cited:

Yukon O.I.C. 2003/67.

Amendments are cited in a similar manner. For example, the 1987 *Equipment Regulations — Motor Vehicles Act*, which was amended in 1987, 1988 and 2000 is cited:

Yukon O.I.C. 1987/86; 1987/191; 1988/131; 2000/50.

(N) NUNAVUT

Regulations of Nunavut are published in the *Nunavut Gazette, Part II* on a monthly basis. Currently it is not being bound annually, but is available online at <http://www.nunavutcourtofjustice.ca/library/gazette>.

(1) Finding Nunavut Regulations

To find Nunavut regulations the only method currently available is to search the *Gazette* online by date. Currently there is no searchable, cumulative index.

(2) Updating Nunavut Regulations

To find the titles of new regulations you can consult the *Gazette, Part II* online, again there is no searchable or cumulative index yet.

(3) Coming Into Force

Unless a different date is specified, Nunavut regulations come into force on the day of registration. This date is indicated in the *Nunavut Gazette* (*Statutory Instruments Act*, R.S.N.W.T. 1988, c. S-13, s. 8, as enacted for Nunavut, pursuant to the *Nunavut Act*, S.C. 1993, c. 28).

(4) Citation

Regulations are cited to a regulation number in the *Nunavut Gazette, Part II*. For example, *the Youth Court Jurisdiction Regulations* filed under the *Justice of the Peace Act* is cited:

Nu. Reg. R-004-2002.

(O) REGULATIONS ONLINE

The easiest way to search for regulations online is through one of the central Canadian portals: <http://www.canlii.org> and <http://www.legis.ca>. Both sites have links to the individual provincial and federal government sites that publish the regulations. Links to P.E.I. and Newfoundland-Labrador statutes are only available on legis.ca. Canlii.org also maintains its own searchable library for statutes and regulations for: Canada (federal), Alberta, Saskatchewan, Manitoba, Ontario, Quebec, New Brunswick, and Nova Scotia. The canlii.org searchable database is a more efficient tool than the provincial or federal websites alphabetical indexes.

Canada	<http://laws.justice.gc.ca/>
British Columbia	<http://www.qp.gov.bc.ca/statreg/>
Alberta	<http://www.qp.gov.ab.ca/>
Saskatchewan	<http://www.qp.gov.sk.ca/>
Manitoba	<http://www.gov.mb.ca/chc/statpub/>
Ontario	<http://www.e-laws.gov.on.ca/>
Quebec	<http://publicationsduquebec.gouv.qc.ca/home.php>
New Brunswick	<http://www.gnb.ca/0062/acts/acts-e.asp>
Nova Scotia	<http://www.gov.ns.ca/legi/legc/>
Prince Edward Island	Not Online
Newfoundland	<http://www.gov.nf.ca/hoa/sr/>
Yukon	<http://www.canlii.org/yk/sta/index.html>
Northwest Territories	<http://www.canlii.ca/nt/sta/>
Nunavut	<http://www.canlii.org/nu/sta/>

2. Subordinate Legislation of the United Kingdom

As mentioned earlier, in the United Kingdom rules and regulations are referred to as "Statutory Instruments" and, as in Canada, all statutory instruments enacted under the authority of a statute must be published within a prescribed period. There are three main sources for the statutory instruments of the United Kingdom.

(A) MAIN SOURCES

(1) Statutory Rules, Orders, and Statutory Instruments (Revised to December 31, 1948)

This is the official source of statutory instruments for the United Kingdom. It is a 25-volume set which revises and consolidates all the statutory instruments in force in the United Kingdom as of December 31, 1948. The set is arranged by subject-matter and the last volume of the set includes indices and tables.

(2) Statutory Instruments

This is the successor to *Statutory Rules, Orders and Statutory Instruments*. Individual volumes are issued every four months. This set also includes indices and tables. A new format was introduced in 1987; refer to the "Preface" (found in Part I, Section I) for a detailed description of the contents.

(3) Halsbury's Statutory Instruments

This multi-volume set covers every statutory instrument of general application in force in England and Wales. The set is arranged by subject-matter. It reprints the text of selected statutory instruments and provides summaries and notations for the others. The set is kept up to date with "reissue" volumes (the title page notes the effective date of reissue) and a set of looseleaf service binders. The cut-off date for materials included in each section of the binders is noted on the tab page or the following page.

The Consolidated Index for *Halsbury's Statutory Instruments* and the "service binders" are the main research tools for finding U.K. regulations.

C. CASE REPORTS

Since the middle of the last century, approximately 200 distinct report series have been published in Canada and the United Kingdom. A few, like the *Chancery Reports*, have been published continuously since that time. Many more flourished for a few years and then ceased publication; nonetheless, they are retained on library shelves because they usually contain judgments which do not appear elsewhere. Throughout this period, as well, most case reports have covered a particular jurisdiction or court. Recently, there has been a rapid growth in case reports exclusively concerned with special areas of the law. The following discussion of case reports is in five parts:

(1)   publication;
(2)   format;
(3)   Canadian case reports;
(4)   English case reports; and
(5)   general rules of citation.

1. Publication

The publication of law reports in Canada is carried out largely by private publishing houses.[29] The publishers gather the relevant written judgments[30] from the various courts soon after they have been delivered and publish them in small groups in paperbound form[31] under a particular name.[32] These unbound parts may be issued weekly, bi-weekly, monthly, or eight to ten times a year. The cases are arranged more or less chronologically. The paperbound parts are later discarded when replaced by bound volumes.

The bound volumes of English and Canadian reports are generally arranged into series or sets, each covering a specific period. One example is the *All England Law Reports* set which consists, at present, of over 166 volumes spanning the period 1936 to 2003. Another example is the *Dominion Law Reports*. At present, this set consists of approximately 577 volumes covering the period 1912 to 2003.[33] A final example is the *Western Weekly Digest*, a short-lived publication which consists of two volumes covering the period 1975 to 1976.

2. Format

Case reports in English and Canadian report series follow the same basic format. The following information will generally be included:

(i)   the full name of the judgment;
(ii)   the date the decision was rendered;
(iii) the court (in multi-jurisdictional reports);
(iv)   the judge or judges;
(v)   the counsel;
(vi)   catchwords (a summary of key facts and legal principles);
(vii) headnote (a summary of facts and the judgment);
(viii) notes (provide cross-reference to other major works);
(ix)   annotation (for selected cases in some reports);
(x)   a list of cases, statutes, rules and authorities cited;
(xi)   the summarized arguments of counsel (in some reports);

---

[29] The *Supreme Court of Canada Reports* and *Federal Court Reports* are two notable exceptions. Both are published by the Queen's Printer.

[30] Not all cases heard in Canada are reported; although, most decisions of superior courts are reported and some report series make a point of reporting lower court judgments which raise interesting points of law.

[31] The release of advance paperbound parts before the publication of bound volumes is a relatively recent practice.

[32] A few examples are *Carswell's Practice Cases*, *Canadian Cases on the Law of Insurance*, *Ontario Law Reports* and *Canada Tax Cases*.

[33] For the purposes of citation, this set is categorized into four series. For further discussion of the citation of the *Dominion Law Reports*, see *infra* at Section C, 3(A)(1).

(xii)   the text of the decision or decisions; and order.

3. Canadian Case Reports

For the purposes of description, Canadian case reports may be classified as follows:

(a)   national reports;
(b)   regional reports;
(c)   provincial reports; and
(d)   subject reports.

The case reports described below are the most important of the modern Canadian case reports.

NOTE: Case reports may also be classified as official, semi-official, and unofficial. Official reports are those published under the authority of the court whose decisions are reported. Unofficial reports are those published without authority by private organizations. Semi-official reports fall midway between the two: they are privately published but have been accorded a measure of authority through custom or sponsorship. The distinction may be important for two reasons. First, where there is a discrepancy among reports, the official report is preferred to the unofficial. Second, when citing collateral reports, the official report should be cited before the semi-official and the semi-official report should be cited before the unofficial. See Appendix VII for a classification of reports in accordance with the above-noted designations.

Case Report Citation

Style of cause (1) then **year (2)** (round brackets for year of case) or [square brackets if the report is indexed by year published], **Volume number (3)** then **Abbreviation of Series (4)** (See Appendix V for a list of abbreviations for major Canadian report series) then **Page number (5)** then **Abbreviation of the court (6)** where the case was heard (see Appendix IV for list of common court abbreviations).

| | 1 | | 2 | 3 | 4 | | 5 | 6 |

E.G. *Apotex Inc. v. AstraZeneca Canada Inc.* (2003), 226 D.L.R. (4th) 422 (F.C.A.).

(A) National Reports

(1) Dominion Law Reports, 1912 to date (cited D.L.R.)

Since 1912, the unofficial *Dominion Law Reports* have provided the most extensive coverage of Canadian cases. The set includes a wide selection of decisions
on all branches of the law from all jurisdictions of Canada. At present, it is published in weekly paperbound parts which are later consolidated in bound volumes. For the purposes of citation, there have been five sets:

    (i)   1912 to 1922. The volumes are numbered consecutively throughout this
           period.

Example:
Re Walker (1919), 49 D.L.R. 415 (Ont. C.A.).

    (ii)   1923 to 1955. The volumes are numbered consecutively throughout
           each year.

Example:
Guay v. Sun Publishing Co., [1953] 4 D.L.R. 577 (S.C.C.).

    (iii)   1956 to 1968. The volumes are numbered consecutively throughout this
           period. This series is distinguished from its predecessors by inserting
           (2d) after "D.L.R.".

Example:
Smuck v. Seburn (1968), 65 D.L.R. (2d) 692 (Ont. H.C.J.).

    (iv)   1969 to 1984. The volumes are numbered consecutively throughout this
           period. This series is distinguished from its predecessors by inserting
           (3d) after "D.L.R.".

Example:
Furber v. Furber (1972), 31 D.L.R. (3d) 642 (B.C.S.C.).

    (v)   1984 to date. The volumes are numbered consecutively throughout this
           period. This series is distinguished from its predecessors by inserting
           (4th) after "D.L.R.".

Examples:
Demeter v. British Pacific Life Insurance Co. (1984), 13 D.L.R. (4th) 318
(Ont. C.A.).
Jabbaz v. Mouammar (2003), 226 D.L.R. (4th) 494 (Ont. C.A.).

There are four important companion publications to the *Dominion Law
Reports*:

(i)   Dominion Law Reports (Second Series) Consolidated Table of Cases;
(ii) Dominion Law Reports Annotation Service (Second and Third Series) and Consolidated Table of Cases (Third Series);
(iii) Dominion Law Reports (Third Series) Index, Volumes 1 to 150; and
(iv) Dominion Law Reports (Fourth Series) Index Annotations and Table of Cases (beginning with Volume 1, 1988).

NOTE: The annotation service acts as a citator for cases reported in the *Dominion Law Reports*. The purpose of the citator is to show whether a reported case has been appealed or judicially considered elsewhere in the set.

These indices are organized according to a unique classification scheme devised by the reports' publisher, Canada Law Book. This scheme lists key headings and subheadings on every topic and appears at the front of every index volume. Thus, when researching the *Dominion Law Reports*, the student should first examine this scheme for the key headings pertaining to the subject under investigation. Once these are known, the student then need only look under these same headings in the index. This will refer the student to pertinent cases. Furthermore, each listing includes a "catchline", which is a short précis of the specific questions decided in each case, in addition to the volume and page number where it can be found.

(2) Supreme Court Reports, 1876 to date (cited S.C.R.)

This set has been the official report series of the Supreme Court of Canada since that court was established in 1875. It contains virtually all the decisions of the Supreme Court of Canada. It is printed in both French and English. For the purpose of citation, it is useful to distinguish three separate publishing periods:

(i)   1876 to 1922. The volumes are numbered consecutively throughout this period and called *Reports of the Supreme Court of Canada* but are referred to as the *Supreme Court Reports*.

Example:
Dominion Fire Insurance Co. v. Nakata (1915), 52 S.C.R. 294.

(ii) 1923 to 1975. The volumes are indicated by the year of publication and are called *Canada Law Reports, Supreme Court* but are referred to as the *Supreme Court Reports*.

Example:
Quebec Asbestos Corp. v. Couture, [1929] S.C.R. 166.

(iii) 1975 to date. The volumes are numbered consecutively through each year and are called *Canada, Supreme Court Reports* but are referred to as *Supreme Court Reports*.

Examples:
Halifax (City) v. S. Cunard & Co., [1975] 1 S.C.R. 458.
R. v. Fliss, [2002] 1 S.C.R. 535.

NOTE: Judgments of the current year are published in paperbound parts (red jacket).

(3) Canada Federal Court Reports,[34] 1971 to date (cited F.C.)

This series has been the official report of the Federal Court of Canada since that court was established in 1971. The *Federal Court Reports* are printed in both French and English and contain virtually all decisions since the Court's inception. A selection of judgments is reported and all judgments not reported are digested.

Examples:
Legault v. Canada (Minister of Citizenship and Immigration), [2002] 4 F.C. 358.
Smythe v. Minister of National Revenue, [1968] 2 Ex. C.R. 189.

(4) Federal Trial Reports, 1986 to date (cited F.T.R.)

This is a series of law reports covering judgments of the Trial Division of the Federal Court of Canada. It is an unofficial publication of the Maritime Law Book Company and is part of the National Reporter System.

Example:
Toys "R" Us (Canada) Ltd. v. Manjel Inc. (2003), 229 F.T.R. 58.

It is serviced with a digest which includes 15 different consolidated indices. The main finding aid is the "Topical Index", found in each volume, which incorporates a key number classification system. A student may find a key number (all points of law in the reports have a key number) by referring to the looseleaf *Master Key Word Index*. This index provides cross-references to the "Topical Index" and replaces the "Key Word Index" in the volumes and digests. Use the *Master Key Word Index* to find a key number. For example, if you are looking for cases on "entrapment", the following entry is in the *Master Key Word Index*:

Entrapment — Criminal Law 205

---

[34] The predecessor of the Federal Court was the Exchequer Court which was established in 1875. From its inception to 1922, decisions of this court were contained in the *Reports of the Exchequer Court of Canada*. From 1922 to 1969 they were contained in the *Canada Law Reports, Exchequer Court*. There are also two volumes for 1970: one called *Canada, Exchequer Court Reports* and the other *Canada Law Reports, Exchequer Court*. Throughout this period they have been usually referred to as the *Exchequer Court Reports*.

The title and key number of "Criminal Law" can be used to search in all reports of the Maritime Law Book Company either manually or by computer.

NOTE: The "Index to Cases Reported, Appeal Notes and Unreported Cases" is a useful companion looseleaf service to the main set.

(5) National Reporter, 1974 to date (cited N.R.)

This is part of the National Reporter System. It contains all of the judgments of the Supreme Court of Canada and all of the judgments of the Federal Court of Appeal. The unofficial *National Reporter* also includes the disposition of all motions for recent leave to appeal to the Supreme Court of Canada. The decisions appear first in paperbound parts and later in bound volumes. Several volumes are issued annually and digests are published for every ten volumes in the set. The digest volumes include brief summaries of reported cases and a consolidation of the various indices which appear in individual volumes.

Each volume of the *National Reporter* includes the following indices:

(i)   "Index to Cases and Motions Reported";
(ii)   "Index to Case Comments";
(iii)   "Index to Unedited/Unreported Cases";
(iv)   "Index to Cases Noticed";
(v)   "Index to Statutes Noticed";
(vi)   "Index to Authors and Works Noticed";
(vii)   "Index to Words and Phrases"; and
(viii) "Topical Index with Topic Numbers".

The most valuable indices for researching a legal issue are the "Topical Index" and the *Master Key Word Index* published in a looseleaf format as a companion volume to all reports in the set. A familiarity with the latter allows the user to find a topic and number which may be used in the "Topical Index" to quickly search all of the digest volumes of the report series, as well as individual volumes which have not been included in a digest, to find cases on a selected point.

NOTE: The same key-word and topical index system is used in all other case reports which form part of the National Reporter System: *Alberta Reports*, *Atlantic Provinces Reports*, *British Columbia Appeal Cases*, *Federal Trial Reports*, *Manitoba Reports (2d)*, *New Brunswick Reports (2d)*, *Newfoundland and Prince Edward Island Reports*, *Nova Scotia Reports (2d)*, *Ontario Appeal Cases*, *Saskatchewan Reports* and *Western Appeal Cases*. The same system applies to *British Columbia Trial Cases*, *New Brunswick Reports (2d) Supp.* and *Ontario Trial Cases*, which are all available electronically.

As a result, the same topic (or subtopic) number may be used to conduct research in all of these reports. For example, given the topic key and number "Contracts — 1205", the user may scan the topical indices in the digest and individual volumes of the *National Reporter* to find cases dealing with "what constitutes an offer?". Then, the user may scan the topical indices in the digest and individual volumes of any one or more of the other case reports mentioned using the same topic and key number to find other cases dealing with "what constitutes an offer?".

All headnotes from these publications are in a computer database called the National Reporter System or "NRS" operated by Quicklaw. All 151 titles and over 25,000 key numbers which cover individual points of law are listed in a separate database called M.L.B. Key Number Database also operated by Quicklaw. A search of these databases by using a word such as "confession" will indicate a key number, which can then be used to search the computer databases, or to search the digest and individual volumes of one or more report series in the set.

(B) REGIONAL REPORTS

(1) Western Weekly Reports, 1911 to date (cited W.W.R.)

This unofficial set contains a wide variety of cases from the four western provinces and the three territories.[35] It is published in weekly paperbound parts which are regularly replaced by bound volumes. For the purposes of citation, there have been five series to date:

(i)   1911 to 1916. The volumes are numbered consecutively throughout this period.

Example:
Heron v. Lalonde (1915), 9 W.W.R. 440 (B.C.C.A.).

(ii)   1917 to 1950. The volumes are numbered consecutively through each year.

Example:
Royal Bank of Canada v. Dodge, [1942] 1 W.W.R. 270 (Alta. S.C.).

(iii)   1951 to 1954. The volumes are numbered consecutively throughout this period. The letters "N.S." are included in the citation of volumes 1 to 13 since this is a new series.

---

[35]   The set also includes judgments of the Supreme Court of Canada and the Federal Court of Canada on appeal from the western provinces and the three territories.

Example:
Prudential Trust Co. v. Cugnet (1954), 11 W.W.R. (N.S.) 634 (Sask. Q.B.).

(iv) 1955 to 1970. The volumes are numbered consecutively throughout this period, continuing from the preceding period. The letters "N.S." are dropped.

Example:
R. v. Ostrove (1967), 60 W.W.R. 267 (Man. Q.B.).

(v) 1971 to date. The volumes are numbered consecutively through each year.

Examples:
Minister of Finance v. Piker, [1973] 1 W.W.R. 169 (B.C.C.A.).
R. v. Fliss, [2002] 4 W.W.R. 395 (S.C.C.).

There are several indices for the following periods: 1951-1970 covering vols. 1 to 75; [1971] vol. 1 to [1980] vol. 6; [1981] vol. 1 to [1985] vol. 6; [1986] vol. 1 to [1988] vol. 6; [1989] vol. 1 to [1991] vol. 6; [1992] vol. 1 to [1994] vol. 10; [1995] vol. 1 to [1996] vol. 10; [1997] vol. 1 to [1998] vol. 10; [1999] vol. 1 to [1999] vol. 12; [2000] vol. 1 to [2000] vol. 12; [2001] vol. 1 to [2001] vol. 11. As well, there is a paperbound *Cumulative Index* for decisions made after the last bound consolidation. This will be later incorporated into a new hardbound consolidated index.

(2) Atlantic Provinces Reports,[36] 1975 to date (cited A.P.R.)

This unofficial set was first published in 1975. It reprints the decisions appearing in the current *New Brunswick Reports, Nova Scotia Reports* and *Newfoundland and Prince Edward Island Reports*. Advance paperbound parts are not published for this set. The parallel series (and the appropriate volume of that series) is provided in each volume of the A.P.R. series.

Examples:
R. v. Bradbury (G.B.) (2002), 618 A.P.R. 82 (Nfld. S.C.).
Smith v. Agnew (2001), 622 A.P.R. 63 (N.B.C.A.).
R.v. Bratzer (2001), 621 A.P.R. 303 (N.S.C.A.).

NOTE: The *Bradbury* case can be found in volume 206 of the Nfld. & P.E.I.R. series, as indicated in volume 618 of the A.P.R. series, at page 82 (the same page number as in A.P.R.). The *Smith* case can be found in volume 240 of the

---

[36] Prior to 1975, coverage of the decisions from the Atlantic provinces was provided by the *Dominion Law Reports* and the *Maritime Provinces Reports* (cited M.P.R.). The latter was published from 1930 to 1968 in 53 volumes.

N.B.R. (2d) series, as indicated in volume 622 of the A.P.R. series, at page 63. The *Bratzer* case can be found in volume 198 of the N.S.R. (2d) series, at page 303.

(3) Western Appeal Cases, 1992 to date (cited W.A.C.)

This unofficial set was first published in 1992 by Maritime Law Book Company. It includes judgments of the Courts of Appeal of Alberta, British Columbia, Manitoba and Saskatchewan. Advance paperbound parts are not published for this set. The parallel series is given in each individual volume in the *Western Appeal Cases*.

Example:
Roumanis v. Scott (1998), 184 W.A.C. 144 (B.C.C.A.).

NOTE: The above case can also be found in volume 113 of the *British Columbia Appeal Cases* (B.C.A.C.), at page 144, as indicated in volume 184 of the W.A.C. series, at page 144.

There are several indices for the following periods: 1992-1993 covering vols. 1-40; 1993-1995 covering vols. 41-80; 1997 covering vols. 81-120; 1996-1998 covering vols. 121-160.

(C) PROVINCIAL REPORTS

(1) British Columbia

(i) British Columbia Law Reports[37] (cited B.C.L.R.)

This unofficial set includes selected cases from the British Columbia Court of Appeal, other British Columbia courts, as well as decisions of the Supreme Court of Canada emanating from British Columbia. It includes, like its sister publications beginning with the *Federal Trial Reports*, discussed at page 58, separate indices and companion digest volumes. For the purposes of citation, there have been three series to date:

First Series, 1976 to 1986. The volumes are numbered consecutively throughout this period. An example citation is:

Shea v. Shea (1983), 47 B.C.L.R. 59 (S.C.).

---

[37] There are a number of earlier case reports which covered selected British Columbia cases, including the *Western Law Reporter*, 1905 to 1916 (cited W.L.R.), and the *British Columbia Reports*, 1867 to 1947 (cited B.C.R.).

Second Series, 1986 to 1995 volume 100. The volumes are numbered consecutively throughout this period. Two example citations are:

British Columbia Government Employee's Union v. Labour Relations Board of British Columbia (1986), 2 B.C.L.R. (2d) 66 (C.A.).

Evans v. Campbell (1993), 77 B.C.L.R. (2d) 211 (C.A.).

Third Series, 1995 to 2002. The volumes are numbered consecutively throughout this period. An example of citation is:

Holsten v. Card (2002), 100 B.C.L.R. (3d) 269 (C.A.).

Fourth Series, 2002 to date. The volumes are consecutively numbered through this period. An example of a citation is:

Xeni Gwet'in First Nations v. British Columbia (2002), 3 B.C.L.R. (4d) 231 (C.A.).

NOTE: The British Columbia Court of Appeal cases are available in a separate Maritime Law Book Company publication, the *British Columbia Appeal Cases*.

(2) Alberta

(i) Alberta Reports,[38] 1977 to date (cited A.R.)

This unofficial set was formerly (until 1986) issued under the authority of the Law Society of Alberta and contains all of the judgments of the Alberta Court of Appeal and selected trial judgments from other Alberta courts. It includes, like its sister publications beginning with the *Federal Trial Reports*, discussed at page 58, separate indices and companion digest volumes. The main volumes are numbered consecutively throughout the set. Two example citations are:

Rufenack v. Hope Mission et al. (2002), 328 A.R. 128 (Surr. Ct.).
R. v. D.J.M. (2003), 327 A.R. 195 (C.A.).

(ii) Alberta Law Reports

This unofficial set contains all of the judgments of the Alberta Court of Appeal and selected trial court judgments including the Court of Queen's Bench, the Surrogate Court and the Provincial Court, as well as judgments of the Supreme Court of Canada emanating from Alberta.

Second Series, 1976 to 1992 (cited Alta. L.R. (2d)). The volumes are numbered consecutively throughout this period. An example citation is:

---

[38] There are a number of earlier case reports which covered selected Alberta cases, including the *Western Law Reporter*, 1905 to 1916 (cited W.L.R.), and *Alberta Law Reports*, 1908 to 1932 (cited Alta. L.R.).

Western Mack Truck (Edmonton) Ltd. v. Heikel (1976), 1 Alta. L.R. (2d) 184 (Dist. Ct.).

Third Series, 1992 to 2002 (cited Alta. L.R. (3d)). This series is also numbered consecutively throughout this period. An example citation is:

Plett v. Blackrabbit (2002), 100 Alta. LR. (3d) 362 (Q.B.).

Fourth Series, 2002 to present (cited Alta. L.R. (4d)). This series is also numbered consecutively throughout this period. An example citation is:

R. v. B. (S.J.) (2003), 5 Alta. L.R. (4d) 207 (C.A.).

(3) Saskatchewan

(i) Saskatchewan Reports,[39] 1979 to date (cited Sask. R.)

This unofficial set includes all of the judgments of the Saskatchewan Court of Appeal and most trial court judgments and selected decisions of the Provincial Courts. It includes, like its sister publications beginning with the *Federal Trial Reports*, discussed at page 58, separate indices and companion digest volumes. Two example citations are:

Desjarlais v. Desjarlais (2002), 230 Sask. R. 34 (Q.B.).
R. v. Romano (L.J.) (2003), 231 Sask. R. 123 (Prov. Ct.).

(4) Manitoba

(i) Manitoba Reports (Second Series),[40] 1979 to date (cited Man. R. (2d))

This unofficial set includes all of the judgments of the Manitoba Court of Appeal and most trial court judgments from the Court of Queen's Bench, selected decisions of the Provincial Court and judgments of the Supreme Court of Canada emanating from Manitoba. It includes, like its sister publications beginning with *Federal Trial Reports*, discussed at page 58, separate indices and companion digest volumes. Two example citations are:

Dyck v. Sidler (2003), 175 Man. R. (2d) 250 (Q.B.).
Petrowski v. Waskul (2003), 173 Man. R. (2d) 237 (C.A.).

---

[39] There are a number of earlier case reports which covered selected Saskatchewan cases, including the *Western Law Reporter*, 1905 to 1916 (cited W.L.R.), and the *Saskatchewan Law Reports*, 1907 to 1931 (cited Sask. L.R.).

[40] There are a number of earlier case reports which covered selected Manitoba cases, including the *Western Law Reporter*, 1905 to 1916 (cited W.L.R.), the *Manitoba Law Reports*, 1884 to 1890 (cited Man. L.R.), vols. 1 to 6, and the *Manitoba Reports*, 1890 to 1967 (cited Man. R.), vols. 7 to 67.

(5) Ontario

(i) Ontario Reports (Second Series),[41] 1974 to 1991 (cited O.R. (2d))

This semi-official set was published under the authority of the Law Society of Upper Canada. It contains cases from the Court of Appeal, the Court of Justice (General Division and Provincial Division), Small Claims Court, as well as summaries of decisions from the Supreme Court of Canada. Companion volumes entitled "Consolidated Index" provide a consolidated alphabetical table of cases and a consolidated subject index to cases found in the individual volumes of the set. An example citation is:

Re Butt (1986), 53 O.R. (2d) 297 (Surr. Ct.).

(ii) Ontario Reports (Third Series), 1991 to date (cited O.R. (3d))

This semi-official set is also published under the authority of the Law Society of Upper Canada. It contains cases from the Court of Appeal of the Ontario Court of Justice (General Division and Provincial Division), as well as summaries of decisions from the Supreme Court of Canada. A companion volume entitled *Consolidated Index* provides a consolidated alphabetical table of cases and a consolidated subject index to cases found in the individual volumes of the set. Two example citations are:

Price v. Sonsini (2002), 60 O.R. (3d) 257 (C.A.).

(iii) Ontario Appeal Cases,[42] 1984 to date (cited O.A.C.)

This unofficial set reports all cases from the Ontario Court of Appeal and the Ontario Divisional Court. It includes, like its sister publications beginning with *Federal Trial Reports*, discussed at page 58, separate indices and companion digest volumes. Two example citations are:

Rubinoff v. Wachsberg (2003), 171 O.A.C. 179 (Sup. Ct. J. (Div. Ct.)).
Shelanu. v. Print Three Franchising (2003), 172 O.A.C. 78 (C.A.).

---

[41] There have been a number of earlier Ontario case reports including the *Ontario Reports*, 1931 to 1973 (cited [year] O.R.), the *Ontario Appeal Reports*, 1876 to 1900 (cited O.A.R.), the *Ontario Law Reports*, 1901 to 1930 (cited O.L.R.), the *Ontario Reports*, 1882 to 1900 (cited O.R.), the *Ontario Weekly Notes*, 1909 to 1932 (cited O.W.N.), and the *Ontario Weekly Notes*, 1933 to 1962 (cited [year] O.W.N.).

[42] An earlier set with a similar name, *Ontario Appeal Reports* (cited O.A.R.) was published between 1876 and 1900.

(6) Québec

(i) Recueils de jurisprudence du Québec, 1986 to date (cited [year] R.J.Q.)

This official set contains judgments of the Cour d'Appel, Cour supérieure, Cour provinciale, Cour des sessions de la paix, and Tribunal de la jeunesse.[43] A "Cumulative Index" is published annually.[44] Two example citations are:

> *Blasser Brothers Inc. S.A. v. Royal Bank of Canada* (C.A.), [2002] R.J.Q. 2307 (C.A.).
>
> *R. v. Doré*, [1992] R.J.Q. 2955 (C.Q.).

(7) New Brunswick

(i) New Brunswick Reports (Second Series),[45] 1969 to date (cited N.B.R. (2d))

This semi-official set, issued under the authority of the Law Society of New Brunswick, includes all of the judgments of the New Brunswick Court of Appeal, most judgments of the Court of Queen's Bench, including selected cases of the Family Division and some decisions of the Provincial Court. It includes, like its sister publications beginning with *Federal Trial Reports*, discussed at page 58, separate indices and companion digest volumes. Two example citations are:

> *Belyea v. Belyea* (1992), 130 N.B.R. (2d) 297 (Q.B.).
>
> *Ryan v. Law Society of New Brunswick* (2003), 257 N.B.R. (2d) 207 (S.C.C.).

---

[43] Before 1986, the *Recueils de jurisprudence du Québec* was published in five parts: *Cour d'Appel* (cited [year] C.A.); *Cour supérieure* (cited [year] C.S.); *Cour provinciale* (cited [year] C.P.), *Cour des sessions de la paix* (cited [year] C.S.P.); and *Tribunal de la jeunesse* (cited [year] T.J.). Prior to 1975, only the first two series were published. The predecessor series, 1892 to 1967, was referred to as *Rapports Judiciares de Québec*. Maritime Law Book Co. commenced a new series in 1987, the *Québec Appeal Cases* (cited Q.A.C.). The set was discontinued in 1995.

[44] The *Cumulative Index* is located at the end of the last volume of each year.

[45] There are a number of earlier case reports which covered selected New Brunswick cases, including *Maritime Provinces Reports*, 1930 to 1968, *Eastern Law Reporter*, 1906 to 1914 (cited E.L.R.), and *New Brunswick Reports*, 1825 to 1929 (cited N.B.R.).

(8) Nova Scotia

(i) Nova Scotia Reports (Second Series),[46] 1969 to date (cited N.S.R. (2d))

This semi-official set is issued under the authority of the Nova Scotia Barristers' Society and includes all of the judgments of the Nova Scotia Court of Appeal and selected judgments from the Nova Scotia Supreme Court, County Courts, Family Courts, and Provincial Courts. It includes, like its sister publications beginning with *Federal Trial Reports*, discussed at page 58, separate indices and companion digest volumes. Two example citations are:

Ward's Estate v. Ward (1985), 68 N.S.R. (2d) 178 (S.C. (A.D.)).

NOTE: Since January 1, 1993, there has been a consolidation of Nova Scotia courts. Thus, a decision of the Court of Appeal would be now cited as *Schaller v. Schaller* (1993), 120 N.S.R. (2d) 82 (C.A.). Formerly, the highest court was referred to as the Supreme Court, Appeal Division, and was cited as (S.C. (A.D.)) (see above).

R. v. Landry (T.) (2003), 214 N.S.R. (2d) 229 (C.A.).

A five-volume companion set, *Nova Scotia Reports, 1965-69* (cited N.S.R.), brings together decisions rendered between 1965 and 1969. There is a single-volume digest[47] which summarizes the cases contained in *Nova Scotia Reports* (1965-69) and the first ten volumes of the *Nova Scotia Reports (2d)*.

(9) Newfoundland and Prince Edward Island

(i) Newfoundland and Prince Edward Island Reports,[48] 1970 to date (cited Nfld. & P.E.I.R.)

This semi-official set, issued under the authority of the Law Society of Newfoundland and the Law Society of Prince Edward Island, includes all of the judgments of the Newfoundland and Prince Edward Island Courts of Appeal, and selected judgments from the Supreme Court of Newfoundland, Trial Division, Newfoundland Family Court, Newfoundland Provincial Court, Prince

---

[46] There have been a number of earlier case reports dealing with selected Nova Scotia cases, including *Maritime Provinces Reports*, 1930 to 1968, *Eastern Law Reporter*, 1906 to 1914, and *Nova Scotia Reports*, 1834 to 1929 (cited N.S.R.).

[47] Referred to as *Digest and Indexes* for volumes 1 to 10 and for *Nova Scotia Reports*, 1965-69, volumes 1 to 5.

[48] There are a number of earlier case reports which covered selected Prince Edward Island cases, including *Eastern Law Reporter*, 1906 to 1914, and *Maritime Provinces Reports*, 1930 to 1968. The latter included Newfoundland cases beginning in 1949.

Edward Island Supreme Court, Trial Division, and the Provincial Court of Prince Edward Island. It includes, like its sister publications beginning with *Federal Trial Reports*, discussed on page 58, separate indices and companion digest volumes. Three example citations are:

> *Lynch v. Lundrigan* (2002), 215 Nfld. & P.E.I.R. 62 (Nfld. S.C.).
> *R. v. Cooper (D.L.)* (2002), 221 Nfld. & P.E.I.R. 143 (Nfld. S.C.).
> *Director of Child Welfare (P.E.I.) v. R.M.* (2003), 226 Nfld. & P.E.I.R. 241 (P.E.I.S.C. (A.D.)).

(10) Northwest Territories

(i) Northwest Territories Reports, 1983 to 1998 (cited [year] N.W.T.R.)

This semi-official set is issued under the authority of the Law Society of the Northwest Territories and contains judgments of the Northwest Territories Court of Appeal, and selected trial court judgments, including the Territorial Court and the Youth Court. It also reports judgments on appeal from the Northwest Territories to the Supreme Court of Canada. The volumes are identified by year. Two example citations are:

> *R. v. Spencer*, [1992] N.W.T.R. 124 (S.C.).
> *Fullowka v. Royal Oak Mines Inc.*, [1998] N.W.T.R. 217 (S.C.).

(11) Yukon Territory

(i) Yukon Reports, 1987 to 1989 (cited Y.R.)

This semi-official set was issued under the authority of the Law Society of the Yukon and contained judgments of the Yukon Court of Appeal and selected trial judgments, including the Yukon Territorial Court and Yukon Supreme Court. It also reported judgments on appeal from the Yukon Territory to the Supreme Court of Canada. The volumes were numbered consecutively. An example citation is:

> *M.B.W. Surveys Ltd. v. Bank of Nova Scotia* (1986), 1 Y.R. 157 (S.C.).

(12) Nunavut

Currently there is no case reporter for Nunavut.

(D) SUBJECT REPORTS

There are nationwide report series in specialized fields. They usually include both decisions of special boards or tribunals, as well as conventional courts which are omitted by other case reports. Some, like the *Labour Arbitration Cases*, contain only the decisions of special tribunals.

Most of the subject case reports contain extensive indices, digests, annotations,[49] and other features designed to assist the user to find cases as well as related legislation and articles more quickly. Many of the cases reported in these series appear as well in national, regional, or provincial case reports.

Appendix III contains the publication periods and the recommended citations for the major subject reports.

4. Canadian Judicial Decisions on the Internet

Judicial decisions from several courts in Canada are now quickly available through the Internet without the need to subscribe to computerized databases. Some of these sites even have search engines which allow for searching by case name or legal topic. One can also subscribe to receive newly released decisions via e-mail from some courts.

These Web sites cannot replace basic library research or searching via commercial databases (see Chapter 4). Only a few superior courts in Canada provide decisions via Web sites, and those sites with a search engine do not search the databases of any of the others. Therefore, one would have to consult each court's Web page to find all relevant cases on a particular topic from each court.

Nevertheless, the following sites provide up-to-date releases from their respective courts, and are welcome additions for the legal researcher:

(A) SUPREME COURT OF CANADA

Offers a searchable database, weekly bulletins, timely releases of Supreme Court of Canada decisions, a free subscription service, and access to the Supreme Court Reports online: The Supreme Court of Canada <http://www.droit.umontreal.ca/doc/csc-scc/en/index.html>.

(B) FEDERAL COURT OF CANADA

Provides access to Federal Court decisions, the Federal Court Rules, a free subscription service, searchable databases online: Federal Court of Canada <http://www.fja.gc.ca/en/cf>.

(C) THE SUPERIOR COURTS OF BRITISH COLUMBIA

Provides access to decisions of the British Columbia Supreme Court and Court of Appeal, a legal "compendium" that describes the laws and judiciary in British

---

[49] There is often extensive commentary on selected cases which is very useful in helping the reader understand the case in the context of earlier law and in terms of perceived trends.

Columbia, and searchable databases online: British Columbia Superior Courts
<http://www.courts.gov.bc.ca>.

(D) ALBERTA COURTS

Contains decisions not only of Alberta's Superior Courts (Court of Queen's
Bench and Court of Appeal), but also includes decisions of the Alberta Provincial Court, which includes Family Court; also provides a searchable database
online: Alberta Courts <http://www.albertacourts.ab.ca>.

(E) ONTARIO COURTS

Provides decisions from the Ontario Court of Appeal, notices and rules from the
Superior Court of Justice and Ontario Court of Justice; no search engine online:
Ontario Courts: <http://www.ontariocourts.on.ca>.

5. English Case Reports

(A) EARLY ENGLISH REPORTS

(1) Nominate Reports

In 1535, law reports began to appear in England in the form which we now
know. This is the period of the "Nominate Reports", which lasted from 1535 to
1865. The "Nominate Reports" is not a specific report series, but rather it is a
broad term describing a multitude of commercial reports prepared by private
reporters. Hundreds of these case reports were published with varying degrees of
completeness and accuracy.

(2) English Reports (cited E.R.)

The *English Reports* series was prepared around the turn of the century by a
group of leading jurists in order to make the great mass of "Nominate Reports"
more accessible. It constitutes a collection of most of the more reliable reports
published between 1378 and 1866. The set consists of 176 volumes of cases
arranged by court and a two-volume *Index of Cases*. Each case is reprinted ver-
batim with the original footnotes. In parenthesis beneath the name of the case,
the editors have provided citations to collateral reports (preceded by "S.C." for
"same case"), to the history of the case, and to subsequent judicial consideration.
The original pagination is indicated in bold type within the text. Some editorial
comment is provided.

(3) Revised Reports (cited R.R.)

The *Revised Reports* were prepared shortly after the *English Reports* and contain a practical selection of case reports from "Nominate Reports" during the period 1785 to 1865. The set consists of 149 volumes of case reports, a one-volume "Table of Cases" and a two-volume "Index Digest". At the beginning of volume 149 there is a "Table of Comparative Reference" which shows the correspondence between the volumes of the original reports and the volumes of the *Revised Reports*. To a great extent, the coverage of the *Revised Reports* duplicates that of the *English Reports*, and, therefore, it is preferable to cite the version in the *English Reports*.

(4) All England Law Reports Reprint (cited All E.R. Rep.)

The *All England Law Reports Reprint* is a recent collection of nominate and commercial reports from the period 1558 to 1935. The set consists of 36 volumes of cases arranged in chronological order and a one-volume *Index* which includes a "Table of Cases". In addition to the judgments, which remain virtually unaltered from the original, each case report includes citation to all parallel reports of the same case and a comprehensive list of cases where the original case has been judicially considered. There is a supplementary series, entitled the *All England Law Reports Reprint Extension Volumes*, covering the period 1861 to 1935. The *Extension Series*, consisting of 17 volumes of cases, a one-volume *Index* and a pamphlet which is a "Table of Cases", is arranged in the same manner as the original series.

(B) MODERN ENGLISH REPORTS

Modern English law reporting began in the mid-nineteenth century with the appearance of several commercial series of case reports. Among those series which have been discontinued, the most important were the *Law Journal Reports* (1822-1949), the *Weekly Reporter* (1853-1906), the *Law Times* (1860-1947), and the *Times Law Reports* (1884-1952).

The most important current reports of a general nature are the semi-official *Law Reports*, the unofficial *Weekly Law Reports* and *All England Law Reports*. There are, of course, many specialized reports currently published in the United Kingdom.

(1) Law Journal Reports (1822-1949) Volumes 1-118

This set consists of approximately 300 volumes containing selected equity and common law court decisions. The set has two parts, an old series and a new series.

(2) The Law Reports

This set is published by the Incorporated Council of Law Reporting for England and Wales and includes cases of interest from the several divisions of the High

Court of Justice. The individual series which constitute *The Law Reports* are named after the division of the High Court of Justice whose decisions they report. Originally there were 11 sets. Owing to the changes in the English system of courts, particularly as a result of the *Judicature Act, 1875*, the component sets have undergone several changes in name and in coverage. From the 11 original series, four current series have evolved. Each of these series is published in monthly parts and regularly consolidated in bound volumes.

The shelving of *The Law Reports* in a law library often leads to confusion for the beginning student. Each current set is shelved with its predecessor sets, many of which have different names. For example, the *Appeal Cases* reports were preceded historically by the *Privy Council Appeals* (1865-75), a seven-volume set of the *English & Irish Appeals* (1866-75), a two-volume set of the *Scotch & Divorce Appeals* (1866-75), and a 15-volume set of *Appeal Cases* (1875-90). Thus, these are shelved before the *Appeal Cases* reports. The same arrangement is applied to the *Chancery Division* reports, *Queen's Bench Division* reports, and *Family Division* reports.

This means that in the overall arrangement of *The Law Reports* very recent volumes of one set (for example, 1994) may be shelved next to the earliest volumes of a second set (for example, 1865).

(3) *Industrial Cases Reports,* 1975 to date (cited [year] I.C.R.)

This report series commenced in 1975 and includes decisions of the Employment Appeal Tribunal, the National Industrial Relations Court, High Court of Justice, Court of Appeal, and House of Lords concerning industrial relations. The predecessors of this series were the *Industrial Court Reports* (1972-74) and the *Reports of Restrictive Practices Cases* (1957-1972).

(4) *Weekly Law Reports*

The semi-official *Weekly Law Reports* (1953 to date) includes every decision from all divisions likely to appear in any general series of reports. Appearing weekly, it constitutes an advance sheet for *The Law Reports* themselves. It also contains decisions which will not appear in *The Law Reports*.[50] Its predecessors were the *Weekly Notes* (1866 to 1952) and the *Times Law Reports* (1884 to 1952).

(5) *All England Law Reports*

The *All England Law Reports* is an unofficial series of weekly reports which began in 1936 and continues to be published to date. It covers, *inter alia*, leading cases in all fields of law decided by the House of Lords, the Privy Council, the Court of Appeal, and all divisions of the High Court.

---

[50] At the end of each year, the *Weekly Law Reports* are usually published in three bound volumes.

CHAPTER 3

Secondary Legal Materials

Secondary legal materials are preliminary research tools that assist the student in finding, evaluating, and understanding primary materials such as statutes and case law. For general research the most important secondary tools are legal encyclopedias and digests. Other useful finding aids include citators, annotators, legal dictionaries, periodical articles, treatises and textbooks.

Encyclopedias are comprehensive multi-volume reference works containing up-to-date statements of the law in essay form. Digests and abridgments are comprehensive, multi-volume reference works which provide digests or summaries of cases.

There are two basic types of legal citators: statute citators and case citators. Statute citators contain the titles of all the statutes for a selected province or for Canada and indicate whether the statutes have been amended or judicially considered. This is illustrated in Table III which is taken from the *Ontario Statute Citator*, R.S.O. 1990 edition. (See also a companion work, *Ontario Statute Annotations*, R.S.O. 1990 edition.)

TABLE III

LEGAL AID SERVICES ACT, 1998

S.O. 1998, Chap. 26

Administered by the Ministry of the Attorney General

In Force
December 18, 1998, except as provided in s. 110; s. 106(2) in force February 1, 1999; Part III, other than s. 18(1), Parts IV, VI and IX, other than ss. 103, 106(2) and 109, in force April 1, 1999.

Amendments
2001, c. 9, Sch. D, s.13; in force June 29, 2001
2002, c. 8, Sch. I, s. 14; to come into force on proclamation
2002, c. 19, s. 1; in force November 26, 2002.

Section 14

Subsec. (1) amended 2002, c. 19, s. 1 by adding after "disadvantaged communities" in the portion before cl. (a) "the need to achieve an effective balance among the different methods of providing legal aid services" and adding the following cl. (a.1):

> **(a.1) entering into agreements with lawyers, groups of lawyers or law firms under which the lawyer, group or law firm provides legal aid services;**

Section 46

O'Sullivan v. Lindley (2000), 100 A.C.W.S. (3d) 390 (S.C.J.) [000/299/151 – 4 pp.]. Costs are recoverable in the same manner and to the same extent as though awarded to an individual who had not received Legal Aid services.

Section 48

Subsec. (4) amended 2001, c. 9, Sch. D, s. 13 by striking out "Consumer and Commercial Relations" and substituting "Consumer and Business Services".

Section 55

Re-enacted 2002, c. 8, Sch. I, s. 14 (to come into force on proclamation).

Source: *Ontario Statute Citator*, April 2003 (Aurora, Ontario: Canada Law Book Inc., 2003).

In the illustration, section 46 is shown as having received judicial consideration, while sections 14, 48 and 55 are shown as having been amended.

Case citators provide lists of cases and indicate subsequent judicial consideration. For example, *The Canadian Abridgment's Thrid Edition* (cited Can. Abr. (3rd)) — *Canadian Case Citations* is a multi-volume set (with hardbound and softcover supplements) which contains lists of all the cases digested in *The Abridgment* which have been applied, considered, distinguished, followed, overruled, referred to, affirmed, reversed, set aside, varied, or, from which leave to appeal was refused or granted in a later decision.

Annotators are similar to case citators in that they indicate subsequent judicial consideration, including the disposition of all leaves to appeal, but they differ from citators in that the cases cited are indexed according to volume and page numbers rather than by case name. See, for example, the *Dominion Law Reports'* .... "Table of Annotations".

Words and Phrases are works which provide citations to cases (and sometimes to statutes) which contain definitions of selected words and/or phrases. Often they include extracts from the actual decision. Legal dictionaries provide definitions of legal terms and common words with special meanings at law, often with reference to judicial authority. The distinction between a dictionary and words and phrases is that the latter provides definitions from the courts (and sometimes from statutes) while the former attempts to define all legal terms whether or not they have been the subject of judicial definition.

The following outline covers the major sources of secondary materials in a law library. The discussion of each major Canadian and English encyclopedia and/or digest is in five parts.

1.   Scope
2.   Time-Frame
3.   Format
4.   Finding Aids
5.   Research Techniques

A. ENCYCLOPEDIAS

1. Canadian

(A) THE CANADIAN ENCYCLOPEDIC DIGEST THIRD EDITION

There are two parts to *The Canadian Encyclopedic Digest*. The first part covers matters relating to Ontario (cited C.E.D. (Ont. 3d)) and the second concerns the prairies and British Columbia (cited C.E.D. (West 3d)).

Scope

The C.E.D. (Ont. 3d) contains a general statement of all the provincial laws of Ontario and the federal laws of Canada. The C.E.D. (West 3d) is identical in scope, but covers provincial legislation for Alberta, British Columbia, Manitoba and Saskatchewan.[1]

Time-Frame

The first edition of *The Canadian Encyclopedic Digest* was published in 1926 and covered then current case and statute law, as well as a selection of earlier laws which the publishers believed were still relevant and would be usefully included in the second edition. The third edition began publication in 1973 and is updated in a looseleaf format. Individual looseleaf volumes are supplied with monthly inserts and provide a continuing present statement of the law. The cut-off date for material included in the various parts of individual volumes is noted on the front of each looseleaf sheet.

---

[1]   Territorial information is occasionally included.

Format

The third edition of *The Canadian Encyclopedic Digest* (Ontario) consists of 34 main volumes and a one-volume *Research Guide and Key*. The *Statutes Concordance* volumes (which include an "Alphabetical Table of Revised Statutes of Ontario") has been published in conjunction with C.E.D. (Ont. 3d).[2] The main volumes contain a statement of law in narrative form, organized under 151 subject titles and alphabetically arranged, and they are annotated with footnote references to case and statute citations.

The arrangement under each subject title in each looseleaf binder is as follows:

Yellow Pages

(a) "Table of Cases" — This section gives citations for cases that are dealt with in the supplement.

(b) "Table of Statutes" (*i.e.*, R.S.C. 1985 and R.S.O. 1990) — Reference to this table helps to update a statement of law which includes references to the specific sections of the statute and paragraph numbers.

(c) "Table of Regulations" — This provides supplementary regulation citations for the main text.

NOTE: These sections are omitted when there has been no change since the last revision.

White Pages

Each title contains the following headings:

(a) "Table of Classification" (otherwise known as "Table of Contents") — This untitled table is found at the beginning of each title. It provides an overview of all the subtopics covered by the given title. References are to paragraph numbers.

(b) "Table of Cases" — This is a consolidation of all the case citations referred to in the main text, as well as to other cases from outside Ontario. References are to paragraph numbers.

(c) "Table of Statutes" — This is a consolidation of all the federal, provincial, and territorial statutes referred to in the footnotes to the discussion of each title. The references are to sections of the statutes and paragraph numbers of the main text.

(d) "Table of Rules and Regulations" — Each main title may or may not include a "Table of Rules" and/or a "Table of Regulations". The

---

[2] The C.E.D. (West 3d) consists of 35 volumes.

references are to sections of the statutes and paragraph numbers of the main text.

(e) General statements of the law, identified by paragraph numbers, are drawn from case and statute law. Refer to the "Table of Classification" to locate the specific topic under the title.

(f) "Index" — This section provides the subject index to the main text, as well as a cross-reference to other relevant subject titles in the C.E.D. (Ont. 3d). Again, each subject can be found by locating the paragraph numbers.

NOTE: Some titles may use other primary sources, and therefore include other miscellaneous tables.

The C.E.D. is kept current by replacement of the looseleaf white pages and by the yellow-page supplements to each title within a volume; each title being updated approximately once a year. Individual titles in the C.E.D. may be brought forward from the cut-off date noted on the looseleaf sheets by referring to *Canadian Current Law* — *Case Law Digests* and *Canadian Current Law* — *Legislation*.

Finding Aids

The Canadian Encyclopedic Digest, Third Edition, Research Guide and Key (hereinafter referred to as *The Key*)

Both the Ontario and Western editions have a one-volume key. This work features five main parts — "Research Guide", "Contents Key", "Statutes Key", "Rules and Regulations Key", and "Index Key". The main text of *The Key* is printed on white pages and is consolidated and republished annually. Supplements to *The Key* are printed on yellow paper and are published throughout the current year. The "Index Key" is updated throughout the year.

CONTENTS KEY

This key contains a list of the subject titles, arranged alphabetically, used in the C.E.D. together with references to the volume and title numbers for each subject. Thus, if the title is known, the "Contents Key" provides a convenient entry point into the main set.

STATUTES KEY

This key contains a consolidation of all provincial, territorial, and federal statutes appearing in the individual "Table of Statutes" for all C.E.D. titles. The cut-off point for material included in the white pages of *The Key* is noted on the first page. New material is published in the yellow-page supplement to *The Key*. Statutes are listed alphabetically, and references are to volume, title, and paragraph numbers, except for Income Tax and Labour Law which also include a reference to part numbers. The "Statutes Key" may assist the student to quickly find a statement of law and a case citation dealing with the desired statutory provision.

RULES AND REGULATIONS KEY

This key contains a consolidation of all provincial, territorial, and federal rules in the "Tables of Rules" with separate alphabetical listings of each, and provincial, territorial, and federal regulations in "Tables of Regulations" with separate alphabetical listings of each for all C.E.D. titles published up to the latest update. New material is published in the yellow-page supplement to *The Key*. The rules are listed alphabetically and references are to volumes, titles, and paragraph numbers within those titles, except for Income Tax and Labour Law which also include a reference to part numbers.

INDEX KEY

This index covers all titles published with cross-references to locate the appropriate entry in the "Index". References are to volume, title, and paragraph numbers within those titles. For new materials refer to the yellow-page supplement.

Research Techniques

First, consult the "Index" in *The Key* for the topic under investigation, unless you know the volume number and title under which your subtopic falls. If the latter, consult the "Index" at the back of the title for the selected volume. This provides a detailed list of subtopics, as well as the relevant paragraph numbers. Locate the relevant paragraph numbers in the white pages. Your research can be updated by referring to the same paragraph numbers in the yellow pages at the beginning of the title. If the paragraph numbers do not appear in this supplement, then there have been no changes to that point of law. Update further by researching current issues of *Canadian Current Law*. The title page to the supplement indicates the cut-off date for material collected from earlier issues of *Canadian Current Law*.

2. English

(A) HALSBURY'S LAWS OF ENGLAND, FOURTH EDITION (CITED AS HALSBURY)

Scope

This work contains a general statement of the laws of the United Kingdom and selected case and statute law of Commonwealth countries. In addition, the law of the European Communities is covered in detail in volumes 51 and 52.

Time-Frame

The first edition of *Halsbury's Laws of England* was published between 1907 and 1917 and consisted of 31 volumes; the second edition consisted of 37 volumes and was published between 1931 and 1942; and, the third edition consisted of 43 volumes published between 1952 and 1964. The fourth edition is the main reference work for students seeking current English law and began publication in 1973. Each volume in the set provides a statement of the law current at the time of publication. The cut-off date for each volume is noted on the "List of Contributors" page. It is updated by the reissue of specific volumes, annually by the publication of the two-volume *Cumulative Supplement*, and monthly by the *Current Service*.

Format

The fourth edition consists of 52 main volumes and several volumes of tables and indices: volume 53 — *Consolidated Tables of Statutes and Statutory Instruments* and *Table of European Communities Material*, volume 54 — *Consolidated Table of Cases*; volumes 55 and 56 — *Consolidated Indexes A-I and J-Z*.

The text is arranged in numbered paragraphs, each of which states the law on a particular topic and provides footnote references to statutes, statutory instruments and case law which serve as authority for the statements made in the text. The main set is kept current by the *Cumulative Supplement* and the *Current Service*. Each volume contains some or all of the following tables: "Table of Statutes", "Table of Statutory Instruments", "Table of European Communities Legislation", "Table of Treaties, Conventions, etc.", "Table of Other Enactments" and "Table of Cases". Each separate title within a volume has a "Table of Contents" which provides subjects and subtopics with reference to paragraph numbers. At the back of each volume is a topical index, as well as an index for "Words and Phrases", and entries in both indices refer to paragraph numbers.

Finding Aids

There are six main finding aids for the fourth edition:

(i)   *Consolidated Index*;
(ii)   Indices to individual volumes;
(iii)   "Tables of Contents" for individual titles;
(iv)   *Cumulative Supplement*;
(v)   *Current Service*; and
(vi)   *Canadian Converter, Third Edition*.

(i) Consolidated Index. This is a multi-volume work listing a great number of topical words which serve as an entry point to general areas of the law and to particular volumes of the main set. References in the work are to volume and paragraph numbers.

(ii) Indices (to Individual Volumes). Individual volumes of the main set contain detailed topical indices to each title included in the volume. For example, the title "Contract" is indexed at the back of volume 9(1), beginning at page 890. References in the indices are to paragraph numbers.

(iii) Tables of Contents. Individual volumes of the main set contain a "Table of Contents" for each title included in the volume. The tables are arranged to emphasize the major subjects within each title. References in the tables are to paragraph numbers.

(iv) Cumulative Supplement. This publication serves as an annual encyclopedia and brings forward the information in the main work. Any changes or additions which affect or relate to a statement or citation in any particular paragraph or in a footnote thereto is noted in the *Supplement* under the same paragraph number and heading or, where it does not directly affect the paragraph of the main work, in a new paragraph placed so as to continue, as far as possible, the scheme of arrangement of the main work. Cases mentioned in the *Supplement* and decided after 1973 are summarized in *Halsbury's Laws of England Annual Abridgment.* The *Supplement* also includes a "Table of Cases", "Table of Statutes", and a "Cumulative Index" which refers to both volume and paragraph numbers. The *Supplement* brings the main work up to date to October 31 preceding its publication. Any developments in the law after this date are then noted in *Current Service* (see *(v)* below).

(v) Current Service. This is a multi-faceted looseleaf work which features a "Monthly Review" and a "Noter-Up". This two-volume work also includes alphabetical lists of "Abbreviations" and "Arrangement of Titles". There are also sections on "Cases", "Statutes", "Statutory Instruments", "Index", "Commencement of Statutes", "Destination Tables", "Personal Injury", "Practice", "Articles", "Words and Phrases" and "European Communities Material". The "Monthly Review" provides summaries of recent reported and unreported judgments and may be used to keep the main volumes up to date in so far as they are not already updated by the annual *Supplement*, as well as to update matters summarized in the *Supplement* itself.

The "Noter-Up" completes the updating of the fourth edition and the *Cumulative Supplement* by supplying the many detailed annotations needed to maintain the accuracy of an encyclopedia. The order of the material is identical to that in the *Supplement* (*i.e.*, the same volume, title, and paragraph order of the main work), to which you should refer first for developments since publication of the original or reissued volumes. It is specified where the material in this "Noter-Up" updates paragraphs in the *Supplement* rather than in the main work. Summaries of statutes, case law and other material are to be found in the "Monthly Reviews" in Binder No. 1, and these are fully tabled and indexed.

(vi) Canadian Converter to Halsbury's Laws of England, Third Edition. This is a multi-volume companion set to *Halsbury's Laws of England, Third Edition.* One volume of the *Canadian Converter* accompanies approximately every five volumes of the main set. The *Canadian Converter* provides Canadian annotations to the text of the main set by listing cases and statutes from the common law jurisdictions of Canada under the corresponding title and paragraph number of the main volumes. The *Canadian Converter* is kept up to date by periodic "replacement" editions.

Research Techniques

A. If the title or subject is unknown:

Step 1:
Consult volume 55 or 56 of the *Consolidated Index* and locate the topic under investigation. Note the relevant volume (in bold type) and paragraph numbers to the main set. Consult the "List of Volumes, Paragraph Numbers and Titles" to determine under which title the subject falls.

NOTE: The *Consolidated Index* is often outdated by reissue volumes. If the subject is not where the index indicated, refer to the "List of Volumes, Paragraph Numbers and Titles" in the *Cumulative Supplement* to find its new location.

Step 2:
Consult the given volume and paragraph numbers and note the references to the authorities which support the statements of law.

Step 3:
Consult the *Cumulative Supplement* and, if available, locate the given volume and the paragraph numbers of particular interest to the topic under investigation. Note any further textual or footnote information.

Step 4:
Consult the "Noter-Up" in the *Current Service* looseleaf binder for any new materials since the publication of the *Cumulative Supplement.*

Example:

To find English cases on the International Convention on Marine Pollution, refer first to volume 56 of the *Consolidated Index* to the fourth edition. There you will find the main heading "MARINE POLLUTION" and the sub-heading "International Convention". The index directs you to volume 52, paragraph 18.212n3 (found on page 828). Next, check the list of titles. The topic falls under the heading "European Community". Look up the paragraph in the main volume. When you next refer to the *Cumulative Supplement*, you will find (under the same volume and paragraph number as in the main set) that you should refer to EC Commission Regulation 2158/93 for the application of the Convention. Lastly, use the same number in the Noter-Up to find the most recent changes.

NOTE: the European Community materials have their own section in the Noter-Up Binder.

Step 5:

Consult the most recent "replacement" volume of the *Canadian Converter, Halsbury's Laws of England, Third Edition* (the green-band set). Subject titles are noted on the spine. Select the book which contains the given subject heading and scan the numbered paragraphs for desired subtopics. References are to the volume and paragraph numbers in the third edition of *Halsbury's Laws of England*. Note the references to case authorities and legislation.

B. If the title or subject is known:

Step 1:

Scan the title names on the spines of individual volumes for the desired title.

Step 2:

Consult the "Table of Contents" for that particular title in the volume and scan the headings and topic listings for the topic under investigation. Note and consult the appropriate paragraph number for the desired textual and footnote information.

Step 3:

Consult the *Cumulative Supplement* and *Current Service* to update the search following steps 3 and 4 in Research Technique "A" above.

Step 4:

Follow the procedure outlined in step 5 in Research Technique "A" above to find Canadian authorities on the topic under investigation.

B. DIGESTS

1. Canadian

The Canadian Abridgment Revised Second Edition (cited Can. Abr. (2nd)) is a comprehensive multi-volume work compiled to assist legal researchers locate cases by a variety of means. It will be replaced over a period of time by a (blue-bound) third edition commencing in December 2002.

Scope

The case digests (the red and black set) contain a digest of "Reported Decisions of Canadian courts, and tribunals since the beginning of law reporting; unreported decisions of courts of appeal since 1987."

Time-Frame

First published in 1809 and continues to date.

Format

The revised second edition of the case digests consists of an original set of multiple volumes each containing digests of case law. The set was published between 1981 and 1993 and is referred to as the "Main Work". The new third edition "Main Work" volumes will gradually replace the second edition "Main Work" volumes commencing as indicated in December 2003. The cut-off date for each "Main Work" volume is noted on the title page.
The digests of case law in *The Abridgment* are organized according to a comprehensive table of classification.

Finding Aids and Research Techniques

The Canadian Abridgment Second and Third Edition Key & Research Guide (hereinafter referred to as the *Abridgment Key*)
To understand the organization and classification system used by the Canadian Abridgment students are urged to carefully review the looseleaf key and research guide which includes the following components:

1. Research Guide — Abridgment Overview
2. Key — Subject Titles Table and Key Classification System
3. Abbreviations

The *Abridgment Key* may also be used as a table of contents to help students gain a perspective of the scope of the subject-matter covered in a selected area of the law, identify legal concepts, and locate case law under selected subject titles and subheadings in hardbound and softcover (supplements) volumes of case digests.

The Canadian Abridgment 2nd and 3rd edition "Main Work" volumes and supplements are serviced with a number of invaluable search tools including the following:

1. Short Guide to the Abridgment
2. Quick Reference Guide
3. General Index
4. Consolidated Table of Cases
5. Words and Phrases (Revised)
6. Index to Canadian Legal Literature
7. Legislation
8. Rules Judicially Considered
9. Canadian Statutes Citations
10. Canadian Case Citations

A number of the research tools that are of particular importance to first-year law students are described below.

Consolidated Table of Cases

Using the *Table of Cases* to Find Legal Digests and Citations
To find a case by case name, refer to the *Consolidated Table of Cases*. This component of *The Abridgment* is the multi-volume gold and black set which arranges cases alphabetically by case name. This set consists of four hardcover volumes, four annual softcover supplements, a quarterly softcover supplement and the monthly case law digests.

NOTE: The hardcover volumes only contain cases dated 1995 or earlier. The softcover volumes are updated annually to reflect new cases. The most recent cases appear in the quarterly and monthly publications.

Step 1:
Refer to the hardcover volume. Search for your case alphabetically. If the case was decided after 1995, searching the hardcover volume is redundant.

Step 2:
Refer to the softcover volume. Search for your case alphabetically.

Step 3:
Refer to the quarterly issue. Search for your case alphabetically.

Step 4:
Refer to the table of cases in the monthly *Current Law — Case Digests* since the most recent quarterly publication. Search alphabetically.

The entry for each case in the table will give the case name (style of cause), any alternate style of cause, the year of the decision, citation(s), the court level of the decision, the result, court level of any higher decision, and the location of the digest. It should be noted that each case is cross-referenced according to the name of the defendant so, if one looked under *Chutorian v. Clark*, the table would direct the reader to see *Clark v. Chutorian*.

Canadian Case Citations

This is a multi-volume set which provides lists of cases showing, *inter alia*, how decisions have been dealt with in subsequent judgments. In particular, the lists show whether a decision has been affirmed, applied, considered, distinguished, followed, not followed or overruled, reversed, varied, referred to, set aside or quashed, or if leave to appeal was refused or granted.

A 22-volume consolidation of all material up until July 1998 has been published under the title *Canadian Case Citations, 1867 — July 1998*. A cumulative supplement and monthly issues of *Canadian Case Citations* cover the period after July 1998.

Finding Cases Which Have Considered a Selected Earlier Case

If a case was decided before July 1998, refer to the main volume of *Canadian Case Citations*, and then refer to any subsequent volumes (including the soft-cover issues) to bring your research up to date. If the date of the case is known to be after July 1998, check only the appropriate supplement volume(s) and monthly issues of *Canadian Case Citations* after the cut-off date noted on the cover of the cumulative supplement to *Canadian Case Citations*.

NOTE: Law libraries which do not have the single-volume consolidation will usually have a 26-volume set referred to as *Cases Judicially Considered* covering the period 1867-1990.

Canadian Statute Citations

The *Canadian Statute Citations* is a multi-volume national statute citator, recording decisions of Canadian courts and tribunals, and noting the statutes and rules of court which have been interpreted or applied in them. This work is the continuation of the publication formerly called *Statutes Judicially Considered*. Bound volumes are issued for a year or for a number of years and the current year is serviced with a softcover supplement.

Finding Cases Which Have Considered a Statute or Section of a Statute for a Given Jurisdiction

Step 1:
Begin your search in the hardcover volume which contains the relevant jurisdiction.[3] The statutes are listed alphabetically by short title.

NOTE: The volumes list statutes considered generally first and then list specific sections of the legislation. As well, be certain that you have located the correct year or revision for your statute; statutes with multiple versions are listed chronologically.

Step 2:
Refer to the softcover supplement following the same steps as for the hardcover.

Step 3:
Refer to the quarterly supplement.

Step 4:
Refer to the monthly editions issued since the most recent quarterly publication. This component of the *Abridgment* also contains a one-volume issue (supplemented by softcover updates) called *Rules Judicially Considered*. This work lists all Canadian jurisdictions alphabetically, and all the rules considered are listed alphabetically therein. A list of foreign rules considered can be found at the beginning of the volume.

NOTE: Foreign rules are listed alphabetically by their English titles.

Canadian Current Law — Legislation

Each issue of *Legislation* contains sections on "Progress of Bills", "Statutes Amended, Repealed or Proclaimed in Force" and "Regulations". Individual issues are collected into a *Legislation Annual*, which began in 1989. In order to track the progress of a bill, check the statutes enacted section of the most recent *Legislation Annual* to see if the desired bill has been enacted in the last year. Look first under a jurisdiction heading and then by name. Update the search by referring to the successive issues of *Canadian Current Law — Legislation* after the most recent *Legislation Annual*.

In order to see whether a selected statute has been amended, repealed, or proclaimed in force, refer to the "Statutes Amended, Repealed or Proclaimed in

---

[3] There are separate volumes for federal legislation and for most provinces. As well, students can search international statutes which have been considered by Canadian courts.

Force" section in the earliest relevant *Legislation Annual*. Look under the appropriate jurisdiction and statute name. Update the research in issues of *Canadian Current Law — Legislation* published after the most recent *Legislation Annual*.

In order to determine if a regulation has been made, repealed, or amended, consult the "Regulations" section in the earliest relevant *Legislation Annual*. Look for the regulation first by the jurisdiction and then by the name of its enabling statute. Update the research by referring to issues of *Canadian Current Law — Legislation* published after the most recent *Legislation Annual*.

Words and Phrases

The blue bound series of *The Abridgment* allows cases to be located by key words or phrases which have been considered or defined by Canadian courts. Each case listed includes an extract from the decision containing the particular word or phrase.

Step 1:
Consult the alphabetical listings in the hardcover volumes. These volumes contain cases up to 1992.

Step 2:
Update your search in the softcover supplement.

Step 3:
Refer to the "Words and Phrases" section of *Canadian Current Law — Case Digests*.

Index to Canadian Legal Literature

The *Index to Canadian Legal Literature* is a multi-volume set which provides references to articles and books, as well as to annotations, case commentary on important judgments, and significant changes in statute law. The Index has five parts:

(1)   "Subject Index";
(2)   "Author Index";
(3)   "Tables of Cases";
(4)   "Table of Statutes"; and
(5)   "Book Review Index".

Using the Subject Index to Find Articles on a Selected Topic
Searching publications from 1985 onwards.

Step 1:
Search each volume alphabetically by Library of Congress[4] titles. Scan the columns for potentially helpful articles.

Step 2:
Update your search in the softcover issues of *Canadian Current Law — Canadian Legal Literature*.

NOTE: For a pre-1985 search, check the subject authorities table in volume 3 of the 1981-1984 series. Go to the *Table of Contents* in the three volumes to find the location of a list of publications.

Searching by statute[5]

Step 1:
Look for your statute under the relevant subject heading for literature written between 1981-1987. For 1988 onwards, consult the *Table of Statutes* in each volume.

Step 2:
To update your search, refer to the table of statutes in *Canadian Current Law — Canadian Legal Literature*.

Online
The Index to Canadian Legal Literature can be found online using Quicklaw (ICLL database).

Canadian Weekly Law Sheet (cited as C.W.L.S.)

The *Canadian Weekly Law Sheet* is a weekly publication providing digests of all Canadian cases reported during that week, some unreported cases, and notes from official gazettes on new statutes, regulations, Royal Assents and proclamations. There are citations to the full text of the cases digested.

All-Canada Weekly Summaries (cited as A.C.W.S.)

This is a weekly looseleaf service of case summaries in civil matters from every jurisdiction in Canada. Every summary is preceded by subject classification and

---

[4]   These titles are more intuitive than those found in *The Abridgment*.

[5]   All other indices follow the same pattern as a search by subject.

key-word entries. There are no citations to the full text of the cases digested. Decisions are usually published within 8-14 weeks after they are rendered. The digests are collected in bound annual volumes, each served with a separate index. For the beginning student, the A.C.W.S. serves primarily as an updating tool in conventional library research. In addition, it may be used as a key-word glossary to prepare computer search strategies in general in the A.C.W.S. (Canada Law Book) database accessed through Quicklaw.

2. English Digests

The Digest: Annotated British, Commonwealth and European Cases (hereinafter referred to as *The Digest*; formerly *The English and Empire Digest*).

Scope

This work provides, in digest form, all the case law of England, together with a considerable body of cases from the courts of Scotland, Ireland, Canada, Australia, New Zealand, and other countries of the British Commonwealth. It also contains extensive annotations denoting every instance in which the case digested was referred to in any subsequent judgment.

Time-Frame

The first edition of *The Digest* was published between 1919 and 1932 in 47 volumes. It was replaced by a 56-volume second (blue-band) edition during the period 1950 to 1970. A third (green-band) edition was started in 1971. The cut-off date for a volume is noted on the page following the title page.

The main volumes of *The Digest* are kept up to date by *Continuation* volumes and an annual *Cumulative Supplement*. The *Supplement* does this, first, by extending the *Consolidated Table of Cases* from the date of publication to the present; second, by indicating where the text of the various titles has been amended or changed by subsequent cases and developments in the law. The main part of the *Supplement* contains new case digests and annotations relevant to the various titles in the main volume. The numbers used in the *Supplement* correspond with those in the main volumes. Small letter suffixes and roman numerals in brackets are appended to the numbers to show that a case or cases in the *Supplement* follow on naturally from the similarly numbered case in the main volumes. Where a new case appropriately appears at the beginning of a digest section, or before an existing case in the *Supplement*, the case is given a capital letter suffix.

Every few years the case digests in the annual *Supplements* are printed in a *Continuation* volume. Eventually, the materials in the latest *Supplement* and *Continuation* volumes are consolidated as reissued or new edition volumes. However, because at any given time only a limited number of titles are consolidated and reissued, all or parts of a *Continuation* volume may continue to be useful.

Format

The current green-band edition of *The Digest* consists of 52 main volumes, organized under 172 titles and several volumes of tables and indices. Each main volume includes:

(i)   a "Table of Contents" which follows the arrangement of the contents of the titles in *Halsbury's Laws of England, Fourth Edition*;

(ii)   a "Table of Cases".

Each entry in *The Digest* contains: (i) cross-references to a general statement of the law in *Halsbury's Laws of England, Fourth Edition*, and to related titles and topics; (ii) digests of English cases in consecutively numbered paragraphs; (iii) annotations to the digest of English cases; (iv) digests of "Scottish, Irish and Commonwealth [including Canada] Cases" (these form part of the consecutive numbering scheme adopted for the digests of English cases).

Finding Aids

There are four main finding aids for *The Digest* — the *Consolidated Index*, the *Consolidated Table of Cases*, the "Tables of Contents" for individual titles of *The Digest*, and the annual *Cumulative Supplement*.

Research Techniques

There are two ways to locate a case in *The Digest*: by subject matter; or by case name.

(i)   When the subject matter is known, scan the spines of the main volume (which are alphabetical) and select the appropriate volume or refer to the list of titles in the *Supplement* to point you to the relevant volume. The *Table of Contents* will help narrow your search within the broader headings.

Another approach is to consult the *Consolidated Index* and search by title. This table will list relevant volumes (in bold type), titles (in italics) and case numbers. This search method may be more helpful when the student has a more specific search topic such as "offer to consumers". The index lists the word "**OFFER**" and contains "consumers" as a subheading. You are then directed to **12(1)** *Contr* 1059. After consulting the list of title abbreviations at the front of volume 12(1), you know to look to paragraph 1059 under the title Contracts.

(ii)   To find a given case name, the digest of a case, and a citation to a report series, consult the *Consolidated Table of Cases*,[6] find the case name in the table, and obtain, as directed, the relevant title and volume number in the main volume:

Brixham Investments Ltd. v. Hansink (1971) (CAN) 12(1) Contr

Then, consult the "Table of Cases" in the main volume to find the case number, *e.g.*, 1558. Note the textual entry and citation.

In order to find cases that are more recent than the last main volume (which can lapse up to ten years), refer to the table of cases at the front of the *Cumulative Supplement*. There you will find the case name, the abbreviated title and a case number. Refer to the list of title abbreviations and turn to that case number for a summary. At the end of the summary, you will be directed to the long version of the decision in a case report series.

To find the various topics under which the case of *Bank of Nova Scotia v. Le Blanc* has been classified, a digest of the case, and a citation to one or more report series, consult the *Consolidated Table of Cases* volume which includes the cases beginning with the letters A-F. At page 171, locate the case and note the references to **8(2) Chos** and **9(2) Coys**. Consult the "Table of Cases" in volume 8(2) and locate case number 289 (referring to the *Bank of Nova Scotia* case), on page 41; consult the "Table of Cases" in volume 9(2) and note that the reference number for the *Bank of Nova Scotia* case is 4697 and is found on page 288.

Current Law (cited C.L.)

Scope

This work contains a comprehensive statement of contemporary English law and a selection of laws from Commonwealth jurisdictions.[7] In addition, it provides an exhaustive compilation of lists of cases and statutes which have been published or referred to in court.

---

[6]   The "Reference Adaptor", located at the back of each volume, shows the change in case numbering following the publication of a reissued volume.

[7]   Prior to 1991, there was a separate edition called *Scottish Current Law Yearbook*.

Time-Frame

Current Law has been published on a monthly basis since 1947 and has covered developments in the law from that date forward.

Format

Current Law is a multi-faceted paperback publication which includes digests of reported and unreported cases, digests of statutes and statutory instruments, commencement dates of statutes and statutory instruments, titles of new books, and citations to articles. The *Current Law Monthly Digests* are consolidated in an annual bound volume, the *Current Law Year Book*, which replaces the paper parts.

Finding Aids

As a first step, consult the "How to Use Current Law" pamphlet. It gives an overview of all the services which *Current Law* provides and instructions on how to use them.

Every issue of *Current Law Monthly Digest* contains a digest of cases, a "Cumulative Table of Cases", a "Cumulative (Subject) Index", a table of "Words and Phrases", a table of "Dates of Commencement — Statutes", a "Statute Citator" and an "Alphabetical Table of Statutory Instruments". The "Table of Cases" provides a list of the names of all the cases reported, judicially considered or otherwise commented upon, during the current year. The *Index* serves the digest portion of *Current Law*. Under each topic heading there is a reference to a month, and a paragraph where the digest of, or notes on, the topic may be found.

A *Current Law Year Book* incorporates each of these tables and finding aids, as well as an "Index of Articles", an "Index of Books" and a "Table of SR & O and SI Affected by Statutory Instruments of [year]". A year book also may contain an index which spans several years. For example, the index in the *1989 Year Book* consolidated the indices for the year books 1987 to 1989. There is also a "Cumulative Subject Index" in the *1976 Year Book* for the period 1947 to 1976, and one in the *1986 Year Book* for the year books 1972 to 1986. The index in the *1992 Year Book* is only for that year. In these indices reference is made to the year book and the paragraph number.

NOTE: When there is no date preceding the paragraph number, that reference is to be found in the *Current Law Consolidation 1947-1951*.

The *Current Law Case Citator* consists of three main volumes — 1947-1976, 1977-1997, 1998-2001 and 2002 to date. The *Current Law Legislation Citator* consists of three volumes — 1947-71, 1972-88 and 1989 to date. These services are updated by the *Current Law Monthly Digest*.

The *Current Law Case Citators* list the name of any case reported since 1947, excepting cases of the current year, and all the report series and journals, if any, in which the case is found. These case citators contain separate headings for England and Scotland. In addition, the case citators indicate, with respect to any case of any date:

(i)   the full name of any case reported between 1947 and 1993;

(ii)   an extensive list of references to the legal reports and journals of each case;

(iii)   the reference to the paragraph in the *Current Law Year Book* where a case is digested; and

(iv)   the history of any case which has been judicially considered, followed, overruled, distinguished or otherwise commented on from 1947 to 1998.

The *Current Law Legislation Citators* include a "Statute Citator", a "Statutory Instruments Citator", an "Alphabetical Table of Statutes" and an "Alphabetical Table of Statutory Instruments". From the *Legislation Citators*, which have been arranged in chronological order, it can promptly be ascertained:

(i)   what public general acts have been passed since 1947;

(ii)   in respect of any act of any date whether it has been repealed, amended or otherwise modified since 1947;

(iii)   in respect of any act of any date, what cases have been decided on it since 1947;

(iv)   in respect of any statute passed between 1947 and 1959, where it is summarized in the *Current Law* volumes and, for any statutes thereafter, the date of the Royal Assent;

(v)   from the "Legislation Not Yet in Force" table it can be determined which acts or sections have received Royal Assent but have not yet been brought into force and for which no commencement date has been fixed; and

(vi)   in respect of any statutory provision, the details of any statutory instrument issued since 1947.

There are also additional services now being offered. The *Current Law Statutes Annotated*, the *European Current Law* which is a monthly guide to recent legal development throughout Europe, and the *Current Law Year Books* 1986 to date on CD ROM.

Research Techniques

(i)   To find case and statute law on a topic under investigation, consult the "Index 1947-76" in the *Current Law Year Book 1976* and scan the columns for the topic under investigation. References in the index are to a paragraph number in a year book or to the *Current Law Consolidation 1947-1951*. Then, consult the year book or *Consolidation* as directed for case and statute notes, and case digests. Next, consult the "Index 1972-1986" in the *Current Law Year Book 1986*, followed by the "Index 1987-1989" in the *1989 Year Book*. Bring the research forward by means of the indices at the back of subsequent year books, as well as the "Cumulative Index" at the back of the most recent issue of *Current Law Monthly Digest*, which provides the month and paragraph references for locating particular cases and statute law.

(ii)   To find a selected case name, in order to ascertain where it has been reported and whether the case has subsequently been judicially considered, refer to the relevant *Current Law Case Citator* (*i.e.*, 1947-1976, 1977-88, 1989 to date) and the "Cumulative Table of Cases" in the most recent issue of *Current Law Monthly Digest*.

(iii)   To find a selected section of a statute, in order to determine if it has been modified or received judicial consideration, refer to the relevant *Current Law Legislation Citator* (*i.e.*, 1947-71, 1972-88, 1989-95, 1996-99, 2000-01 and 2002 to date) and to the "Statute Citator" section in the most recent issue of *Current Law Monthly Digest*. If the consolidation of *Current Law Legislation Citator* for the last calendar year is not published at the time of your research, consult the "Statute Citator" section in the December issue of *Current Law Monthly Digest* and then refer to the most recent monthly digest.

C. CASE CITATORS

1. Canadian

The Canadian Abridgment, Second Edition, Canadian Case Citations

The Abridgment provides an extensive citation service for Canadian cases. The work is described, *above*, at page 83.

Dominion Law Reports, Annotation Service

This publication provides a table of cases which have been judicially considered or disposed of on appeal from any decision reported in the *Dominion Law*

Reports. The period covered is noted on the title page. The annotations are listed under the D.L.R. volume and page number where the original case was reported. The nature of the disposition or consideration is indicated by abbreviations which are explained in the introduction. The work is described, above, at page 56.

NOTE: Several other works offer citations or annotations to Canadian cases. These include:

(i)   the *All England Law Reports* index volumes;
(ii) all the report series published by Maritime Law Book Company. Each volume of the individual report series (referred to on page 59) and;
(iii) Western Legal Publication (W.L.P.) database on Quicklaw.

2. English

There are a number of English publications which provide case citations and annotations, including the *All England Law Reports* index volumes, *The Law Reports* index volumes, *The Digest*, and *Current Law Case Citator*. These have been described in detail in the foregoing materials.

D. STATUTE CITATORS

Canadian Statute Citators (includes an issue for each province/territory as well as a federal issue)
Canada Statute Citator
Selected Provincial Citator Services

E. WORDS AND PHRASES

1. Canadian

The Encyclopedia of Words and Phrases, Legal Maxims

J. Gardner, ed., *Words and Phrases, Legal Maxims* (Toronto: Thomson Canada (Carswell), 1986).

The fourth edition of this work, in looseleaf binders, covers definitions provided by Canadian courts between 1825 and 1985. Under each word or phrase, definitions are listed according to the hierarchy of the courts. This work offers the most comprehensive coverage of Canadian judicial definitions. It is updated by cumulative supplements.

The Canadian Abridgment, Second Edition, Words and Phrases (Revised)

This is a compilation of individual words and phrases which have been defined or interpreted by a court. *Words and Phrases* are set out in alphabetical order, together with one or more citations to cases which have considered the word or phrase. For a full description on using *Words and Phrases*, see the section on *The Abridgment* in this chapter.

NOTE: Other sources of words and phrases include the *Western Weekly Reports* and all the report series published by Maritime Law Book Company.

2. English

Words and Phrases Legally Defined

J.B. Saunders, ed., *Words and Phrases Legally Defined,* 3rd ed. (London: Butterworths, 1995).

Words and Phrases Legally Defined provides judicial definitions from decisions in the House of Lords, the Privy Council and the superior courts of England, Canada, Australia and New Zealand. Under each word or phrase, there is an explanatory note followed by extracts from cases.

NOTE: Other sources of words and phrases include the *Current Law Year Book* and *Current Law Monthly Digest*, the index volumes to *The Law Reports*, the *All England Law Reports*, *Halsbury's Laws of England*, and *The Digest*.

F. DICTIONARIES

In addition to the standard dictionaries of the English language, a legal dictionary is invaluable to anyone involved in the law. Legal dictionaries provide definitions of legal words and phrases and ordinary words and phrases expressly defined by the courts. The following publications are usually available in a university law library:

Stroud's Judicial Dictionary of Words and Phrases

J.S. James, ed., *Stroud's Judicial Dictionary of Words and Phrases,* 6th ed. (London: Sweet & Maxwell, 2000).

Published in its sixth edition in 2000, it consists of three volumes. Definitions are annotated with references to English cases and statutes and to Commonwealth cases. The set is kept up to date by a softcover cumulative supplement.

Jowitt's Dictionary of English Law

J. Burke, ed., *Jowitt's Dictionary of English Law*, 2nd ed. (London: Sweet & Maxwell, 1977).

E. Williams, ed., *Second Supplement to Jowitt's Dictionary of English Law*, (London: Sweet & Maxwell, 1985).

Published in 1977, this is a two-volume work with annotations to English statutes, cases and standard textbooks. It is now in its second edition and is updated by a hardcover cumulative supplement published in 1985.

Osborn's Concise Law Dictionary

L. Rutherford & S. Bone, eds., *Osborn's Concise Law Dictionary*, 9th ed. (London: Sweet & Maxwell, 2001).

Published in its ninth edition in 2001, this is a "user friendly" single-volume work which provides selected annotations to English statutes and cases.

Mozley & Whiteley's Law Dictionary

H.N. Mozley, *Mozley & Whiteley's Law Dictionary*, 12th ed. by E.R. Hardy Ivamy (London: Butterworth & Co., 2001).

This single-volume work is now in its 12th edition. It provides definitions of legal terms and phrases of the past and present, as well as expositions of the law.

Black's Law Dictionary

J.R. Nolan & J.M. Nolan-Haley, *Black's Law Dictionary*, 7th ed. by West Publishing Company Editorial Staff (St. Paul: West Publishing, 1999).

Published in its seventh edition in 1999, *Black's Law Dictionary* is an exhaustive one-volume work with annotations to American cases and to older English cases and commentaries.

Canadian Law Dictionaries

J. Yogis, *Canadian Law Dictionary*, 5th ed. (New York: Barron's Educational Series, 2003).

R.S. Vasan, ed., *The Canadian Law Dictionary* (Don Mills, Ontario: Law and Business Publications, 1980).

D.A. Dukelow & B. Nuse, *The Dictionary of Canadian Law*, 2nd ed. (Scarborough, Ontario: Thomson Professional Publishing Canada, 1994).

G. CITATION RULES FOR CANADIAN LEGAL MATERIALS

McGill Law Journal, *Canadian Guide to Uniform Legal Citation*, 5th ed. (Toronto: Thomson Canada (Carswell), 2002).

C. Tang, Guide to Legal Citation & Sources of Citation Aid: A Canadian Perspective, 2nd ed. (Toronto: Thomson Canada (Carswell), 1988).

H. RESEARCH GUIDES

M.A. Banks *et al.*, *Banks on Using a Law Library: A Canadian Guide to Legal Research*, 6th ed. (Toronto: Thomson Canada (Carswell), 1994).

E.M. Campbell *et al.*, *Legal Research Materials and Methods*, 4th ed. (Sydney: The Law Book, 1996).

J.R. Castel & O.K. Latchman, *The Practical Guide to Canadian Legal Research*, 2nd ed. (Toronto: Thomson Canada (Carswell), 1996).

P. Clinch, *Using a Law Library*, 2nd ed. (London: Blackstone Press, 2001).

J. Dane & P.A. Thomas, *How to Use a Law Library*, 4th ed. (London: Sweet & Maxwell, 2001).

E.M.A. Kwaw, *The Guide to Legal Analysis, Legal Methodology and Legal Writing* (Toronto: Emond Montgomery Publications, 1992).

D.T. MacEllven & M.J. McGuire, *Legal Research Handbook*, 4th ed. (Markham, Ontario: Butterworths Canada Ltd., 1998).

I. LEGAL PERIODICALS

Legal periodicals contain collections of varied writings on the law published at regular intervals (monthly, quarterly, etc.). The typical periodical contains several articles on subjects of current interest (often in considerable detail), book reviews, and "comments" on important recent cases. There are two types of periodicals: those of a general nature covering any legal subject (*e.g., The Canadian Bar Review, Yale Law Journal*) and those of a specialized nature (*e.g., Criminal Law Quarterly*). Some periodicals devote whole issues to an exhaustive discussion of one subject in its various aspects, such as town planning or juvenile delinquency.

Although most periodicals publish their own indices, the search for periodical literature most usefully begins with a general index. The most comprehensive is the *Index to Legal Periodicals* published for the American Association of Law Libraries. Commencing in 1908, it covers major articles, notes, case comments, and book reviews from periodicals published in the United States, Canada, the United Kingdom, Australia and New Zealand. The work is indexed by subject and author and currently includes a table of case comments and a book review index. It appears monthly, with quarterly and annual cumulations since its commencement, and triennial cumulations beginning in 1926. Legal articles in non-legal journals may be located in the *Index to Periodical Articles Related to Law*, which has been published since 1958. In addition, there is an *Index to Foreign Legal Periodicals*, published annually since 1960.

There are three major Canadian sources of legal periodical literature: the *Index to Canadian Legal Literature*, the *Canadian Abridgment, Third Edition*, the *Index to Canadian Legal Periodical Literature* and *Current Law Index*.

CHAPTER 4
Computerized Legal Research

For today's law students it is hard to believe that computerized research was first introduced to most Canadian law schools in the early 1980s. In a relatively short period of time computerized legal research has become the mainstay of legal research. It continues to evolve in the sources available and the methods used.

Although it has not replaced paper based research, it has become an important component of law school and law office libraries. Many law schools and legal libraries no longer carry paper copies of large sections of material, (American and English jurisprudence in particular) while electronic services such as Quicklaw and WestlaweCarswell work at making worldwide legal materials easily accessible.

Virtually every legal research problem has some aspect which is more quickly and more thoroughly dealt with through computerized research. As with all research methods, the real benefit comes from understanding the advantages and disadvantages, the variety of sources available and training on the use of particular electronic services, so that you can choose the most efficient, thorough and cost effective way to meet your research needs.

Computerized legal research offers a number of important features including:

(i)   convenience;
(ii)   speed of retrieval;
(iii) accuracy;
(iv)   access to a larger volume of material; and
(v)   currency.

Traditionally, the single most important component of any computerized legal retrieval system is speed. For example, in less than one minute, Quicklaw or WestlaweCarswell or the National Reporter System (Maritime Law Book) can search for a phrase in more than one million cases stored in their databases. By contrast, an equivalent search by conventional library methods using the paper versions (if available) could take hours.

In recent years, there has been an impressive growth in the number and types of legal databases available in Canada. These databases range from free resources available through CANLII, and most governments across Canada, to CD ROM subscriptions found in most law libraries, to pay as you go subscriptions through Quicklaw, WestlaweCarswell and the National Reporter System of Maritime Law Book.

While the computer's speed and ability to find volumes of information will readily be apparent to the beginning student, its value in expanding traditional research techniques, and providing the most germane material available will be less evident. Becoming familiar with the sources of material available will assist you to chose the best source for your particular needs. As an example, Quicklaw and Westlaw*e*Carswell provide access to vast numbers of cases, commentaries and legislation; however, particular governmental sites often provide legislation in a form which better allows the user to check for a particular type of provision.

The following provides some examples of research options and capabilities that are available for computerized legal research. We have divided our sources into those which provide solely legislative material, those which provide legislative material and case law, and those which include commentaries, and texts.

NOTE: This chapter is intended to be an introduction to the electronic sources available, and to provide information on what we believe to be the best resources available to law students. For a more detailed discussion of computer/electronic research, see Aleksandra Zivanovic, *Guide to Electronic Research*, 2nd ed. (Markham, Ont.: LexisNexis Butterworths, 2002).

A. STATUTORY MATERIAL

1. Canada

The easiest way to access statutory material online is through one of the two central Canadian portals: <http://www.canlii.org> and <http://www.legis.ca>. Both of these central sites have links to both national sites and the individual provincial sites. Legis.ca is a site developed and maintained by the department of justice that specializes in legislation and has links to: statutes, regulations and bills. Canlii.org maintains its own searchable database of statutes and regulations for a selection of provinces and is a more efficient search tool than the alphabetical listing that exists on the provincial sites. We have provided a detailed discussion of Canlii.org below.

Canada (federal)

Statutes and Regulations	<http://laws.justice.gc.ca/>
Status of Bills	<http://www.parl.gc.ca/common/index.asp>
Bar Society Web site	<www.cba.org>
CanLII Searchable	Yes

British Columbia

Statutes and Regulations	<http://www.qp.gov.bc.ca/statreg/>

Status of Bills	<http://www.legis.gov.bc.ca/>
Bar Society Web site	<http://www.lawsociety.bc.ca/>
CanLII Searchable	No

British Columbia provides a free online electronic library at <http://www.bcpl.gov.bc.ca/ell/> that includes links to case law, statutes and regulations.

Alberta

Statutes and Regulations	<http://www.qp.gov.ab.ca/>
Status of Bills	<http://www.assembly.ab.ca/>
Bar Society Web site	<http://www.lawsocietyalberta.com/>
CanLII Searchable	Yes

Saskatchewan

Statutes and Regulations	<http://www.qp.gov.sk.ca/>
Status of Bills	<http://www.legassembly.sk.ca/>
Bar Society Web site	<http://www.lawsociety.sk.ca/>
CanLII Searchable	Yes

Manitoba

Statutes and Regulations	<http://www.gov.mb.ca/chc/statpub/>
Status of Bills	<http://www.gov.mb.ca/leg-asmb/>
Bar Society Web site	<http://www.lawsociety.mb.ca/>
CanLII Searchable	Yes

Ontario

Statutes and Regulations	<http://www.e-laws.gov.on.ca/>
Status of Bills	<http://www.ontla.on.ca/>
Bar Society Web site	<http://www.lsuc.on.ca/>
CanLII Searchable	Yes

Quebec

Statutes and Regulations	<http://publicationsduquebec.gouv.qc.ca>
Status of Bills	<http://www.assnat.qc.ca/>
Bar Society Web site	<http://www.barreau.qc.ca/>
CanLII Searchable	Yes

New Brunswick

Statutes and Regulations	<http://www.gnb.ca/0062/acts/acts-e.asp>
Status of Bills	<http://www.gnb.ca/legis/index.asp>
Bar Society Web site	<http://www.lawsociety.nb.ca/>
CanLII Searchable	Yes

Nova Scotia

Statutes and Regulations	<http://www.gov.ns.ca/legi/legc/>
Status of Bills	<http://www.gov.ns.ca/legislature/>
Bar Society Web site	<http://www.nsbs.ns.ca/>
CanLII Searchable	Yes

Prince Edward Island

Statutes	<http://www.gov.pe.ca/law/statutes/[1]>
Status of Bills	<http://www.assembly.pe.ca/>
Bar Society Web site	No Site
CanLII Searchable	No

Newfoundland

Statutes and Regulations	<http://www.gov.nf.ca/hoa/sr/>
Status of Bills	<http://www.gov.nf.ca/hoa/>
Bar Society Web site	<http://www.lawsociety.nf.ca/>
CanLII Searchable	No

Yukon

Statutes and Regulations	<http://www.canlii.org/yk/sta/>
Status of Bills	<http://www.gov.yk.ca/leg-assembly/>
Bar Society Web site	<http://www.lawsocietyyukon.com/default.asp>
CanLII Searchable	No

Northwest Territories

Statutes and Regulations	<http://www.canlii.ca/nt/sta/>
Status of Bills	<http://www.assembly.gov.nt.ca/>
Bar Society Web site	<http://www.lawsociety.nt.ca/>
CanLII Searchable	No

---

[1] P.E.I. Regulations are not published online.

Nunavut

Statutes and Regulations	<http://www.canlii.org/nu/sta/>
Status of Bills	<http://www.assembly.nu.ca/>
Bar Society Web site	<http://lawsociety.nu.ca/members.html>
CanLII Searchable	No

2. United States

Cornell University Law School's Legal Information Institute, LII Web site, <http://www.law.cornell.edu/> offers the user free access to statutory and case authority for the U.S. in addition to international material. The site offers the user the ability to search by subject area, jurisdiction or for a particular document. In addition to traditional legal material, the Law Source by Jurisdiction option provides links to legal dictionaries, and embassies. The mission statement for the site includes the following goal, "To make law more accessible not only to U.S. legal professionals but to students, teachers, and the general public in the U.S. and abroad."

3. United Kingdom

Her Majesty's Stationary Service, a free access government Web site found at, <http://www.hmso.gov.uk/> delivers a wide range of services to the public, information industry and government relating to access and re-use of government information. The site offers, but is not limited to information and access to U.K. legislation, Gazettes and copyright. The site is straightforward and easy to use, the legislation and explanatory notes are broken down by jurisdiction, and are searchable.

B. CASELAW, STATUTORY MATERIAL, COMMENTARIES AND TEXTS

In the last couple of years, there has been a trend where the electronic legal services have been combining with a large publishing company. The underlying idea being that by combining resources instead of duplicating them, each is able to provide a better, faster and more comprehensive service at a better price. Quicklaw, Butterworths and LexisNexis have combined into one large legal information company, as have Westlaw, Carswell and Thomson Publishing. The effect, from my perspective, has been what was intended. Each organization seems to have improved in all of the areas that they intended. All of the electronic services are currently available, free of charge to Canadian law schools. If your school doesn't currently offer one of the services, and you are interested, contact the company directly. They are usually happy to sign you up and offer training.

A. Quicklaw and LexisNexis

Quicklaw, one of the first computerized legal research databases, has undergone major changes. Quicklaw is now packaged with LexisNexis as companion services. The major difference between the two is that Quicklaw continues to focus on Canadian content, while LexisNexis focuses on American, United Kingdom, Australian and some European content.

Both services offer access to authoritative primary and secondary legal material. The particular ones offered are far too numerous to list, but of particular interest to law students may be the fact that LexisNexis has the All English Reports, and Shepard's, (a citation service conceptually similar to *The Abridgment*), while Quicklaw offers comprehensive Canadian case law reporting, through the inclusion of Canada Law Book's summary services (*All Canada Weekly Summaries*, *Weekly Criminal Bulletin* and *Canadian Labour Arbitration Summaries*) linked to the full text of the judgments.

Each of the services has its own interface, although they intend to integrate them into one within the next two years.

Access to LexisNexis is available through the Internet at <http://www.lexisnexis.ca>. Quicklaw is available at <http://www.quicklaw.com>, and offers a downloadable interface or an online interface. The advantage of the online interfaces is that you can access the service from any computer with Internet access. If you intend to use Quicklaw from home, we recommend downloading the software, because it makes searching faster.

In the last few years Quicklaw has changed its interface so that you do not have to do traditional Boolean searches. You can simply type the party, words, level of court, judge and or year that you are looking for into the form, select whether you require all or some of them to be in the document. The form is pretty self-explanatory for any computer literate person; however, narrowing your search so as to locate the best search results requires some training. For those who are experienced with Boolean searching, Quicklaw allows you the option of performing a straight Boolean search.

A particularly useful tool to a first year law student in narrowing his or her search is the topical database selection. After you sign on, you will be asked for a client identifier, and then taken to a database selection screen. By clicking on "Canada", then, "Topical Collections of Caselaw Commentaries & Statutory Materials" you will be taken to an alphabetical topical index. Once you select a particular subject you will then be able to continue to narrow the sources that you are searching before you even get to the key word searching stage. By going through this process, you can significantly improve your search results.

Also of note is the fact that Quicklaw has numerous leading texts available and searchable through its normal interface. By going through the topical database selection mentioned above, you can select texts and/or commentaries only, and then search for particular terms. The availability of texts indexed by subject, and searchable on line, (at home) is an invaluable tool to a first-year law student.

As suggested above, the ability to key word search commentaries on a particular legal subject is one of the best tools Quicklaw offers to first-year students. The following is an example of a search based on the Fact Scenario at the beginning of the book:

After signing in and providing a client identifier, you will be taken to a screen that looks like this:

...**What's New?**   Check Announcements, including . . .

- Nova Scotia Human Rights Board of Inquiry: Johnson v. Halifax Regional Police Service, now available: (NSHR) (Announcement).

- Butterworths Construction NetLetter™ (BCST) (Announcement).

- Canada Regulations and Rules of Court (SOR) (Announcement).

- Butterworths Sentencing NetLetter™ (BSEN) (Announcement).

Database Directory
Supreme Court of Canada Service

- Now available:
  15 rulings on applications for leave to appeal released Thursday, January 8. No appeal judgments are expected.

LAW/NET Legal Update Service

Click on "Database Directory" to be taken to,

Quicklaw provides access to 2500 databases in the following collections. All collections are available to Quicklaw users.

- Canada
- Commonwealth
  - Africa
  - Australia
  - Caribbean
  - Malaysia

- European Union
- Ireland
- United Kingdom
- United States
- Quicklaw News and Announcements

By clicking on "Canada" you will be taken to a page which includes this:

Canada
  Legal Databases

- Statutory Materials
- Court and Tribunal Decisions
    - Supreme Court of Canada
    - LAW/NET Legal Update Service
    - Federal and National Collection
    - Provincial and Territorial Collections
    - *NetLetters*™ (Current awareness services)
- Topical Collections of Caselaw, Commentary and Statutory Materials
- Commentary (Law Journals, Texts, Newsletters, Press Releases, Indexes)
- Case Citators
- Legal Directories

Then by clicking on "Topical Collections of Caselaw, Commentary and Statutory Materials" you will be taken to a page which includes the following subject headings:

- Health Law
- Human Rights Law
- Immigration Law
- Insolvency Law
- Insurance Law
- Intellectual Property Law
- International Law
- Labour Law (Unionized employees)
- Landlord & Tenant Law
- Legal Profession

Click on "Insurance Law" to get to a list of subheadings.

Commentary

• Insurance Law Commentary, a global of journals, articles, papers and newsletters. For a list of present contents: <u>scope JOUR</u>	<u>ISPA</u>	1990 to date

The following titles also are included:

o Lexpert Articles on Recent Legal Developments	<u>LEXD</u>	2000 to date
o Nelligan O'Brien Payne Newsletters	<u>NPNL</u>	1992 to date
o Practical Strategies for Advocates Programmes	<u>PSAP</u>	1990 to date
o LAW/NET Corporate, Commercial, Insurance	<u>LNCO</u>	1990 to date

Click on the ISPA link from the "Commentary" section. You will now be at the final screen which looks like the one below. From here, you simply input your key words. We have used "assume!" and "risk" then selected "all words 'near' each other" from the drop down tab to the right of the box.

Boolean Search

Ranking: | statistical, newest first ▼ | **Automatic plurals:** | off ▼ |

Search for:

Title:		any of these words ▼
Author:		any of these words ▼
Citation:		any of these words ▼
Text:		any of these words ▼
Any field:		any of these words ▼

Find by citation   Help on Quicklaw query syntax

SEARCH   **CLEAR**

After clicking the "Search" button, you will be taken to your results page. On the left is a list of the case names. By clicking on a case name, the text of the case or commentary will come up on the right. Read the intro to the document to see if it is directly on point. Sometimes you will be able to rule out a document without going further, but usually you will need to look further. By clicking on the words "locate next" located on the green bar at the top of your screen, you can skip to each point that your search terms appear in the document.

Time spent learning how to search effectively is time well spent. As law students and later lawyers, good research skills will be one of your best assets. Contact your student Quicklaw representative, (if your school has one) and ask about training or contact Quicklaw directly.

2. Westlaw*e*Carswell

Carswell electronic services, Thomson Publishing and Westlaw have combined to form the other major source of legal information in Canada. The corporate goal is to utilize the Westlaw*e*Carswell online platform in conjunction with Thomson's international legal publishing empire to make one-stop shopping for world-wide legal information and services.

*e*Carswell has created its own computerized research database. Through this system, one can search "Criminal Source", "Family Source", "Insolvency Source" or "Securities Source". These sites contain both case law and all Canadian legislation relevant to those specific areas of law. For a more general approach to case law research, "Law Source" contains all Carswell publications as well as all officially reported cases since 1986 and unreported decisions from 1996 onward.

*e*Carswell has also acquired the rights to distribute Westlaw, a major American resource, in Canada.

All of the electronic services are integrated into one online interface which allows you to switch from Westlaw, to Law Source to Insolvency Source by clicking on tabs located at the top of the interface. You also have the option of customizing or creating new tabs at any time. These services are available, free of charge to Canadian law students, so if your school does not currently provide access, contact your local Carswell representative through their Web site at <http://www.carswell.com>, in the top right hand corner of the window, you just click on "Find a Carswell Rep".

The Westlaw*e*Carswell and Quicklaw/LexisNexis services seem comparable in content, while each offers its own particularly useful tools. Conducting the same search on both systems often gets different results, and for that reason, using both is the best way to ensure that you are finding the best legal information available.

For a first-year law student, the one stop shopping approach of the Westlaw*e*-Carswell interface makes the whole process a little easier. For Canadian content, students will likely be using the Law Source tab, so I will restrict my comments on features to that particular service.

One of the best features available to a first-year student, is the online Abridgment available through Law Source. Through the online Abridgment, you can scroll through an alphabetical index of legal subject areas, and then click on each to allow for further specification. When you take the process to the last click, it will show summaries of cases which have impacted on that particular area of the law. The main advantage, is that you don't have to know an area of law in detail to be able to identify the relevant issues in that area, and to access the relevant cases. Law Source offers an online form for conducting key word searches. Unlike Quicklaw, you do need to be familiar with Boolean searching, but there is a help button which explains the process, and a Boolean connector quick reference guide.

The following is an example of an Abridgment search based on the Fact Scenario at the beginning of the book.

After signing in and providing a client identifier, you will be taken to the main screen. On the left hand side of the screen, you will see the following:

BROWSE TABLES OF CONTENTS

<u>Canadian Abridgment Digests</u>
<u>CED</u>
<u>Legislation</u>
<u>Rules Concordance</u>
<u>LawSource Directory</u>

Click on "Canadian Abridgment Digests" which will take you to an alphabetical list of subject areas including:

☐ ⊞ I1 Income tax

☐ ⊞ I3 Injunctions

☐ ⊞ I4 Insurance

☐ ⊞ I5 Intellectual property

☐ ⊞ I6 International Law

☐ ⊞ J1 Judges and courts

By clicking on the plus symbol beside "Insurance" you will open a list of sub-categories:

☐ ⊟ **I4 Insurance**

☐ ⊞ I Regulation of insurance industry

☐ ⊞ II Agents, brokers and adjusters

☐ ⊞ III Contracts of insurance

☐ ⊞ IV Principles of interpretation and construction

☐ ⊞ V Insurable interest

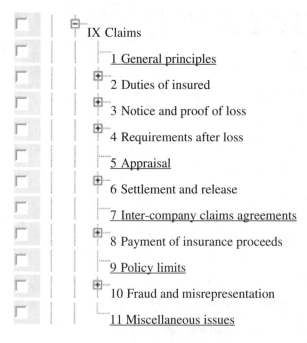

☐ ⊞ VI Contract of indemnity

☐ ⊞ VII Extent of risk (exclusions)

☐ ⊞ VIII Disclosure of risk

☐ ⊞ IX Claims

☐ ⊞ X Actions on policies

☐ ⊞ XI Principles applicable to specific types of insurance

☐ ⊞ XII Marine insurance

☐ ⊞ XIII No-fault automobile insurance

☐ XV Miscellaneous issues

From within this list, if you click on the plus symbol beside "Claims" you will open a list of further sub-categories:

☐ ⊟ IX Claims

☐   1 General principles

☐   ⊞ 2 Duties of insured

☐   ⊞ 3 Notice and proof of loss

☐   ⊞ 4 Requirements after loss

☐   5 Appraisal

☐   ⊞ 6 Settlement and release

☐   7 Inter-company claims agreements

☐   ⊞ 8 Payment of insurance proceeds

☐   9 Policy limits

☐   ⊞ 10 Fraud and misrepresentation

☐   11 Miscellaneous issues

You may click on any of the underlined words at anytime to be taken to summaries of the relevant cases in that area, or by clicking on any plus symbol you will be taken to a list of sub-categories within that sub-category.

As mentioned above, Law Source also allows for key word searches in addition to locating a particular case. Features including, searching within a search can assist the speed and accuracy of your results. Contact your student representative, (if your school has one) or contact Westlaw*e*Carswell for training. We note that training is also provided over the phone.

3. Maritime Law Book

Maritime Law Book provides computerized research capabilities along with its bound editions. The site was overhauled in 2003 and re-launched in late December with a new user friendly interface. The site is easy to use and allows for key word searches where the user can then skip to the key words as they appear in the document (similar to that of Quicklaw and Westlaw*e*Carswell).

Although its database may not be as large as that of Quicklaw or Westlaw*e*-Carswell the site offers case reporters from all of the Canadian jurisdictions and allows the user to do a Key Number Search which takes full advantage of the Maritime Law Book Key Number System. The Key Number Search allows the user to choose a subject area, and then breaks that subject down into all of the issues within that area. This is particularly useful to a law student, because it essentially lists all of the issues within a given area of the law, and links each issue to case law. The Maritime Law Book Key Number Search is very easy to use and provides an exceptional level of issue breakdown. It essentially allows a person with little or no knowledge of a particular legal area to go through each of the Key Numbers (specific issues) and decide if they apply.

The following is an example of a Key Number Search based on the Fact Scenario at the beginning of the book,

From the main page at <http://www.mlb.nb.ca>, simply click on "Key Number Search" located near the top of the left hand side of the page. You will be taken to a screen with an alphabetical list of subject areas which are listed on the left hand side of the page. Simply go down the list to locate the general area in which you are interested.

   ...

Habeas Corpus
Health
Highways
Hospitals

Income Tax
Indians, Inuit and Metis
Infants
Injunctions
Insurance
Interest
International Law

Joint Ventures
  ...

When you click on "Insurance" a list of sub headings (Key Numbers) will come up on the right hand side. A portion of which reads:

INSURANCE: ACCIDENT AND SICKNESS INSURANCE (3501 - 3700)

EXCLUSIONS (3581 - 3600)

3581 General

3582 What constitutes

3585 Noncompliance with statutory requirements

3586 Death caused or contributed to, directly or indirectly, by disease

3588 Pre-existing condition

3589 Abuse of medication, drugs or alcohol

INSURANCE: ACCIDENT AND SICKNESS INSURANCE (3501 - 3700)

DEFENCES (3601 - 3620)

3601 General

3607 Statutory exclusions

3608 Other insurance

3610 Commission of criminal offence by insured

3611 Intentional self-infliction of an injury or illness

3614 Bars to defences, incontestable clauses

By clicking on any of the Key Numbers, you are taken to a list of cases which may be sorted by number of hits, or other criteria. To view any of the cases, you simply click on either the case name or the "View Document" button.

The ease of use and extensive issue breakdown of the Key Number section makes this site great for someone who is not familiar with the issues surrounding a particular area. Maritime Law Book provides full access to all Canadian law students, and will provide training at any school if requested. Even if you don't sign up for the site, you can access the Key Number Search function, although you will not be able to see the full text of the decisions.

4. CANLII

CanLII is part of the LII group of free public services, maintained and developed by Cornell University that links to statutes and regulations as well as having a searchable case law section that is indexed by the court where the decision came from. CanLII was developed as an initiative of the Federation of Law Societies of Canada (an umbrella organization of Canada's 14 law societies) and provides access to case law and primary legal sources through the Internet without requiring the user to download any software.

CanLII is designed to be, and is, fairly user friendly. It uses the SINO search engine system which allows the user to conduct searches using typical language (*i.e.* "general and leg and damages"). Although based on Boolean searching like the search engines of Quicklaw and WestlaweCarswell, SINO is significantly different. In my opinion, time spent reviewing the search tips located on the site, is time well spent.

Both legislation and case law are searchable and offer the ability to locate your search terms within each document.

One downside to CanLII is that there is no consistency in scope offered by each collection.

Features: User friendly search engine
Search term locator built into the site
Full text of decisions
Decisions available in French and English.
Free public access

CHAPTER 5

Legal Writing

In many law offices the first test of an articling clerk will be his or her ability to write a clear and useful memorandum of law. This is no less true for the beginning law student. Often, the beginning clerk or student will have great difficulty in arranging legal material in the order that will be most helpful to the reader. Indeed, in some instances, the considerable efforts expended in the research process are wasted because of a poorly presented paper. Where there is a deficiency, it can be mastered only with a great deal of practice.

No one can lay down a detailed formula for presenting materials. The organization of a paper will vary depending on the nature of the problem. Also, since an office memorandum is written for the use of another member of the firm, its form will depend, in part, on the instructions given by the person concerned. Typically, the paper will be informal and structured with headings and subheadings to enable the reader to quickly find a discussion of a particular question. The following suggested scheme may serve as a model of an office memorandum of law.

A. WRITING A MEMORANDUM

1. Title

If litigation has commenced, use the title of the proceedings, *e.g.*,

Between

    Lisa Smith

                                           Plaintiff

    -and-

    ABC Insurance Company, a body corporate

                                        Defendant

If litigation has not yet commenced, use the following title: ....

TO: Senior Partner
FROM: Articling Clerk
DATE: June 1, 2004
RE: Refusal of ABC Insurance Company to pay Accidental Death Benefits
            to our client, Lisa Smith

2. Facts

State the most material facts in one or two short paragraphs. The finer details should be discussed in the main body of the memorandum as the student applies the principles of law, culled from the research, to the particular facts of the problem under investigation.

3. Statement of the Questions Presented or Raised by the Facts

This part of the memorandum should give a clear statement of the main issues to be resolved. A statement of the narrower issues will normally be included in the body of the paper at the beginning of each new section.

4. Introduction

This is usually one or two paragraphs long and serves to orient the reader to the general field or fields of law to be discussed. It may also include a brief statement of the answer. Further, when there is concern about the exclusion of a discussion of a particular topic (which does not directly help to resolve the problem), it may be useful to explain your reasons in the introduction.

5. Discussion

Each issue formulated (under 3, above) should be developed in sequence. Present the authorities on which the conclusion rests, remembering that the purpose of the memorandum is to explore and evaluate both sides of a question. Therefore, the student should give equal attention to cases and other authorities that tend to support the client's position as to those cases and authorities that do not. The main purpose of a memorandum is to provide a reliable statement of law. It is not generally conceived as a forum for opinion, persuasive argument, or the writer's notions about what the law should be. It does, however, require the student to distinguish cases and to draw inferences from particular cases to the problem under investigation. As well, it may, when the authorities are in conflict or when little or no law can be found, require commentary on social or policy considerations.

6. Conclusion

The conclusion should include a brief summary of the main points and an evaluation of the strengths and weaknesses of the case law in terms of providing an answer to the legal issues of the question you have been asked to answer. If the research suggests that the law is unclear on a point, this should be acknowledged.

7. Recommendations

In some instances, it is appropriate for a memorandum to include a recommendation of action to be taken or strategy to be pursued. Usually, this relates directly to the contemplated litigation and may include commentary on the need for more information or on how to support the client's position. It may also include a suggestion to guide the future conduct or policies of the client.

SAMPLE MEMORANDUM

TO: Senior Partner

FROM: Articling Clerk

DATE: April, 1, 2004

RE: Mrs. Smith's Insurance Claim

Statement of Facts

Mr. Smith was 35 years old at the time of his death. He was a successful accountant and his wife was pregnant with their first child. According to his wife, Mr. Smith had many friends and appeared to be happy with their marriage and excited for the birth of his child. In his spare time, Mr. Smith enjoyed participating in "extreme" activities such as bungee-jumping and skydiving. Mrs. Smith said that her husband rarely drank alcohol, however when he did, he had a tendency to "overdo it" and become extremely intoxicated. On these occasions, Mrs. Smith could recall him attempting foolish and risky activities, however, she would not characterize her husband as having a drinking problem.

After his wife had become pregnant, Mr. Smith bought a handgun for the protection of his family. He had taken his gun to a shooting range on several occasions and would regularly clean it at the kitchen table.

On the night of Thursday, August 14, 2003, Mr. Smith and his wife had a disagreement. Mrs. Smith recalled that the fight had been about the family's finances, which, according to her husband, were worse than he had previously let on to her. Mrs. Smith did not feel that this fight was a serious one, and the following evening Mrs. Smith left the home on an overnight visit to her parents'. When she returned on the morning of Saturday, August 15, 2003, she found her husband's body slumped over the kitchen table. Mrs. Smith recalled seeing a large amount of blood around her husband's head and on the floor around him, and saw his gun on the floor beside him. On the table, she saw an open bottle of liquor, some broken glass, and her husband's gun cleaning supplies. Mr. Smith's body was cremated two days later. After contacting her husband's life insurance provider, ABC Insurance Company, Mrs. Smith was notified that they were refusing to pay benefits under his Accidental Death Benefit Policy because they did not consider his death to be an accident.

Statement of Issues Raised by the Facts

1.   What is the proper interpretation of an accidental death provision in a life insurance policy?
2.   Was Mr. Smith's death accidental?

Introduction

The central focus of this memorandum is to determine what constitutes "accidental death" for the purposes of an insurance policy and it will be in two parts. The first contains an examination of judicial treatment of the proper interpretation of an accidental death provision in a life insurance policy. The second will examine all of the relevant factors to be taken into consideration when determining whether or not a death can properly be classified as "accidental". This analysis is followed by a conclusion and recommendations.

Discussion

Proper Interpretation of "Accidental Death"

The leading authority in this area of the law is the very recent decision in *Martin v. American International Assurance Life Co.*[1] In that decision, the Supreme Court explicitly rejected a narrow conception of "accidental death".

> It follows that death is not non-accidental merely because the insured could have prevented death by taking greater care, or that a mishap was reasonably foreseeable in the sense used in tort law. Nor does a death that is unintended become "non-accidental" merely because that person was engaged in a dangerous or risky activity...the jurisprudence assigns a generous meaning to "accidental" in the absence of language to the contrary in the insurance policy.[2]

The Court further determined that insurance policies must be interpreted "...in a way that gives effect to the reasonable expectations of the parties".[3] This means

---

[1]   [2003] S.C.J. No. 14, 2003 SCC 16.
[2]   *Ibid.*, at para. 20.
[3]   *Ibid.*, at para. 12.

not only taking into consideration the expectations of the insurer, but also those of the insured.

The Appropriate Test to Determine "Accidental Death"

The pivotal question to ask in any inquiry into whether a death can be considered "accidental" is to determine whether the insured expected to die as a result of his or her behaviour. This can be done by looking at the circumstances surrounding the death, including what the insured said and did, or failed to do.[4] This analysis is intended to be a very holistic one, taking into account the action causing the injury, and all the circumstances leading up to and surrounding it.[5] And while it has already been established that this expectation is not to be measured to the same standard as reasonable expectation in tort law, the decision in *Martin* noted that where the expectations of the insured are unclear, it will be open to the court to consider whether a reasonable person in the position of the insured would have expected to die.[6]

Factors Altering the Application of the Test

i) Risky Behaviour

The presence of an open bottle of liquor and broken glass on the table beside Mr. Smith's body suggests that he may have been intoxicated at the time of his death. Because Mr. Smith had a history of risk-taking behaviour, particularly when drinking, it is necessary to address how his potentially being intoxicated could alter the appropriate test to be applied. Mrs. Smith specifically indicated that while Mr. Smith rarely drank alcohol, when he did, he had a tendency to "overdo it" and become extremely intoxicated. While in this state, she could recall him engaging in foolish and risky behaviour, including walking along balcony ledges, and on one occasion jumping off the roof of a friend's house into a swimming pool.

Canvassing the relevant case law, the Court in *Martin* identified two types of cases. The first involves people engaging in high risk activities either for the psychological gratification of doing so, or to impress others with their bravado. The second involves a rescuer who puts him or herself in the way of death.[7] For the first set of cases, the court maintained that the question must be answered from the perspective of the insured, regardless of the high risk nature of the

---

4   *Supra* note 1 at para. 21.
5   *Bertalan Estate v. American Home Assurance Co.* (2001), 196 D.L.R. (4th) 445 at para. 6, 25 C.C.L.I. (3d) 16, [2001] 4 W.W.R. 401, 149 B.C.A.C. 244, [2001] I.L.R. I-3958 (C.A.).
6   *Supra* note 1 at para. 21.
7   *Ibid.*, at paras. 25-28.

activity.[8] For the second, death was characterized as the result of a tragic, accidental sequence of events, and thus accidental itself, supporting recovery.[9]

In explicitly rejecting a narrow interpretation of "accidental death", the Court by extension rejected the proposition that risky behaviour contributing to the circumstances surrounding the death precludes a finding of accidental death. The decision to "court death" does at some point become equivalent to an intention to die,[10] however it does not change the application of the test.

> The test does not change for cases involving conduct that brings with it a high risk of death; the test remains whether the death was designed or expected. The first question is always "What did the insured, in fact, expect?" If we cannot be sure, as is often the case, then we may ask what a reasonable person endowed with the factual beliefs of the insured and placed in the circumstances of the insured would have expected.[11]

In any situation, the unique circumstances, as well as the individual policy wording will prove to be determinative in this analysis. It should also be noted that narrowly framed exclusionary clauses will bear heavily on the outcome of any analysis.[12]

ii) Probability of Suicide

In situations where the circumstances surrounding the death are questionable and where the probability of suicide exists as the only other probable alternative to accidental death, a different set of factors must be considered. In the situation at issue, Mr. Smith had been fighting with his wife, was experiencing some financial difficulties, and was expecting a new baby, all factors contributing to a high stress level. This knowledge, combined with the circumstances of his death could potentially indicate suicide.

There is a long-standing legal presumption against a finding of suicide. The Supreme Court of Canada in *London Life Insurance Co. v. Lang Shirt Co. (Trustee of)*[13] referred to this well-established presumption as early as 1929. This presumption was reaffirmed in the 1945 decision of *New York Life Insurance Co. v. Ross Estate.*[14] Originally, the presumption arose as a branch of the evidentiary presumption against the imputation of a crime, as suicide was considered to be a criminal act.[15] The removal of attempted suicide from the Canadian *Criminal*

---

[8] *Supra* note 1 at para. 27.

[9] *Ibid.*, at para. 28.

[10] *Ibid.*, at para. 23.

[11] *Ibid.*, at para. 23.

[12] *Candler v. London & Lancashire Guarantee & Accident Co. Of Canada* (1963), 40 D.L.R. (2d) 408 at 11 and 18 (Ont. H.C.).

[13] [1929] S.C.R. 117 at 7.

[14] [1945] S.C.R. 289 at 7-8.

[15] *Ibid.*, at 8, also see *London Life*, *supra* note 13 at 7.

Code removed this basis for the presumption; however, it remains that unless proven to the contrary, the presumption against suicide remains operational.[16]

This presumption was discussed in some detail by the Newfoundland Court of Appeal in the decision of *Greening v. Commercial Union Assurance Company*, providing the following commentary with regards to the nature of the presumption:

> Similarly, in my opinion, presumption against suicide has both a substantive and procedural aspect. Its substantive impact arises because in invoking the presumption, it effectively places on the side of the party claiming accidental death the affirmative and clear assumption that the deceased dies accidentally. Since it is so placed upon the scales by operation of law, and not as a deduction from conflicting evidence, it represents a substantive premise of a clear and unequivocal nature. Indeed, no proof need be adduced by the proponent of accidental death other than occurrence of the death itself since death by accident is taken as axiomatic truth but liable to rebuttal. It follows that clear and cogent rebuttal evidence is required to tip the balance of probabilities sufficiently to justify a finding of suicide.[17]

The substantive nature of the presumption is that it shifts the evidentiary burden of having to prove suicide from the plaintiff to the defendant. The procedural aspect of the presumption is discussed as follows:

> On the other hand, the presumption does have procedural aspects as well. It does allocate the burden of proof to the person alleging suicide. Where the circumstances of death are equally consistent with accident as suicide, the presumption becomes operative and accidental death is to be assumed. That burden is to be satisfied on the balance of probabilities. I would reiterate, however, that the discharge of the onus cast by the presumption requires that probability to be demonstrated by clear and cogent evidence of substantial civil weight.[18]

The type of "clear and cogent evidence" required would be the actual circumstances pertaining to the death.[19] In this case, the court was unable to, having regard to the evidence adduced, say with certainty how the death at issue had occurred, and as such, was unable to find that the presumption against suicide could be rebutted.

The nature of this presumption was also discussed in very concise terms by Justice Fraser of the Alberta Court of Queen's Bench in the decision in *Sherstone v. Westroc Inc.*[20] In that decision, it was very clear that where a policy is payable on accidental death, it is the responsibility of the plaintiff only to establish the death. The onus then shifts to the defendant to rebut that presumption, by clear and cogent evidence on a balance of probabilities, that the deceased

---

[16] *Greening*, *infra* note 17 at 4.

[17] *Greening v. Commercial Union Assurance Company*, [1988] I.L.R. 1-2300 at 5 (NL.C.A.).

[18] *Ibid.*, at 6.

[19] *Supra* note 13 at 8.

[20] [2001] A.J. No. 640, 2001 ABQB 414.

committed suicide.[21] Applying the decision in *Greening*, Mason J. of the Alberta Court of Queen's Bench in the *Beischel v. Mutual of Omaha Insurance Co.* decision further indicated that the degree of probability required by the defendant must be commensurate with the seriousness of the allegation of suicide.[22] This evidentiary requirement was cited from the Supreme Court decision in *Hanes v. Wawanesa Mutual Insurance Company*[23] and further supports the need to perform an analysis of all the relevant circumstances surrounding each individual death. The presumption and its attendant evidentiary burdens has also been discussed and applied in Nova Scotia courts.[24]

Conclusion

The Supreme Court in *Martin* has clearly rejected a narrow conception of accidental death indicating that the term should be taken to mean accidental death resulting as a result of both deliberate and accidental means. While external factors such as risky behaviour should be taken into consideration when performing this analysis, the central question to ask is whether or not the deceased expected to die as a result of his or her actions.

In situations where the cause of death is questionable, such as in the situation at issue, the relevant case law in Canada has clearly identified a presumption against a finding of suicide. In this type of context, it is clearly incumbent upon the defendant insurer to prove, on a balance of probabilities commensurate with the allegation of suicide, that the deceased was responsible for his or her own death. If unable to do so, the presumption becomes operative, necessitating a finding of accidental death, therefore falling within the bounds of an accidental death benefits policy.

Recommendations

Based on Mrs. Smith's recollection of events, her description of her husband's character, his regular patterns of behaviour with regard to his gun, and his frame of mind at the time of his death, it can be argued that ABC Insurance Company would be unable to rebut the strong presumption against a finding of suicide. However, it should be noted that Mr. Smith was also under financial stress at the time of his death. His proclivity towards high-risk recreational activities, coupled with his pattern of risky behaviour while intoxicated, as well as the actual wording of his insurance policy are all important factors to be considered when making a determination of accidental death in this situation. However, the

---

[21] *Supra* note 20, at paras. 58-62.
[22] *Beischel v. Mutual of Omaha Insurance Co.*, [1991] A.J. No. 757 at para. 21, 122 A.R. 325.
[23] [1963] S.C.R. 154.
[24] *MacInnes v. London Life Insurance Co.*, [1979] N.S.J. No. 602 at para. 59, 33 N.S.R. (2d) 326, 57 A.P.R. 326, S.H. No. 11274 (S.C.T.D.).

evidentiary burden rests with ABC Insurance to do so. The very recent Supreme Court decision in *Martin* is quite similar to Mr. Smith's situation factually, and the weight of the law articulated in that decision would seem to lie in Mrs. Smith's favour which may suggest success if she were to choose to pursue a course of litigation against her late husband's insurer.

B. GENERAL RULES OF STYLE

As mentioned above, the organization of a paper will depend on the nature of the problem and the intended audience. There are, however, rules of grammar, rules concerning the reference to other material, and many guidelines for writing. The ability to accurately and effectively convey a message through the written word is an integral part of the legal profession, and one worth improving. The following pages are designed to be of assistance with the most common issues facing law students, but are not intended to be exhaustive. For general tips on legal writing try: Constance Rooke, *A Grammar Booklet for Lawyers, or, How not to dangle your participles in public* (Ontario: The Law Society of Upper Canada, 1991); and Martha Faulk and Irving M. Mehler, *The Elements of Legal Writing* (New York: MacMillan, 1994).

1. Citation

A citation is a reference to other published material and it is important that a student be able to cite legal materials without error. The need for accuracy is the primary reason for acquiring citing skills. A legal writer gives the citation of the material alluded to primarily to enable the reader to find that material and to personally examine it. This rationale leads to the oft-heard rule: a correct citation is one that leads, without ambiguity, to the primary source.

Students should follow a consistent method of citation. Certain guiding principles are laid down in this manual. (It is not suggested, however, that there is only one "correct" way to give a legal citation.) Whenever a point is not covered, the citation system used by the *Canadian Bar Review* is a good model. Reference may also be made to C. Tang, *Guide to Legal Citation and Sources of Citation Aid: A Canadian Perspective*, 2nd ed. (Scarborough, Ontario: Thomson Canada (Carswell), 1988); and *Canadian Guide to Uniform Legal Citation*, 5th ed. (Scarborough, Ontario: Thomson Canada (Carswell), 2002). Useful information pertaining to the citation of books, periodicals, and American material generally may be found in the current (15th) edition of Harvard Law Review's *The Bluebook: A Uniform System of Citation*.

When citing cases, statutes, regulations or other materials, a full citation is necessary. The citation for a case, statute or other legal material appears in a footnote or in the body of a memorandum. Always cite primary material before secondary material.

Never quote from secondary material when a primary source is available, except when you need a broad generalization to set the stage for detailed consideration. Unless you have no alternative, do not depend on a textbook or a legal periodical for a citation or for the interpretation of a case or statute. However, if you must do so, be sure to acknowledge the fact in a footnote.

2. Footnoting

Usually citations appear in footnotes. The general practice followed by most legal texts and law journals is to place footnotes at the bottom of each page. A few publications place citations at the end of chapters or articles (called "references" or "endnotes"). In many law offices it is common practice to include citations in the body of a memorandum, often in parenthesis, following a statement from the authority cited. Many Canadian law schools prefer the use of footnotes in student papers. If in doubt, assume that citations are to be placed in footnotes at the bottom of each page.

The most common practice is to raise the footnote number half a space in the text. Usually footnotes are numbered consecutively throughout an article, memorandum or each chapter of a book.

The names of cases and titles of books are usually italicized (and sometimes in bold-face type as well) in published text or underlined in typescript, as are the titles of statutes, although some publishers do not italicize titles of statutes. (Italicize references to the titles of all statutes in published material, even though the titles of acts appearing in the official statute volumes may not, themselves, be italicized.) The titles of periodical articles are usually placed in quotation marks, although sometimes titles are italicized in published material. This manual recommends placing the titles of articles in quotation marks.

If a particular passage in a case, article, or book is quoted or cited as authority, the page or pages on which it appears are indicated by the use of "at 00" or "at 00-00".

[11] J.C. Smith, "The Unique Nature of the Concepts of Western Law" (1968), 46 Can. Bar Rev. 191 at 195.

[12] *Osborne v. Canada (Treasury Board)* (1991), 82 D.L.R. (4th) 321 at 331 (S.C.C.).

[13] M.P. Furmston, *Cheshire, Fifoot and Furmston's Law of Contract*, 12th ed. (London: Butterworths, 1991) at 115.

Legal writing of all kinds tends to be heavily footnoted. Since law is built on a system of authoritative pronouncements, propositions put forward are commonly supported by the citation of authority. However interesting a writer's opinions may be, a lawyer, because of his or her training, will want to assess the extent to which the ideas are based on authority, particularly when in the process of forming a professional opinion. Indeed, lawyers often use articles or memoranda merely as a means of discovering relevant cases or statutes. Thus, footnoting of authorities will make your legal writing more useful. Even more important, plagiarism must be carefully avoided. All direct quotes, paraphrases and borrowed ideas must be acknowledged by footnote references.

In legal writing, footnotes are frequently used for purposes other than the citation of authorities. They may be used to introduce subsidiary points, to deal with conflicting views, and generally, for the discussion of matters that interrupt the flow of the main argument.

3. Quotations

Quotation Marks and Indentation

Any passage quoted directly from other writings that is less than 50 words should normally be enclosed in quotation marks, but not set off from the text. If it is more than 50 words (or if it is a legislative provision, irrespective of length) it should normally be indented on both sides of the page and single-spaced without quotation marks. (The latter is called a "block quote".) Where it is necessary to change the quotation for the flow of the argument, the altered portion should be placed in square brackets. Where only part of a passage is reproduced by the author, the first letter of the passage being quoted should be capitalized and placed in square brackets. If quoted material contains an error, place "sic" in square brackets (*i.e.*, [sic]) after the word(s).

Omissions

The omission of words from a quoted passage should be indicated by the ellipsis signal (three dots). The following rules will apply:

(1) The ellipsis is not used at the beginning of a sentence or after the period at the end of a final quoted sentence.

(2) When quoting a phrase from a text or when using quoted material as a phrase the ellipsis is not used before or after the phrase which is quoted.

Example:
The Supreme Court of Canada decided that the award of $300,000 arising out of a breach of the wrongful dismissal was not "[a debt]...for services performed for the corporation" for which the directors of Wabasso would be liable and that section 114 "is [there] to ensure that certain sums, including

wages, are paid to employees in the event the corporation becomes bankrupt or insolvent". (*Crabtree v. Barrette* (1993), 10 B.L.R. 1 (S.C.C.), quoting A. Bohemier and A-M. Poliquin, "Réflexion sur la protection des salariés dans la cadre de la fuillite on de l'insolvabilité" (1988), 48 R. du B. 75, at 81).

(3)   When omitting material from within a quoted phrase or sentence use an ellipsis.

Examples:

(i)   Phrase

"[A]ccording to traditional wisdom, Parliament always was...concerned with protecting employees" where a company declared bankruptcy or insolvency.

(ii)   Sentence

"The parameter which is at the heart of the appeal is therefore not the concept of wages, but the expression 'debts...for services performed by the corporation'."

(4)   When words are omitted from the beginning of a quoted sentence capitalize the first letter and place it in square brackets unless it is capitalized in the source text.

Example:

"[O]ne can see and read object code as a series of 0s and 1s when the same has been printed out by a computer...no programmer can find those 0s and 1s on looking at any part of the computer's hardware or software for they are but electrical impulse."

(5)   When words are omitted from the end of a quoted sentence the ellipsis is used following the final punctuation to show the omission.

Example:

"To the extent the individual features of the Macintosh interface are licensed or are unprotectible they are together...with the protectible features, claimed as copyrightable arrangement — a 'look and feel' which constitutes protectible expression apart from its individual elements...."

(6)   When words are omitted between the end of the sentence and additional quoted material the ellipsis is used together with punctuation at the end of a new sentence. An ellipsis is not used to indicate that the text which follows a period or other final punctuation that concludes a final quoted sentence was not included in the quoted passage.

Example:
"Southam has not denied that it failed to meet the delivery schedule stipulated in the contract....[T]here was a breach of the contract in this respect which frustrated the commercial purpose of the contract."

Paragraph Structure

In a block quote, the paragraph structure of the original material is retained by indenting the first sentence of each paragraph. If the first word of the quoted paragraph is not the first word of the original paragraph, however, no indentation is shown. Also, if material is omitted at the beginning of the first paragraph, no indentation or ellipsis should occur. If material is omitted from the beginning of the second or subsequent paragraphs, this is indicated by indentation and by an ellipsis.

If there is a substantial omission of a paragraph or more, four dots should be inserted in its place, leaving a double space between the dots and the paragraphs above and below.

Example:
"Defamation can be conveyed in any number of styles. What matters is the tendency of the utterance, not its form. Ridicule, *e.g.*, is a familiar weapon for attacking reputation, as by juxtaposing the plaintiff's portrait with that of a gorilla in a magazine article or by publishing a photo of him in what appears to be an obscene posture. On the other hand, if a statement is made as a harmless joke and so understood, its defamatory barb may thereby disappear.

...

[D]efamation is confined to only those that strike at character or reputation."

If you wish to draw attention to certain words in a quoted passage, you should italicize those words and include the explanation "[Emphasis added]" at the end of the passage. Any other modifications (such as a change from upper to lower case or vice versa or the substitution of one or more words) in the quoted passage should likewise be noted.

Example:
The report goes on to say that "drastic changes to the current procedure are *not* necessary at this time". [Emphasis added]

4. Introductory Signals

"Introductory Signals" is the term applied, in the Harvard Law Review's *A Uniform System of Citation*, to words or symbols used to introduce the citation of an authority in a footnote. The signal indicates the degree of support afforded the proposition in the text by the authority cited. No signal is used where the footnote simply identifies the source of a quote or gives the citations of the case or statute named in the text, nor is the signal used where the cited authority directly supports the proposition in the text.

The signals set out in *A Uniform System of Citation* to support a proposition advanced are the following:

[No signal necessary]

Example:
The doctrine of ancient lights is worthy of examination as it does demonstrate that "the law can recognize and protect a natural resource that supplies significant benefits to individuals". M. Freeman, "Securing Solar Access in Maine" (1980), 32 Me. L. Rev. 439, at 440.

NOTE: In the above example, no signal is required as the cited authority directly identifies the source of the quotation and states the proposition.

e.g.,   This indicates there are other authorities that state the proposition; "*e.g.,*" which is italicized and followed by a comma, is also frequently used in combination with other signals:

See, *e.g.*
But see, *e.g.*
Example:
The recognition by the Superior Courts in both British Columbia and Nova Scotia of the need for caution in dispensing with a parent's consent is consistent with recent developments in English law. *E.g.*, P. Seago & A. Bissett-Johnson, *Cases and Materials on Family Law* (London: Sweet and Maxwell, 1976), at 418-481; A. Bissett-Johnson, "Step-Parent Adoptions" (1978), 41 Mod. L. Rev. 96; B. Hoggett, "Adoption by Step-Parents" (1973), 117 Sol. J. 606.

Accord   "*Accord*" is used when two or more cases state or clearly support the statement, but the text quotes or refers to only one; the others are then introduced by "*accord*". "*Accord*" is also apt to show that the law of another jurisdiction is in accord with the law of the jurisdiction cited.

Example:
Contracting parties cannot exclude an antecedent right to sue in tort unless an intention to do so is clearly expressed in the contract. *Edgeworth Construction v. N.D. Lea & Assoc.* (1993), 17 C.C.L.T. (2d) 101 (S.C.C.). *Accord BG Checo Int'l v. B.C. Hydro* (1993), 14 C.C.L.T. (2d) 233 (S.C.C.) and *Central Trust Co. v. Rafuse*, [1986] 2 S.C.R. 147.

See This indicates that an examination of the material cited will support the proposition put forth, although the proposition is not put forth explicitly in that material.

Example:
Lord Denning's sometimes cavalier attitude to precedent and his attachment to general principles of fairness for resolving contractual disputes appear very attractive to trial judges. See *McKenzie v. Bank of Montreal* (1975), 55 D.L.R. (3d) 641 (Ont. H.C.).

See also This indicates material that might profitably be examined by the reader because it provides additional support for the proposition in the text.
Example:
Despite the fact that several communities attempt to use zoning to "freeze" land, the practice has run into trouble in the courts. See *Re Corporation of District of North Vancouver Zoning ByLaw 4277*, [1973] 2 W.W.R. 260 (B.C.S.C.); see also *Regina Auto Court v. Regina (City)* (1958), 25 W.W.R. (N.S.) 167 (Sask. Q.B.).

Cf. This indicates that the material cited lends support to the proposition in the text, although directed to a different point.

Example:
An obligation of confidence under the law relating to breach of confidence may arise from a condition precedent of confidentiality between a private company and the Crown to which the company has submitted a proposal to develop Alpine Ski facilities. *Pharand Ski Corp. v. Alberta* (1991), 7 C.C.L.T. (2d) 225 (Alta. Q.B.). *Cf. LAC Minerals Ltd. v. Int'l Corona Resources*, [1989] 2 S.C.R. 574 (holding that the acquisition of property by one company as a result of information given in contemplation of a possible joint venture amounted to a breach of confidence at common law).

The following signals contradict a proposition advanced:

Contra This indicates that the material cited directly contradicts the proposition in the text.

Examples:
The application of the doctrine of *ex turpi causa non oritur actio* to tort actions was accepted by the British Columbia Court of Appeal in *Hall v. Hebert* (1991), 6 C.C.L.T. (2d) 294. *Contra Gala v. Preston* (1991), 172 C.L.R. 243 (Aust. H.C.) and *Pitts v. Hunt*, [1990] 3 All E.R. 344 (C.A.).

The Court of Appeal in *Metall and Rohstoff AG v. Donaldson Lufkin & Jenrette Inc.*, [1989] 3 All E.R. 14 (C.A.), gave a narrow application to the tort of civil conspiracy in requiring proof in every case that the predominant intention of the conspirators was to injure the plaintiff. See *Allied Arab Bank Ltd. v. Hajjar* (No. 2), [1988] 3 All E.R. 103 (Q.B.D.). *Contra Lonrho plc v. Fayed*, [1991] 3 All E.R. 303 (H.L.) (holding that if the conspirators used unlawful means to injure the business interests of the plaintiff it was no defence to say that their predominant purpose was to advance a legitimate business interest).

But see   This indicates that the cited authority supports a proposition contrary to the main proposition.

Example:
King v. University of Saskatchewan, [1969] S.C.R. 678, seems to lay down the general principle that a later, properly conducted appeal can cure an earlier defective hearing. But see *Leary v. National Union of Vehicle Builders*, [1971] 1 Ch. 34 (holding that, as a general rule, a failure of natural justice in the trial body cannot be cured by a sufficiency of natural justice in the appellate body).

But *cf.*   This indicates contradiction, but is not as strong as "but see". The cited authority supports a proposition analogous to the contrary of the main proposition.

Example:
These arguments seem strongly to support the idea that defects in a hearing should not be curable by properly conducted appeals. But *cf. Calvin v. Carr*, [1979] 2 W.L.R. 755 (P.C.) (suggesting that in some circumstances an appeal might cure an earlier defect).

In addition to the above signals, "see generally" is commonly used to indicate useful background material related to the proposition. "Compare" (which is used with the connectives "with" or "and") may also be used to contrast sources that support or illustrate a proposition in the text. "Compare" differs from "*cf.*" in that the former requires comparison of two or more references which, standing alone, could not support the proposition.

Examples:
For a good discussion of China's development in the late nineteenth century, see generally J. Chesneaux *et al.*, *China from the Opium Wars to the 1911 Revolution* (New York: Pantheon Books, 1977).

Prior to the Court of Appeal's decision in *Lewis v. Averay*, [1972] 1 Q.B. 198, the English law on mistaken identity favoured a distinction between mistake as to identity and mistake as to attributes. However, in application the distinction often produced conflicting decisions in situations where the facts were clearly indistinguishable. Compare *Phillips v. Brooks Ltd.*, [1919] 2 K.B. 243, with *Ingram v. Little*, [1961] 1 Q.B. 31 (C.A.).

5. Repeated References

One source or authority may be cited more than once. In fact, it is common in legal writing to refer repeatedly to the same case or other source referring, perhaps, to different pages each time. The first reference to a source is given a full citation in a footnote. A subsequent footnote reference to that source is not given a full citation. It merely refers back to the initial footnote citation.

A citation to a repeated reference consists of the name of the source, or a shortened version of the name, and a cross-referencing signal, such as *supra* or *ibid.*, to direct the reader to the footnote giving the full citation of the source. If a shortened version of the source is to be used, the reader should indicate this in square brackets at the end of the full citation by the use of the word "hereinafter" for legislation or cases.

Examples:
Alberta Oil Sands Technology and Research Authority Act, R.S.A. 1980, c. O-6 [hereinafter *Oil Sands Act*].
Rights of the Aboriginal Peoples of Canada, Part II of the Constitution Act 1982 (U.K.), being Schedule B to the *Canada Act, 1982*, R.S.C. 1985, App. II, c. 44 [hereinafter cited as *Aboriginal Rights*].
R. v. Skinner (1985), 58 N.R. 240 (S.C.C.) [hereinafter cited as *Skinner*].
A.G. Guest, ed., *Chitty on Contracts*, 26th ed. (London: Sweet & Maxwell, 1989) [hereinafter cited as *Chitty*].

Where the citation includes parallel references to other cases, it may be useful to indicate which source is being referred to in subsequent footnote references with the use of the expression "cited to...".
Taylor v. Co-operative Fire & Casualty Co. (1984), 35 Alta. L.R. (2d) 77, 57 A.R. 328, 10 C.C.L.I. 284 (Q.B.) [hereinafter *Co-op* cited to Alta. L.R.].

If a secondary source is referred to more than once, the shortened citation may refer to the author's name, in which case the writer need not indicate "hereinafter" or "hereinafter cited as". Alternatively, the writer may refer to the shortened version of the title of the work.

Examples:

[1]   S.M. Waddams, *The Law of Damages* (Toronto: Canada Law Book, 1983).

[5]   S.M. Waddams, *supra* note 1 at 36.

or

[2]   R.M. Fernandes, *Marine Insurance Law of Canada* (Toronto: Butterworths, 1987) [hereinafter *Marine*].

[6]   *Marine, supra* note 2 at 45.

The simplest way to cross-reference is by using, in footnotes, the words "*supra*" for that which has gone before and "*infra*" for that which comes after. Note that the words are italicized.

Examples:

[7]   *R. v. Skinner* (1985), 58 N.R. 240 (S.C.C.).

[12]   *Skinner, supra* note 7 at 243.

Where the author is directing the reader to a footnote appearing later in the work, the footnote might state:

[1]   *Infra* note 6.

In some instances the writer may simply wish to refer to material discussed later in the work. In this instance, the term "below" should be used.

[2]   For a discussion of the citation and footnoting of legal literature see Section 6, below.

"*Ibid.*" (*Ibidem*, in the same place) may be used where there is no intervening footnote between the first and second references to a source. It takes the place of the name and citation of a case, or of the author, title and citation of an article or book. "*Ibid.*" can appear after the original full citation, or after the use of "*supra*", or following the use of another "*ibid.*" in a footnote. It should not be used as the first citation on a page. If the writer directs the reader to a page reference which is not the same as the preceding note, this must be indicated.

Examples:

[16]   *McLean v. Pettigrew*, [1945] S.C.R. 62 at 63.

[17]   *Ibid.*

or

[33]   *Watteau v. Fenwick*, [1893] 1 Q.B. 346.

[34]   *Ibid.* at 348-350.

6. The Citation and Footnoting of Legal Literature

By the time most students enter law school they have adopted a workable system of footnoting material derived from periodicals, books and other sources. Legal citation, however, may differ in some respects from the practice recommended in other disciplines. The following examples are representative of common usage in Canada for the citation of books and articles.

Books

With respect to both books and articles do not capitalize all the letters in the title. It is common in Canada to use upper and lower case letters. Titles of books are italicized (and may also appear in bold-face) in printed text. Normally, a subtitle need not be cited as part of a title unless it imparts clarifying substantive information. Abbreviations are not acceptable unless employed in the actual text.

When citing a book in a piece of legal writing, it is helpful to place in brackets, before the date of publication, the place of publication, as well as the publisher's name. Generally, references to definite articles, abbreviations such as "Inc.", "Ltd.", "Co.", and, also, the words "publishing" or "publisher", which may appear on the title page, are omitted.

Example:
G.J. Borrie, *Elements of Public Law* (London: Sweet & Maxwell, 1967).

When there are two or three authors, list the initials and surnames of each separating the last two with an ampersand (&).

Examples:
D.A. Dukelow & B. Nuse, *Dictionary of Canadian Law* (Scarborough, Ontario: Thomson Canada (Carswell), 1991).
M.O. Price, H. Bitner & S.R. Bysiewicz, *Effective Legal Research*, 4th ed. (Boston: Little, Brown and Co., 1979).

A work of more than three authors may be designated by the initials and surname of the first author followed by "*et al.*", which is followed by a comma:

B. Cass *et al.*, *Why So Few? Women Academics in Australian Universities* (Sydney: Sydney University Press, 1983).

In Canadian legal writing it is the usual practice to include a reference to the name of an editor or editors, followed by the abbreviation "ed." or "eds." and a comma.

Example:
R. St. J. Macdonald, G.L. Morris & D.M. Johnston, eds., *Canadian Perspectives on International Law and Organization* (Toronto: University of Toronto Press, 1974).

In some books, the name of the original author has become part of the title. Reference should be made also to the current editor or editors.

Example:
A.G. Guest, ed., *Chitty on Contracts*, 26th ed. (London: Sweet & Maxwell, 1989).

Where the name of the original author is retained, separate from the title, the name of the editor is commonly placed after the edition reference.

Example:
R.E. Megarry, *Manual of the Law of Real Property*, 6th ed. by D.F. Hayton (London: Stevens & Sons, 1982).

Periodical Articles

In citing articles appearing in periodicals, the year of the volume (in round brackets) is placed immediately after the name of the article and before the volume number, name of the periodical and page number. It is common to give the author's initials and last name in citing articles, as is the case with books. The title of an article is often placed in quotation marks (unlike the title of a book which is italicized in printed text) and many publishers place a comma after the title if the year appears in square brackets and omit the comma if the year appears in round brackets. The abbreviations for legal periodicals are not italicized. Information on the details of publication are not included when referring to a periodical.

The major legal periodicals are contained in several sources; consult the *Index to Canadian Legal Literature*, the *Index to Canadian Periodical Literature*, *Black's Law Dictionary*, *Osborn's Concise Oxford Law Dictionary* and the latest edition of *The Bluebook: A Uniform System of Citation*.

Examples:
C. Boyle, "The Battered Wife Syndrome and Self-Defence: *Lavallee v. R.*" (1990), 9 Can. J. of Fam. L. 171.
S. Boyd, "Child Custody and Working Mothers" in K. Mahoney & S. Martin, eds., *Equality and Judicial Neutrality* (Toronto: Carswell, 1987) at 168.

If a particular periodical employs a calendar year system rather than a volume number, the year is placed in square brackets.

Examples:

T.R.S. Allan, "Legislative Supremacy and the Rule of Law", [1985] Camb.
L.J. 111 at 113.

P. Birks, "Personal Restitution in Equity", [1988] Lloyd's Mar. and Com.
Quart. 128 at 132.

The rules governing multiple authors are the same for periodicals as for textbooks.

Examples:

E. Abner, M.J. Mossman & E. Pickett, "A Matter of Simple Justice: Assess-
ing the Report of the Royal Commission on the Status of Women in
Canada" (1990), 22 Ottawa L. Rev. 573.

J. Bonta *et al.*, "The Characteristics of Aboriginal Recidivists" (1992), 34
Can. J. Crim. 15.

CHAPTER 6

Writing a Brief

In Chapter 5 we provided general suggestions for legal writing, with an emphasis on writing a memorandum. While writing memoranda will likely be the first, and most common task assigned to articled clerks, a close second will probably be drafting a Brief for a judge in Chambers. Many of the skills discussed in relation to writing a memorandum continue to be applicable, although there is a definite style change.

The goal in writing a memorandum is to find and layout the applicable legal principles from the most relevant and authoritative courts that can be found. Identify the issues from the facts you are given, to provide a neutral statement of the law for each issue, and anticipate and provide information on other issues which may come up.

The goal in writing a Brief is to use the facts as they have been provided, to identify and address each of the relevant legal issues, and to craft the two together in as persuasive a manner as is possible (while not misstating the facts or the law).

A Chambers' Brief is prepared and filed with the court in advance of the court date; most Chambers' Applications are less than one hour, although Special Chambers may extend well beyond an hour. Unlike a trial, a Chambers' Application is restricted to a question of law. Evidence is put before the court by way of Affidavit. All documentation before the court is led as exhibits to the Affidavits filed on the particular Application.

NOTE: Cross examination on Affidavit evidence is usually allowed.

Normally, there is no cross examination on Affidavit evidence, because, as stated above, an Application is restricted to a determination of law, not of fact. If the relevant facts are yet to be determined, then the matter will not proceed by way of Application.

The form of a Chamber's Brief may vary from law office to law office but is often written in the form of a letter to the judge hearing the matter.

A. WRITING A CHAMBERS BRIEF

1. Address

If you know who will be hearing the Application, then address the Brief to that person by name, otherwise use the following style,

The Honourable Justice in Chambers on July 1, 2004, 9:30 a.m.
The Law Courts
1815 Upper Water Street
Halifax, Nova Scotia B3J 1S7

2. Title

Although you could use the style of cause, often the matter is referred to by stating the parties and the court number in the following manner,

RE: Lisa Smith, Applicant v. ABC Insurance Company, Respondent
S.H. No. 111111

3. Introduction

This is where you state who you represent, why you are writing to the court, and under what authority the Application is being made. An introduction might read:

My Lord:

I represent the Plaintiff in the above noted matter, Lisa Smith, and ask that you please consider this letter as the pre-Chambers Brief of the Applicants on this Application for Summary Judgment pursuant to Rule 13.01 of the *Nova Scotia Civil Procedure Rules*. The Application is currently scheduled to be heard by you in Chambers on July 1, 2004.

4. Authority for the Application

Cite the provision under which the application is being made. The idea is not to get into the merits of the Application, you are simply stating the provision, and referring to cases which establish any relevant criteria.

5. Argument Summary

Before getting into the substance of the brief, it is a good idea to preview your main argument. By providing a list of the main points, you will assist the judge in identifying the important legal principles and facts as he or she reads the brief. You are essentially previewing your argument. This manual suggests an actual list of points, rather than a paragraph. A list will help you to formulate your argument, and will provide a quick reference for the reader.

6. Facts

Unlike a memorandum, all of the relevant facts should be outlined at the beginning of your brief. Often times, you are cobbling together facts from the Affidavits of several individuals. Make sure that you know the facts, as stated in the Affidavits before you start drafting. The goal is to tell the story in a way that makes it easy to follow, and in a way which highlights the facts that support your position. Do not misstate, or embellish what has been stated in the Affidavits, simply highlight the parts which support your position. For ease of reference, this manual recommends that you number each paragraph in the Facts section. The Facts section might read:

Factual Background

The relevant facts set out in the affidavits of Lisa Smith, and Mr. Coroner, filed on this Application, are briefly summarized as follows:

1.   The Applicant, Lisa Smith is the widow of the late Joseph Smith.

2.   Joseph Smith, (hereinafter "Joe") was a thirty-five (35) year-old accountant, who, with his wife was expecting the birth of his first child at the time of his death.

        ...

7. Statement of the Legal Issues

This part of the Brief should give a clear statement of the main issues to be resolved. A statement of the sub-issues will normally be included in the body of the paper at the beginning of each new section.

8. Law and Argument

Each issue formulated (under the Facts section, above) should be developed in sequence. Organization is the key to having a persuasive brief. You need to organize your issues and argument in a way that is easy to follow and persuasive, especially where the Brief is longer than five (5) pages. Present the authorities on which the conclusion rests, remembering that the purpose of the Brief is to demonstrate that the law supports your client's position, or to acknowledge that the law does not support your client's position, and argue that the law should change. If there are decisions of high-level courts which do not support what you are asking the court to do, you should address them, because your opponent will. Try to demonstrate why cases which do not support your position are distinguishable on the facts.

If there is a Supreme Court of Canada decision or a decision from the Court of Appeal in your jurisdiction, which is on point, you must bring it forward and try to deal with it.

This manual recommends that you flesh out why the particular cases are or are not relevant. Chambers judges have to read volumes of material daily. They may not have as much time as they, or you would like to review your Brief and the cases referred to within it. If there is a particular point which you want them to get, spell it out. On this point, do it well the first time! If you feel like coming back to a point raised earlier in your Brief, you didn't explore it fully the first time. Repeating the same thing over and over is not effective, it is simply repetitive. If there is a legal test which must be met, make sure that you actually demonstrate that you meet the test, (word for word). Don't presume that the judge will read between the lines. Remember that your writing should be straightforward and direct. Your writing needs to be authoritative and convincing.

Finally, remember that the judge doesn't care what your opinion is. He or she cares what the law is, and cares how, (you submit) the law applies to your client's situation.

9. Conclusion

The conclusion should include a brief summary of your main arguments and should include a statement of what you want. Clearly state what relief your client is seeking, including costs.

SAMPLE BRIEF

The following is a Brief based on the Factual Scenario found at the beginning of this manual, and has been prepared simply to offer a sample. In a real proceeding with similar facts, there would be numerous factual determinations which would require determination by a trial judge. In order to provide a sample, the problem has been designed to eliminate many of the factual issues.

Additionally, this Brief is premised on having additional facts, which were not known at the time that the original memorandum (found in Chapter 5) was written.

SAMPLE

June 24, 2004

The Honourable Justice in Chambers on July 1, 2004, 9:30 a.m.
The Law Courts
1815 Upper Water Street
Halifax, Nova Scotia B3J 1S7

    RE: Lisa Smith, Applicant v. ABC Insurance Company, Respondent
    S.H. No. 111111

My Lord/Lady:

I represent the Plaintiff in the above noted matter, Lisa Smith, and ask that you please consider this letter as the pre-Chambers Brief of the Applicants on this Application for Summary Judgment currently scheduled to be heard by you in Chambers on July 1, 2004.

Application Pursuant to Rule 13.01[1]

This Application for Summary Judgment is made pursuant to Rule 13.01 of the *Nova Scotia Civil Procedure Rules* which reads as follows:

> 13.01 After the close of pleadings, any party may apply to the court for judgment on the ground that:
> (a)   there is no arguable issue to be tried with respect to the claim or any part thereof;
> (b)   there is no arguable issue to be tried with respect to the defence or any part thereof;
> (c)   the only arguable issue to be tried is as to the amount of any damages claimed.

In the 1999 case of *Guarantee Co. of North America v. Gordon Capital Corp.*, the Supreme Court of Canada observed at paragraph 27 that the test for summary judgment is as follows:

---

[1]   *Guarantee Co. of North America v. Gordon Capital Corp* (1999), 178 D.L.R. (4th) 1 (S.C.C.).

The appropriate test to be applied on a motion for summary judgment is satisfied when the applicant has shown that there is no genuine issue of material fact requiring trial, and therefore summary judgment is the proper question for consideration by the court. Once the moving party has made this showing, the respondent must then establish his claim as being on with a real chance of success.

The leading Nova Scotia authority for interpretation of Summary Judgment is *Bank of Nova Scotia et al. v. Dombrowski*,[2] wherein the Appeal Division wrote beginning at paragraph 18:

> Rule 13 has its antecedents in Order 14 of the English Supreme Court Rules. As stated in the Supreme Court Practice (1976), Vol. 1 at p. 136 the purpose of 0.14 is to enable the plaintiff to obtain summary judgment without trial if he can prove his claim clearly, and if the defendant is unable to set up a bona fide defence, or raise an issue against the claim which ought to be tried... The defendant is bound to show that he has some reasonable ground of defence to the action.
>
> ....
>
> The issue may, I believe, be summarized as being whether there is a fair issue to be tried, based on some reasonable ground of defence.

The comments of the court in *Dombrowski*, echo those of earlier cases like *Carl B. Potter Ltd. v. Antil Canada Ltd. and Mercantile Bank of Canada*,[3] wherein the Appeal Division cited with approval the decision in *Royal Bank of Canada v. Malouf*,[4] for the following authority:

> It is well settled that the provisions of Rule 127 are not to be used to strike out a defence, unless it is very clear that the defendant has no substantial defence to submit to the Court; but when a Judge is satisfied, not only that there is no defence, but no fairly arguable point to be presented on behalf of the defendant, it is his duty to give effect to the Rule and to allow the plaintiff to enter judgment for his claim...**Moreover, in order to resist an application under the Rule, it is not sufficient for the defendant to say that he has a good defence on the merits; the defence must be disclosed, and sufficient facts must appear to show that there is a bona fide defence, or at least, as stated by Jessel, M.R., in** *Anglo – Italian Bank v. Wells, supra*, **"a fairly arguable point to be argued on behalf of the defendant:"** [emphasis added]

Summary of Argument

The Applicant's argument on this Application may be summarized as follows:

---

[2] *Bank of Nova Scotia et al v. Dombrowski* (1977), 23 N.S.R. (2d) 532 (S.C. (A.D.)) [hereinafter "*Dombrowski*"].

[3] *Carl B. Potter Ltd. v. Antil Canada Ltd. and Mercantile Bank of Canada* (1976), 15 N.S.R. (2d) 408 [hereinafter "*Potter*"].

[4] *Royal Bank of Canada v. Malouf*, [1932] 2 W.W.R. 526 at para. 9 (Sask. C.A.).

I.   The Defendant, Respondent on this Application, denied the Plaintiff, Applicant benefits under the provisions of an accidental death benefits policy, claiming that the death of Joseph Smith was not accidental.

II.   Before denying the claim, the Defendant, ABC Insurance Company, carried out no good faith investigation concerning the death of Joseph Smith.

III.   There is a legal presumption against suicide.

IV.   The Onus to prove that Joseph Smith's death was not accidental lies with the Defendant insurance company.

V.   There is no direct or forensic evidence to substantiate the Defendant insurance company's Defence.

VI.   Based on the foregoing, the Applicant, Lisa Smith requests Summary Judgment.

Facts

The relevant facts set out in the affidavit of Lisa Smith, filed on this Application, are briefly summarized as follows:

1.   The Applicant, Lisa Smith (hereinafter "Lisa") is the widow of the late Joseph Smith.

2.   Joseph Smith, (hereinafter "Joe") was a thirty-five (35) year-old accountant, who, with his wife Lisa Smith, (hereinafter "Lisa") was looking forward to the birth of their first child at the time of his death.

3.   Joe was found dead by his wife, Lisa when she returned home on the morning of August 15, 2003 after spending the night at her parents' home.

4.   When Joe was found, he was slumped over his kitchen table. On the table beside Joe was an open bottle of rum, a broken glass, and Joe's gun cleaning supplies.

5.   Joe apparently died of a gun shot wound to the head (although no autopsy was performed to confirm). He had a bullet wound to his forehead. The wound was slightly off center, to the right, and appeared to be at an upward angle.

6. There is no evidence to suggest that anyone else was in the Smith home at the time of Joe's death.

7. The police concluded that Joe's death was a suicide, and did so without the aid of a forensic scientist, or an autopsy. Furthermore, no tests were conducted to establish Joe's blood alcohol level at the time of his death.

8. Joe was cremated on August 22, 2003.

9. On August 29, 2003, after finding a copy of Joe's life insurance policy, Lisa contacted ABC Insurance Company.

10. Joe had taken out the life insurance policy in April of 1998, and had maintained it since that time.

11. On September 8, 2003, without conducting an investigation, and relying on the police report, ABC Insurance Company (hereinafter "ABC") denied coverage under Accidental Death Benefit Provision of Joe's life insurance policy.

12. Specifically, ABC wrote, "We extend our deepest condolences on your loss...unfortunately, your husband's death was not accidental, and therefore does not fall within the coverage of his policy."

13. The wording of the Accidental Death Benefit Provision of Joe's policy reads,

    > Subject to this provision's terms, the Company will pay the amount of the Accidental Death Benefit upon receipt of due proof that the Life Insured's death resulted directly, and independently of all other causes, from bodily injury solely through external, violent and accidental means.

14. There is no direct evidence to suggest that Joe committed suicide. ABC relies solely on the findings of the police.

15. There was no forensic testing to indicate that Joe committed suicide.

16. There is no evidence to suggest that Joe was contemplating suicide.

17. Joe purchased his gun within weeks of finding out that Lisa was pregnant (six months prior to his death). He cited the need to protect his family as the reason for his purchase.

18. Joe was known to clean his gun at the kitchen table in conjunction with attending a shooting range for target practice.

Issues

1. What is the proper interpretation of an accidental death provision in a life insurance policy?

2. Was Mr. Smith's death accidental?

3. Does this Application meet the test for Summary Judgment?

Law and Argument

The Applicant submits that the determination of what constitutes "accidental death" within the accidental death provisions of Joseph Smith's policy with ABC Insurance Company is a two-part process. First an examination of judicial treatment and interpretation of accidental death provisions in a life insurance policy. Second the examination of the relevant factors to be taken into consideration when determining whether or not a death can properly be classified as "accidental".

Proper Interpretation of "Accidental Death"

The leading authority in this area of the law is the recent decision of the Supreme Court of Canada in *Martin v. American International Assurance Life Co.*[5] In the unanimous decision of all nine judges; Chief Justice McLachlin writing for the Court explicitly rejected a narrow conception of "accidental death".

> It follows that death is not non-accidental merely because the insured could have prevented death by taking greater care, or that a mishap was reasonably foreseeable in the sense used in tort law. Nor does a death that is unintended become "non-accidental" merely because that person was engaged in a dangerous or risky activity...the jurisprudence assigns a generous meaning to "accidental" in the absence of language to the contrary in the insurance policy.[6]

The Court further determined that insurance policies must be interpreted "...in a way that gives effect to the reasonable expectations of the parties".[7] Chief Justice McLachlin went on to explain that this means not only taking into consideration the expectations of the insurer, but also those of the insured.

The Appropriate Test to Determine "Accidental Death"

The Respondent submits that, as per the decision in *Martin*, the pivotal question to ask in any inquiry into whether a death can be considered "accidental" is to

---

[5] *Martin v. American International Assurance Life Co.*, [2003] S.C.J. No. 14, 2003 SCC 16 [Hereinafter *Martin*].

[6] *Ibid.*, at para. 20.

[7] *Ibid.*, at para. 12.

determine whether the insured expected to die as a result of his or her behaviour. This is done by examining the circumstances surrounding the death, including what the insured said and did, or failed to do.[8] The analysis is intended to be a holistic approach which takes into account the action causing the injury, and all the circumstances leading up to and surrounding it.[9] The deceased's expectation is not measured to the same standard as reasonable expectation in tort law. The decision in *Martin* noted that where the expectations of the insured are unclear, it is open to courts to consider whether a reasonable person in the position of the insured would have expected to die.[10]

Factors Altering the Application of the Test

    i)   Risky Behaviour

The Defence filed by the Respondent on this Application states Mr. Smith was intoxicated at the time of his death. The Defence further states that Mr. Smith had a history of risk-taking behaviour, particularly when drinking. The question then becomes, whether these statements if substantiated alter the appropriate test to be applied.

    The only evidence before this court is the Affidavit of Mrs. Smith, which indicates that while Mr. Smith rarely drank alcohol, when he did, he had a tendency to "overdo it" and become extremely intoxicated. The test requires an examination of his intention. Mrs. Smith indicated that while in this state, she could recall him engaging in foolish and risky behaviour, including walking along balcony ledges, and on one occasion jumping off the roof of a friend's house into a swimming pool. At best, in the present situation the Defendant could argue that there was a chance that he engaged in risky behavior if they could establish that Mr. Smith was intoxicated.

    The concept of risky activities was discussed in *Martin,* wherein the Court identified two types of cases. The first involves people engaging in high risk activities either for the psychological gratification of doing so, or to impress others with their bravado. The second involves a rescuer who puts him or herself in the way of death.[11] For the first set of cases, the court maintained that the question must be answered from the perspective of the insured, regardless of the high risk nature of the activity.[12] For the second, death was characterized as the result of a tragic, accidental sequence of events, and thus accidental itself, supporting recovery.[13]

---

[8] *Supra* note 5, at para. 21.

[9] *Bertalan Estate v. American Home Assurance Co.* (2001), 196 D.L.R. (4th) 445 at para. 6, 25 C.C.L.I. (3d) 16, [2001] 4 W.W.R. 401, 149 B.C.A.C. 244, [2001] I.L.R. I-3958 (C.A.).

[10] *Supra* note 5 at para. 21.

[11] *Ibid.*, at paras. 25-28.

[12] *Ibid.*, at para. 27.

[13] *Ibid.*, at para. 28.

In explicitly rejecting a narrow interpretation of "accidental death", the Court by extension rejected the proposition that risky behaviour contributing to the circumstances surrounding the death precludes a finding of accidental death. As per *Martin*, the decision to "court death" does at some point become equivalent to an intention to die,[14] however it does not change the application of the test.

> **The test does not change for cases involving conduct that brings with it a high risk of death; the test remains whether the death was designed or expected.** The first question is always "What did the insured, in fact, expect?" If we cannot be sure, as is often the case, then we may ask what a reasonable person endowed with the factual beliefs of the insured and placed in the circumstances of the insured would have expected.[15] [Emphasis added]

The Defendant has no way to establish that Mr. Smith was intoxicated at the time of his death. Even if the Defendant could establish that Mr. Smith was intoxicated and therefore prone to risky behaviour, his past behaviour demonstrates that this behaviour was linked to attempting to impress others, not that he was courting death, or contemplating suicide.

In the case at bar, the wording of the policy in question is an exact match of the policy considered in *Martin*, and therefore, I submit, there is no question concerning the appropriate test.

ii) Probability of Suicide

Where the circumstances surrounding the death are questionable and where the probability of suicide exists as the only other probable alternative to accidental death, a different set of factors must be considered. In the situation at bar, although there is evidence to suggest that the family was experiencing some financial difficulties, Mr. Smith was a successful accountant whose business and income were growing with each year. Most importantly, the Smiths were expecting a new baby within weeks of Joe's death.

I submit that there is insufficient forensic, or other evidence to determine whether Mr. Smith's death was suicide, and that there is little or no probability that his death was a suicide given his attitude toward impending fatherhood.

There is a long standing legal presumption against a finding of suicide. The Supreme Court of Canada in *London Life Insurance Co. v. Lang Shirt Co. (Trustee of)*[16] referred to this well-established presumption as early as 1929. This presumption was reaffirmed in the 1945 decision of *New York Life Insurance Co. v. Ross Estate*.[17] Originally, the presumption arose as a branch of the evidentiary presumption against the imputation of a crime, as suicide was considered to be a

---

[14]   *Supra* note 5, at para. 23.

[15]   *Ibid.*, at para. 23.

[16]   [1929] S.C.R. 117 at 7.

[17]   [1945] S.C.R. 289 at 7-8.

criminal act.[18] The removal of attempted suicide from the Canadian *Criminal Code* removed this basis for the presumption; however, it remains that unless proven to the contrary, the presumption against suicide remains operational.[19]

This presumption was discussed in some detail by the Newfoundland Court of Appeal in the decision of *Greening v. Commercial Union Assurance Company*, providing the following commentary with regards to the nature of the presumption:

> Similarly, in my opinion, presumption against suicide has both a substantive and procedural aspect. Its substantive impact arises because in invoking the presumption, it effectively places on the side of the party claiming accidental death the affirmative and clear assumption that the deceased dies accidentally. Since it is so placed upon the scales by operation of law, and not as a deduction from conflicting evidence, it represents a substantive premise of a clear and unequivocal nature. Indeed, no proof need be adduced by the proponent of accidental death other than occurrence of the death itself since death by accident is taken as axiomatic truth but liable to rebuttal. It follows that clear and cogent rebuttal evidence is required to tip the balance of probabilities sufficiently to justify a finding of suicide.[20]

The substantive nature of the presumption is that it shifts the evidentiary burden of having to prove suicide from the plaintiff to the defendant. The procedural aspect of the presumption is discussed as follows:

> On the other hand, the presumption does have procedural aspects as well. It does allocate the burden of proof to the person alleging suicide. **Where the circumstances of death are equally consistent with accident as suicide, the presumption becomes operative and accidental death is to be assumed... That burden is to be satisfied on the balance of probabilities. I would reiterate, however, that the discharge of the onus cast by the presumption requires that probability to be demonstrated by clear and cogent evidence of substantial civil weight.**[21] [Emphasis added]

The type of "clear and cogent evidence" required would be the actual circumstances pertaining to the death.[22] In this case, the court was unable to, having regard to the evidence adduced, say with certainty how the death at issue had occurred, and as such, was unable to find that the presumption against suicide could be rebutted.

The nature of this presumption was also discussed in very concise terms by Justice Fraser of the Alberta Court of Queen's Bench in the decision in *Sherstone v. Westroc Inc.*[23] In that decision, the court was very clear that where a policy is payable on accidental death, it is the responsibility of the plaintiff only

---

[18] *Supra* note 17, at 8; see also, *London Life*, *supra* note 16 at 7.

[19] *Greening v. Commercial Union Assurance Company*, [1988] I.L.R. 1-2300 at 4 (NL. C.A.).

[20] *Ibid.*, at 5.

[21] *Ibid.*, at 6.

[22] *Supra*, note 17 at 8.

[23] [2001] A.J. No. 640, 2001 ABQB 414.

to establish the death. The onus then shifts to the defendant to rebut that presumption, by clear and cogent evidence on a balance of probabilities, that the deceased committed suicide.[24] Applying the decision in *Greening*, Mason J. of the Alberta Court of Queen's Bench in the *Beischel v. Mutual of Omaha Insurance Co.* decision further indicated that the degree of probability required by the defendant must be commensurate with the seriousness of the allegation of suicide.[25] This evidentiary requirement was cited from the Supreme Court decision in *Hanes v. Wawanesa Mutual Insurance Company*[26] and further supports the need to perform an analysis of all the relevant circumstances surrounding each individual death. The presumption and its attendant evidentiary burdens has also been discussed and applied in Nova Scotia courts.[27]

Conclusion

The Supreme Court in *Martin* has clearly rejected a narrow conception of accidental death indicating that the term should be taken to mean accidental death resulting as a result of both deliberate and accidental means. While external factors such as risky behaviour should be taken into consideration when performing this analysis, the central question to ask is whether or not the deceased expected to die as a result of his or her actions.

In situations where the cause of death is questionable, the relevant case law in Canada clearly identifies a presumption against a finding of suicide. In this context, it is clearly incumbent upon the defendant insurer to prove, on a balance of probabilities commensurate with the allegation of suicide, that the deceased was responsible for his or her own death. If unable to do so, the presumption becomes operative, necessitating a finding of accidental death, therefore falling within the bounds of an accidental death benefits policy.

Based on Mrs. Smith's recollection of events, her description of her husband's character, his regular patterns of behaviour with regard to his gun, and his frame of mind at the time of his death, I respectfully submit that ABC Insurance Company is unable to rebut the strong presumption against a finding of suicide. The evidentiary burden rests with ABC Insurance Company. The very recent Supreme Court decision in *Martin* is quite similar to Mr. Smith's situation factually, and the wording of the policy identical.

Relying on the forgoing, the Applicant respectfully submits that there exists no fairly arguable point, such that the Defendant, ABC Insurance Company could rebut the presumption against suicide, and thereby be entitled to deny benefits under the policy. Accordingly, the Applicant, Plaintiff, requests that this

---

[24] *Supra* note 23, at paras. 58-62.

[25] *Beischel v. Mutual of Omaha Insurance Co.*, [1991] A.J. No. 757 at 21, 122 A.R. 32 (Q.B.).

[26] [1963] S.C.R. 154.

[27] *MacInnes v. London Life Insurance Co.*, [1979] N.S.J. No. 602 at para. 59, 33 N.S.R. (2d) 326, 57 A.P.R. 326, S.H. No. 11274 (S.C. (T.D.)).

honourable court grant this Application for Summary Judgment and further requests costs on this Application.

ALL OF WHICH IS RESPECTFULLY SUBMITTED

Mr. or Mrs. Lawyer

CHAPTER 7

Writing a Factum

Few documents written to a court will be read as many times or as thoroughly as a Factum. Generally, the judges of the Court of Appeal will read Facta at least three times, once weeks before the appeal is to be heard, a second time within days of the appeal, and a third time, before writing the decision. For this reason, the time and effort put into writing them is time well spent.

Good writing style remains important, whether for a memorandum, Brief, or Factum, however, the purpose and use of each document will influence the structure and tone of each document. The first thing to remember when writing a Factum is that you're your goal is to persuade. There is less flexibility with the structure a Factum than with a Brief, which for the student may provide some comfort.

Remember that an appeal is based on arguing that the lower court judge got it wrong. An appeal court will not overturn a decision just because they would have come to a different decision. Most appeals are based on arguing that the wrong legal principles were applied, although some are based on appealing findings of fact. In both situations, the appeal relies on the court record, and will involve examination of the decision and transcript of the lower court decision. Do not paraphrase, or summarize either document. All references should be exact quotes, and should provide the paragraph and/or line number where the quoted material can be found.

Like writing a memorandum the goal is to find, and layout the applicable legal principles from the most relevant and authoritative courts that can be found. In a Factum however, those principles will often be stated succinctly with reference to only two or three authorities. Often, the leading Supreme Court of Canada case, the leading decision of the Court of Appeal to which you are appealing, and the most on point case that can be found comprise the authority provided for each issue.

Your Factum should be double spaced and left justified, while all references to authorities, the decision being appealed, or the transcript, should be single spaced and right justified.

A. WRITING A FACTUM

1. Cover

The front page of a Factum should, at a glance, inform the reader on the parties, the lawyers, and on whose behalf, it has been filed. Facta are colour coded, so that the reader/judge can locate the Factum of either party at a glance, buff or yellow for the Appellant, green or blue for the Respondent. From top to bottom, the front page has the style of cause for the proceeding, denotes which party has filed the Factum, and then provides contact information on the lawyers involved. Most Facta look like the following example:

2003   C.A. No. 111112

IN THE NOVA SCOTIA COURT OF APPEAL

BETWEEN:

ABC Insurance Company, a body corporate registered to do
business in Nova Scotia

APPELLANTS

and –

Lisa Smith

RESPONDENT

FACTUM OF THE RESPODENT

Ian Chetum	Joe Lawyer
Doey Chetum & How	Joe Lawyer & Associates
123 Main Street	345 Right Avenue
Halifax, NS B3J 2X2	Halifax, NS B3J 2V1
Solicitor for the Appellant	Solicitor for the Respondent
Tel: (902) 555-1212	Tel: (902) 555-1313
Fax: (902) 555-1213	Fax: (902) 555-1314

---

2. Index

The index simply provides the page references for the beginning of each section of the Factum as follows:

3. Part I, Statement of Facts

The numbering of pages begins with this section. From this point forward, only the backs of pages should be used for your Factum. When you open a Factum, the right hand page should always be blank, thereby allowing the judges space to make notes.

Each fact in a Statement of Facts should form a separate numbered paragraph, and must refer to the place in the decision or transcript where it may be found. Make sure that your statement of facts is a statement of the facts as found by the judge. Do not take liberties in the way you state your facts. If there are additional facts which you believe are important, and on which the judge did not comment you can include them and refer to where they are found in the transcript. If you are appealing a finding of fact by the judge, you must clearly indicate that the judge found "X" however, you submit that the testimony before the court supports "Y", and refer to those sections of the transcript which support your position.

Location references for your facts should be right justified on a separate line directly below the fact which they support.

A typical Statement of Facts might begin as follows:

PART I

STATEMENT OF FACTS

1.   This Factum replies to the Appellant's Appeal of the decision of the Honourable Justice I. M. Right, whereby His Lordship:

    i.   Granted the Plaintiff's motion for Summary Judgment; and
   ii.   Awarded costs to the Plaintiff.

Decision of I. M. Right
Appeal Book Tab 5, at p. 15.

2.   On April 1998, Joseph Smith purchased life insurance from the Appellant ABC Insurance Company.

Insurance Policy
Appeal Book, Tab P, p. 40.

---

4. Part II, Statement of Issues

The issues are as set out in the Appellant's Notice of Appeal. The Respondent should use the same issues in the same order as they appear in the Appellant's Factum. The idea is to address the Appellant's argument head on. For ease of reference for the court, it is best if you maintain the issues in the same order as the Appellant, as per the following example:

PART II

STATEMENT OF ISSUES

13. The Appellant's Factum set out the following grounds of appeal:

   1.   Whether the Learned Chambers Judge erred in law in the Application of Civil Procedure Rule 13.01 in that he applied the wrong test to an application for summary judgment brought by the Plaintiff;

   2.   Whether the Learned Chambers Judge erred in law in finding that there was no arguable issue with respect to the interpretation or application of the accidental death coverage provided to Lisa Smith by ABC Insurance Company's policy.

   3.   Whether the Learned Chambers Judge erred in law in finding that the threshold was met with respect to the Plaintiff's application for summary judgment.

---

5. Part III, Argument

Brevity will serve you well. A Factum should be no more than 30 pages, unless the issues are particularly complex. Remember that these are 30 double spaced pages, with large indented quotes. For this reason, and because, you can assume that the court will have read your Factum carefully; you can and should, be direct and to the point in stating your position. In the words of Justice Goodfellow of the Nova Scotia Supreme Court, superfluous verbiage will not assist your argument.

Use headings and sub-headings to help make your argument clear. When referring to case authorities, place the full name of the case within the text, and then place the full cite for the case directly after the paragraph in which it is referenced. Almost every paragraph in your argument section should cite authority for the proposition put forward, and should provide a specific page, and/or paragraph reference for each argument.

Finally, your argument should be arranged to correspond to the issues as they are arranged in your Statement of Issues section; paragraph numbers should continue sequentially, from the Statement of Facts section.

6. Part IV, Relief Sought

This section should briefly state what relief your client is seeking, whether requesting that the lower court decision be affirmed, varied, or overturned, you should always include a comment on costs.

7. Appendix "A", List of Authorities

This section is simply a list of all case authorities cited in the Factum in the order in which they appear. Number each of the authorities beginning from number 1.

8. Appendix "B", List of Statutory Authorities

This section is a list of all statutory authorities referred to in the Factum. Numbering of this list begins where the List of Authorities ends.

B. SAMPLE FACTUM

The following is a Factum based on the Factual Scenario found at the beginning of this manual, and has been prepared simply to offer as a sample. It is premised on the Plaintiff, Lisa Smith having won an application for Summary Judgment, and now responding to an appeal of that order by ABC Insurance Company.

SAMPLE

2004   C.A. No. 111112

IN THE NOVA SCOTIA COURT OF APPEAL

BETWEEN:

ABC Insurance Company, a body corporate registered to do
business in Nova Scotia

APPELLANTS

and –

Lisa Smith

RESPONDENT

FACTUM OF THE RESPONDENT

Ian Chetum	Joe Lawyer
Doey Chetum & How	Joe Lawyer & Associates
123 Main Street	345 Right Avenue
Halifax, NS B3J 2X2	Halifax, NS B3J 2V1
Solicitor for the Appellant	Solicitor for the Respondent
Tel: (902) 555-1212	Tel: (902) 555-1313
Fax: (902) 555-1213	Fax: (902) 555-1314

INDEX

PART I

STATEMENT OF FACTS

3.   This Factum replies to the Appellant's Appeal of the decision of the Honourable Justice I. M. Right, whereby His Lordship:

   i.   Granted the Plaintiff's motion for Summary Judgment; and

   ii.   Awarded costs to the Plaintiff.

> Decision of I. M. Right
> Appeal Book Tab 5, at p. 15.

4.   On April 1998, Joseph Smith purchased life insurance, from the Appellant ABC Insurance Company [hereinafter the "Policy"].

> Insurance Policy
> Appeal Book, Tab P, p. 40.

5.   The Policy included a death benefits provision, which, like the policy continued in force until the time of Joseph Smith's death.

> Insurance Policy
> Appeal Book, Tab P, p. 45.

6.   The wording of the Accidental Death Benefit Provision of the Policy reads,

> Subject to this provision's terms, the Company will pay the amount of the Accidental Death Benefit upon receipt of due proof that the Life Insured's death resulted directly, and independently of all other causes, from bodily injury solely through external, violent and accidental means.

> Insurance Policy
> Appeal Book, Tab P, p. 42.

7.   The Applicant, Lisa Smith (hereinafter "Lisa") is the widow of the late Joseph Smith.

> Affidavit of Lisa Smith
> Appeal Book, Tab 7, paragraphs 3-5.

8.   At the time of his death, Joseph Smith, [hereinafter "Joe" was a thirty-five (35) year-old accountant, who, with his wife was looking forward to the birth of his first child.

> Affidavit of Lisa Smith
> Appeal Book, Tab 7, paragraphs 4-17.

9.   Joe was found dead by his wife, Lisa when she returned home on the morning of August 15, 2003 after spending the night at her parents' home.

> Affidavit of Lisa Smith
> Appeal Book, Tab 7, paragraphs 16-18.

10. Joe was found, slumped over his kitchen table with an open bottle of rum, a broken glass, and his gun cleaning supplies all on the table beside him.

Affidavit of Lisa Smith
Appeal Book, Tab 7, paragraphs 16-18.

11. Joe died of a gun shot wound to the head.

Affidavit of Bob the Police Officer
Appeal Book, Tab 8, paragraphs 4-8.

12. There was no evidence to suggest that anyone else was in the Smith home at the time of Joe's death.

Affidavit of Bob the Police Officer
Appeal Book, Tab 8, paragraphs 15-22.

13. Without the aid of a forensic scientist, or an autopsy, the police concluded that Joe's death was a suicide. There is no evidence in relation to Joe's blood alcohol level at the time of his death.

Affidavit of Bob the Police Officer
Appeal Book, Tab 8, paragraphs 23-28.

14. There is no way to gain additional evidence from Joe's body, as he was cremated on August 22, 2003 (one week after his death).

Affidavit of Bob the Police Officer
Appeal Book, Tab 8, paragraph 29.

15. On August 29, 2003, after finding a copy of Joe's life insurance policy Lisa contacted ABC Insurance Company.

Affidavit of Lisa Smith
Appeal Book, Tab 7, paragraph 21.

16. On September 8, 2003, without conducting an investigation, and relying on the police report, ABC Insurance Company (hereinafter "ABC") denied coverage under Accidental Death Benefit Provision of Joe's life insurance policy, writing, "We extend our deepest condolences on your loss...unfortunately, your husband's death was not accidental, and therefore does not fall within the coverage of his policy."

Affidavit of Lisa Smith
Appeal Book, Tab 7, paragraphs 23-25.

Affidavit of Clem the Claims Adjuster
Appeal Book, Tab 8, paragraphs 4-16.

17. There is no direct evidence to suggest that Joe committed suicide. ABC relies solely on the findings of the police.

18. There was no forensic testing to indicate that Joe committed suicide.
Affidavit of Bob the Police Officer
Appeal Book, Tab 8, paragraph 22.

19. There is no evidence to suggest that Joe was contemplating suicide.

20. Joe purchased his gun within weeks of finding out that Lisa was pregnant. He cited the need to protect his family as the reason for his purchase.
Affidavit of Lisa Smith
Appeal Book, Tab 7, paragraphs 7-9.

21. Joe was known to clean his gun at the kitchen table in conjunction with attending a shooting range for target practice.
Affidavit of Lisa Smith
Appeal Book, Tab 7, paragraphs 8-11.

22. On December 1, 2003, the Respondent commenced an action seeking specific performance of the Policy, in addition to general and punitive damages.
Originating Notice and Statement of Claim
Appeal Book, Tab 1.

23. On January 1, 2004, the Appellant filed a defence, pleading *inter alia*, that Joseph Smith's death did not result from external means.
Defence
Appeal Book, Tab 2, para 8.

24. On April 1, 2004, the Respondent made application for Summary Judgment.
Interlocutory Notice and Application
Appeal Book, Tab 3.

25. On July 2, 2004, Justice I. M. Right granted summary judgment, ordering ABC to specifically perform its obligations under the Policy, ordering $50,000.00 in punitive damages against ABC, and ordering costs against ABC fixed at $2,000.00.
Order of Mr. Justice Right dated July 2, 2004
Appeal Book, Tab 5.

PART II

STATEMENT OF ISSUES

26. The Appellant's Factum set out the following grounds of appeal:

a. Whether the Learned Chambers Judge erred in law in the Application of Civil Procedure Rule 13.01 in that he applied the wrong test to an application for Summary Judgment brought by the Plaintiff;

b. Whether the Learned Chambers Judge erred in law in finding that there was no arguable issue with respect to the interpretation or application of the accidental death coverage provided to Joseph Smith by ABC Insurance Company's policy.

c. Whether the Learned Chambers Judge erred in law in finding that the threshold was met with respect to the Plaintiff's application for Summary Judgment.

PART III

ARGUMENT

A. The Standard of Review

27. On a question of law, the standard of review by an appellate court is correctness; an appellate court may replace the opinion of the trial judge with its own.

Housen v. Nikolaisen
[2002] 2 S.C.R. 235 at para. 8.

28. On findings of fact, absent a palpable and overriding error in the understanding of the evidence, an appellate court should not interfere with the trial judge's findings.

St-Jean v. Mercier
[2002] S.C.R. 491 at para. 36.

29. The decision under appeal is a discretionary interlocutory order. This Honourable Court has held on many occasions that it will not interfere with discretionary orders unless wrong principles of law have been applied, or if a patent injustice would result.

30. The Alberta Court of Appeal in *Shuchuk v. Wolfert* recently examined the issue of the appropriate standard of review for appeals from summary judgment

orders stating at para 9:

> The standard of review on an appeal of a summary judgment decision made by a Court of Queen's Bench Justice *de novo* from a Master's Order is correctness on questions of law and palpable and overriding error on questions of fact. On a summary judgment decision, which is discretionary, great deference is given.

> *Shuhuk v. Wolfert*
> 2003 ABCA 109, leave to appeal to S.C.C.
> refused [2003] CarswellAlta 1653.

31. The Respondent submits that the decision of the Learned I. M. Right in Chambers is correct in its findings of fact, and application of law, and further submits that this Honourable Court should not interfere with his decision to grant summary judgment.

B. The Merits of the Appeal

Issue #1 – Whether the Learned Chambers Judge erred in law in the Application of Civil Procedure Rule 13.01 in that he applied the wrong test to an application for summary judgment brought by the Plaintiff

32. Rule 13.01 of the Nova Scotia *Civil Procedure Rules* states, *inter alia*:

> 13.01 After the close of pleading, any party may apply to the court for judgment on the ground that:
>
> 1. there is no arguable issue to be tried with respect to the claim or any part thereof;
>
> 2. there is no arguable issue to be tried with respect to the defence or any part thereof; or
>
> 3. the only arguable issue to be tried is the amount of any damages claimed.

33. The leading Nova Scotia authority for the interpretation of Summary Judgment Rule is *Bank of Nova Scotia et al. v. Domrowski*, wherein the Appeal Division wrote beginning at paragraph 18 that:

> Rule 13 has its antecedents in Order 14 of the English Supreme Court Rules. As stated in the Supreme Court Practice (1976), Vol. 1 at p. 136 the purpose of 0.14 is to enable the plaintiff to obtain summary judgment without trial if he can prove his claim clearly, and if the defendant is unable to set up a *bona fide* defence, or raise an issue against the claim which ought to be tried ... The defendant is bound to show that he has some reasonable ground of defence to the action.
>
> ....

The issue may, I believe be summarized as being whether there is a fair issue to be tried, based on some reasonable ground of defence.

Bank of Nova Scotia et al. v. Dombrowski
(1977), 23 N.S.R. (2d) 532 (S.C. (A.D.)).

34. In *Ocean Contractors Ltd. v. Acadia Construction Ltd. et al.*, on an application for Summary Judgment, Justice Saunders wrote:

> On an application for summary judgment the plaintiff is bound to prove by affidavit its entitlement as alleged in the Statement of Claim. *The burden then moves to the defendant to satisfy the Court either that it has a legitimate defence or that it has a fairly arguable point to raise in defence.* [Emphasis added]

Ocean Contractors Ltd. v. Acadia Construction Ltd. et al.
(1991), 107 N.S.R. (2d) 366 at 371 (S.C. (T.D.))

35. In the well quoted case of *Carl B. Potter Ltd. v. Antil Canada Ltd. and Mercantile Bank of Canada*, the Appeal division referred approvingly at paragraph 9, to the following passage from *Royal Bank of Canada v. Malouf*:

> It is well settled that the provisions of Rule 127 are not to be used to strike out a defence, unless it is very clear that the defendant has no substantial defence to submit to the Court; but when a Judge is satisfied, not only that there is no defence, but no fairly arguable point to be presented on behalf of the defendant, it is his duty to give effect to the Rule and to allow the plaintiff to enter judgment for his claim...*Moreover, in order to resist an application under the Rule, it is not sufficient for the defendant to say he has a good defence on the merits; the defence must be disclosed, and sufficient facts must appear to show that there is a bona-fide defence or at least, as stated by Jessl, M. R., in Anglo – Italian Bank v. Wells, supra, "a fairly arguable point to be argued on behalf of the defendant":...*

Carl B. Potter Ltd. v. Antil Canada Ltd. and Mercantile Bank of Canada
(1976), 15 N.S.R. (2d) 408 (S.C. (A.D.)).

Royal Bank of Canada v. Malouf
[1932] 2 W.W.R. 526 (Sask. C.A.)

36. In *Guarantee Co. of North America v. Gordon Capital Corp. et al.*, the Supreme Court of Canada wrote that the test for Summary Judgment is as follows:

> The Appropriate test to be applied on a motion for summary judgment is satisfied when the application has shown that there is no genuine issue of material fact requiring trial, and therefore summary judgment is a property question for consideration by the court. *Hercules Management Ltd. v. Ernst & Young*, [1997] 2 S.C.R. 165 (S.C.C.) at para. 15; *Dawson v. Rexcraft Storage & Warehouse Inc.* (1998), 164 D.L.R. (4th) 257 (Ont. C.A.) at pp. 267-68; *Irving Ungerman Ltd. v. Galanis* (1991), 4. O.R. (3d) 545 (Ont. C.A.) at pp. 550-51. Once the moving party has made this showing, *the respondent must then "establish his claim as being one with a real chance of success." Hercules*, supra at para 15. [Emphasis added]

Guarantee Co. of North America v. Gordon Capital Corp. et al.
[1999] 3 S.C.R. 423 at para. 27.

37. The party applying for Summary Judgment bears the initial burden of proving that there is no arguable issue for trial, once met, the opposing party then bears the burden of establishing that his claim has a real chance of success.

38. In the case at bar, Justice I. M. Right correctly adopted the test set out by the Supreme Court of Canada in *Guarantee Co. of North America* and *Hercules Management*, writing:

> Starting with Carl B Potter Limited, Nova Scotia developed an approach to Plaintiff's summary judgment applications by which the Plaintiff was required to clearly prove the claim. Then the Defendant was called upon to demonstrate a point reasonably to be presented in defence.
>
> The Court will consider summary judgment only where the moving party establishes that, "there is no genuine issue of material fact requiring trial", and that the threshold having been met by the Applicant, the Respondent fails to, "establish his claim as being one with a real chance of success."

Decision of I. M. Right
Appeal Book, Tab 4, p. 16.

39. The Respondent submits that, Justice I. M. Right was correct in the test to be applied.

Issue #2 – Whether the Learned Chambers Judge erred in finding that there was no arguable issue with respect to the interpretation or application of the accidental death coverage provided to Joseph Smith by ABC Insurance Company's policy.

40. The Applicant submits that the determination of what constitutes "accidental death" within the accidental death provisions of Joseph Smith's policy with ABC Insurance Company is a two-part process. First an examination of judicial treatment and interpretation of accidental death provisions in life insurance policies. Second the examination of the relevant factors to be taken into consideration when determining whether or not a death can properly be classified as "accidental".

Proper Interpretation of "Accidental Death"

41. The leading authority in this area of the law is the recent decision of the Supreme Court of Canada in *Martin v. American International Assurance Life Co.* In the unanimous decision of all nine judges; Chief Justice McLachlin writing for the court explicitly rejected a narrow conception of "accidental death" writing:

It follows that death is not non-accidental merely because the insured could have prevented death by taking greater care, or that a mishap was reasonably foreseeable in the sense used in tort law. Nor does a death that is unintended become "non-accidental" merely because that person was engaged in a dangerous or risky activity...the jurisprudence assigns a generous meaning to "accidental" in the absence of language to the contrary in the insurance policy.

> *Martin v. American International Assurance Life Co.*
> [2003] S.C.J. No. 14 at para. 20, 2003 SCC 16.

42. The Court further determined that insurance policies must be interpreted "...in a way that gives effect to the reasonable expectations of the parties". Chief Justice McLachlin went on to explain that this means not only taking into consideration the expectations of the insurer, but also those of the insured.

> *Martin v. American International, supra*, at para. 12.

The Appropriate Test to Determine "Accidental Death"

43. The Respondent submits that, as per the decision in *Martin*, the pivotal question to ask in any inquiry into whether a death can be considered "accidental" is to determine whether the insured expected to die as a result of his or her behaviour. This is done by examining the circumstances surrounding the death, including what the insured said and did, or failed to do.

> *Martin v. American International, supra*, at para. 21.

44. The analysis is intended to be a holistic approach which takes into account the action causing the injury, and all the circumstances leading up to and surrounding it.

> *Bertalan Estate v. American Home Assurance Co.*
> 2001 BCCA 131 at para. 6, 86 B.C.L.R. (3d) 1.

45. The deceased's expectation is not measured to the same standard as reasonable expectation in tort law. The decision in *Martin* noted that where the expectations of the insured are unclear, it is open to courts to consider whether a reasonable person in the position of the insured would have expected to die.

> *Martin v. American International, supra*, at para. 21.

Factors Altering the Application of the Test

i)   Risky Behaviour

46. The Defence filed by the Respondent on this Application states Mr. Smith was intoxicated at the time of his death. The Defence further states that Mr.

Smith had a history of risk-taking behaviour, particularly when drinking. The question then becomes, whether these statements if substantiated alter the appropriate test to be applied.

47. The only evidence before this court is the Affidavit of Mrs. Smith, which indicates that while Mr. Smith rarely drank alcohol, when he did, he had a tendency to "overdo it" and become extremely intoxicated. The test requires an examination of his intention. Mrs. Smith indicated that while in this state, she could recall him engaging in foolish and risky behaviour, including walking along balcony ledges, and on one occasion jumping off the roof of a friend's house into a swimming pool.

Affidavit of Lisa Smith
Appeal Book, Tab 7, paras. 15-34.

48. Based on all of the evidence before this court, if the Defendant could establish that Mr. Smith was intoxicated, the best that they could argue is that there was a chance Joe engaged in risky behaviour.

49. The concept of risky activities was discussed in *Martin* wherein the Court identified two types of cases. The first involves people engaging in high risk activities either for the psychological gratification of doing so, or to impress others with their bravado. The second involves a rescuer who puts him or herself in the way of death. For the first set of cases, the Court maintained that the question must be answered from the perspective of the insured, regardless of the high risk nature of the activity. For the second, death was characterized as the result of a tragic, accidental sequence of events, and thus accidental itself, supporting recovery.

Martin v. American International, supra, at paras. 25-28.

50. In explicitly rejecting a narrow interpretation of "accidental death", the Court by extension rejected the proposition that risky behaviour contributing to the circumstances surrounding the death precludes a finding of accidental death. As per *Martin*, the decision to "court death" does at some point become equivalent to an intention to die, however it does not change the application of the test.

> **The test does not change for cases involving conduct that brings with it a high risk of death; the test remains whether the death was designed or expected.** The first question is always "What did the insured, in fact, expect?" If we cannot be sure, as is often the case, then we may ask what a reasonable person endowed with the factual beliefs of the insured and placed in the circumstances of the insured would have expected.
> [Emphasis added]

Martin v. American International, supra, at para. 23.

51. The Defendant has no way to establish that Mr. Smith was intoxicated at the time of his death. Even if the Defendant could establish that Mr. Smith was

intoxicated and therefore prone to risky behaviour, the only evidence led on his past behaviour demonstrates that this behaviour was linked to attempting to impress others, and not that he was courting death, or contemplating suicide.

Affidavit of Lisa Smith
Appeal Book, Tab 7, paragraphs 19-34.

52. In the case at bar, the wording of the policy in question is an exact match of the policy considered in *Martin*, and therefore, I submit, there is no question concerning the appropriate test.

ii) Probability of Suicide

53. Where the circumstances surrounding the death are questionable and where the probability of suicide exists as the only other probable alternative to accidental death, a different set of factors must be considered. In the situation at bar, although there is evidence to suggest that the family was experiencing some financial difficulties, Mr. Smith was a successful accountant whose business and income were growing with each year. Most importantly, the Smiths were expecting a new baby within weeks of Joe's death.

Martin v. American International Assurance Life Co., at paras. 23-25.

54. I submit that there is insufficient forensic or other evidence to determine whether Mr. Smith's death was suicide, and that there is little or no probability that his death was a suicide given his attitude toward impending fatherhood.

Affidavit of Bob the Police office
Appeal Book, Tab 8, paras. 7-18.

55. There is a long-standing legal presumption against a finding of suicide. The Supreme Court of Canada in *London Life Insurance Co. v. Lang Shirt Co. (Trustee of)* referred to this well-established presumption as early as 1929.

London Life Insurance Co. v. Lang Shirt Co. (Trustee of)
[1929] S.C.R. 117 at 7.

56. This presumption was reaffirmed in the 1945 decision of *New York Life Insurance Co. v. Ross Estate*. Originally, the presumption arose as a branch of the evidentiary presumption against the imputation of a crime, as suicide was considered to be a criminal act.

New York Life Insurance Co. v. Ross Estate
[1945] S.C.R. 289 at 7-8.
see also, *London Life, supra* at 7.

57. The removal of attempted suicide from the Canadian *Criminal Code* removed this basis for the presumption; however, it remains that unless proven to the contrary, the presumption against suicide remains operational. This presumption was discussed in some detail by the Newfoundland Court of Appeal in the decision of *Greening v. Commercial Union Assurance Company*, providing the following commentary with regards to the nature of the presumption:

> Similarly, in my opinion, presumption against suicide has both a substantive and procedural aspect. Its substantive impact arises because in invoking the presumption, it effectively places on the side of the party claiming accidental death the affirmative and clear assumption that the deceased dies accidentally. Since it is so placed upon the scales by operation of law, and not as a deduction from conflicting evidence, it represents a substantive premise of a clear and unequivocal nature. Indeed, no proof need be adduced by the proponent of accidental death other than occurrence of the death itself since death by accident is taken as axiomatic truth but liable to rebuttal. It follows that clear and cogent rebuttal evidence is required to tip the balance of probabilities sufficiently to justify a finding of suicide.

> *Greening v. Commercial Union Assurance Company*
> [1988] I.L.R. 1-2300 at 5 (Nfld. C.A.).

58. The substantive nature of the presumption is that it shifts the evidentiary burden of having to prove suicide from the plaintiff to the defendant. The procedural aspect of the presumption is discussed as follows:

> On the other hand, the presumption does have procedural aspects as well. It does allocate the burden of proof to the person alleging suicide. **Where the circumstances of death are equally consistent with accident as suicide, the presumption becomes operative and accidental death is to be assumed. That burden is to be satisfied on the balance of probabilities. I would reiterate, however, that the discharge of the onus cast by the presumption requires that probability to be demonstrated by clear and cogent evidence of substantial civil weight.**
> [Emphasis added]

> *Greening v. Commercial Union Assurance Company*
> [1988] I.L.R. 1-2300 at 6 (Nfld. C.A.).

59. The type of "clear and cogent evidence" required would be the actual circumstances pertaining to the death. In this case, the court was unable to, having regard to the evidence adduced, say with certainty how the death at issue had occurred, and as such, was unable to find that the presumption against suicide could be rebutted.

> *Greening v. Commercial Union Assurance Company*
> [1988] I.L.R. 1-2300 at 8 (Nfld. C.A.).

60. The nature of this presumption was also discussed in very concise terms by Justice Fraser of the Alberta Court of Queen's Bench in the decision in *Sherstone v. Westroc Inc.*

> *Sherstone v. Westroc Inc.*
> [2001] A.J. No. 640, 2001 ABQB 414.

61. In that decision, the Court was very clear that where a policy is payable on accidental death, it is the responsibility of the plaintiff only to establish the death. The onus then shifts to the defendant to rebut that presumption, by clear and cogent evidence on a balance of probabilities, that the deceased committed suicide.

Sherstone v. Westroc Inc.
[2001] A.J. No. 640 at paras. 58-62, 2001 ABQB 414.

62. Applying the decision in *Greening*, Mason J. of the Alberta Court of Queen's Bench in the *Beischel v. Mutual of Omaha Insurance Co.* decision further indicated that the degree of probability required by the defendant must be commensurate with the seriousness of the allegation of suicide.

Beischel v. Mutual of Omaha Insurance Co.
[1991] A.J. No. 757 at 21, 122 A.R. 32 (Q.B.).

63. This evidentiary requirement was cited from the Supreme Court decision in *Hanes v. Wawanesa Mutual Insurance Company* and further supports the need to perform an analysis of all the relevant circumstances surrounding each individual death. The presumption and its attendant evidentiary burdens has also been discussed and applied in Nova Scotia courts.

Hanes v. Wawanesa Mutual Insurance Company
[1963] S.C.R. 154.

MacInnes v. London Life Insurance Co.
[1979] N.S.J. No. 602 at para. 59, 33 N.S.R. (2d) 326.

Issue #1 – Whether the Learned Chambers Judge erred in law in finding that the threshold was met with respect to the Plaintiff's application for Summary Judgment.

64. The test for Summary Judgment is clear; the moving party must meet the threshold of demonstrating to a court that there is no arguable issue to be tried.

65. Based on the fact that the Appellant has no evidence to substantiate their claim that Joseph Smith's death was designed or expected, as per *Martin*, and the fact that there is a legal presumption against suicide, the Respondent respectfully submits that there is no arguable issue to be tried. Accordingly, the Respondent submits that the Honourable Justice Right was correct in concluding that the threshold was met.

PART IV

RELIEF SOUGHT

66. The Respondent requests that this Appeal be dismissed with costs and that the July 2, 2004 Order of the Honourable Justice Right be affirmed.

ALL OF WHICH IS RESPECTFULLY SUBMITTED this 1st day of September, 2004.

_____

Joe Lawyer
Joe Lawyer & Associates
345 Right Avenue
Halifax, NS B3J 2X2
Solicitor for the Respondent
Tel: (902) 555-1212
Fax: (902) 555-1213

TO: The Registrar

AND TO: Ian Chetum
Doey Chetum & How
123 Main Street
Halifax, NS B3J 2V1
Solicitor for the Appellant
Tel: (902) 555-1313
Fax: (902) 555-1314

APPENDIX "A"

LIST OF AUTHORITIES

1. *Housen v. Nikolaisen,* [2002] 2 S.C.R. 235.

2. *St-Jean v. Mercie,* [2002] S.C.R. 491.

3. *Shuhuk v. Wolfert,* 2003 ABCA 109, leave to appeal to S.C.C. refused [2003] CarswellAlta 1653.

4. *Bank of Nova Scotia et al. v. Dombrowski,* (1977), 23 N.S.R. (2d) 532 (S.C. (A.D.)).

5. *Ocean Contractors Ltd. v. Acadia Construction Ltd. et al.*, (1991), 107 N.S.R. (2d) 366 (S.C. (T.D.)).

6. *Carl B. Potter Ltd. v. Antil Canada Ltd. and Mercantile Bank of Canada* (1976), 15 N.S.R. (2d) 408 (S.C. (A.D.)).

7. *Royal Bank of Canada v. Malouf,* [1932] 2 W.W.R. 526 (Sask. C.A.).

8. *Guarantee Co. of North America v. Gordon Capital Corp. et al.,* [1999] 3 S.C.R. 423.

9. *Martin v. American International Assurance Life Co.* [2003] S.C.J. No. 14, 2003 SCC 16.

10. *Bertalan Estate v. American Home Assurance Co.*, 2001 BCCA 131, 86 B.C.L.R. (3d) 1.

11. *London Life Insurance Co. v. Lang Shirt Co. (Trustee of)*, [1929] S.C.R. 117.

12. *New York Life Insurance Co. v. Ross Estate*, [1945] S.C.R. 289.

13. *Greening v. Commercial Union Assurance Company*, [1988] I.L.R. 1-2300 (Nfld. C.A.).

14. *Sherstone v. Westroc Inc.,* [2001] A.J. No. 640, 2001 ABQB 414.

15. *Beischel v. Mutual of Omaha Insurance Co.*, [1991] A.J. No. 757, 122 A.R. 32 (Q.B.).

16. *Hanes v. Wawanesa Mutual Insurance Co.*, [1963] S.C.R. 154.

17. *MacInnes v. London Life Insurance Co.*, [1979] N.S.J. No. 602, 33 N.S.R. (2d) 326 (S.C. (T.D.)).

APPENDIX "B"

LIST OF STATUTORY AUTHORITIES

18. Nova Scotia *Civil Procedure Rule* 13.01

Chapter 8

General Rules of Citation

Because of the multiplicity of case reports and the variety in publication there is no single method of legal citation. The following "rules" cover most of the important points.

A. RULE 1: THE FORM OF CITATION

A complete case citation consists of:

(i)   the style of cause (or name of the parties) in italics;

NOTE: The name of an individual is not given in full; use the surname only. If there are multiple individuals give the surname of the first adversary party on each side. Do not use the words "and others" or "*et al.*". A criminal case is usually cited as *R. v. Jones.*

(ii)   "*v.*" separating the names of the opposing parties.[1] When writing in English never use "c." instead of "*v.*", even if citing a case reported in French;

(iii) the year of the decision;[2]

(iv)   the volume number (if any);

(v)   the abbreviated title of the case report;

(vi)   the series;

(vii) the page at which the report begins;

(viii) the specific page reference where the relevant text material appears (if any); and

(ix)   the abbreviated name of the jurisdiction and court (unless it is obvious from the name of the report series).

---

[1] It is bad form when speaking to say "versus"; always say "A against B" or "A and B".

[2] Usually a volume of case reports includes several cases from the prior year. If so, the recommended practice is to cite the year of the decision in round brackets even if another year is indicated on the spine of the volume. The citation, in this case is for a 2002 case indexed in a 2003 reporter: *Martin v. American International Assurance Life Co.* (2002), [2003] S.C.J. No. 14 (S.C.C.). If the year is necessary to find the volume, include the year which appears on the spine in square brackets. Note that some publishers indicate the appropriate citation for the volume on the title page.

Examples:

Bank of Montreal v. Faclaris (1984), 13 D.L.R. (4th) 245 at 247 (Ont. H.C.J.).

Bradbury v. Mundell (1993), 13 O.R. (3d) 269 (Gen. Div.).

Sidoroff v. Joe (1992), 76 B.C.L.R. (2d) 82 at 84 (C.A.).

In these examples, the plaintiff's surname has been placed first in the report of the trial and the defendant's surname appears second.[3]

In the first example, the decision was reported in 1984 in the 13th volume of the *Dominion Law Reports (Fourth Series)*. The report begins on page 245, the quoted passage is on page 247, and the decision was handed down by the Ontario High Court of Justice.

In the second example, the decision was reported in 1993 in the 13th volume of the *Ontario Reports (Third Series)*. The report began on page 269 and the decision was handed down by the General Division of the Ontario Court of Justice.

In the third example, the decision was reported in 1992 in the 76th volume of the *British Columbia Law Reports (Second Series)*. The report begins on page 82, the quoted passage is on page 84, and the decision was handed down by the British Columbia Court of Appeal.

Capitalize the first letter of a party name and the first letter of all words other than prepositions, connectives and the like. (Omit given names and initials of individuals, except when they appear in the name of a company.) If the style of cause appears in the body of a memorandum or other text material, it is not repeated in the footnote citation.

B. Rule 2: Style of Cause

1. The use of "*sub nom.*"

Where a case is reported under different names it may be necessary for clarity to indicate this to the reader by use of the explanatory phrase "*sub nom.*". "*Sub nom.*" is placed in brackets with the name.

Example:

Walton v. Hebb, [1985] 1 W.W.R. 122, (*sub nom. Re Walton and Attorney General of Canada*) 13 D.L.R. (4th) 379 (N.W.T.S.C.).

---

[3]   The practice on appeal is not uniform. In some reports the appellant's name (the one who appeals to the higher court) appears first on appeal while in other reports the plaintiff's name remains first regardless of which side appeals. The Canadian Law Information Council has developed a standard for identification of cases by name. Under the new standard a case keeps the same name as used in the original proceeding through all appeal levels.

The case of *Dalton and MacDonald* which appears in the Western Weekly Reports as In *Re Dalton and MacDonald Estate*, and in the British Columbia Law Reports as In *Re Testator's Family Maintenance Act and the Estate of Donald Alexander MacDonald* may be cited as follows:

Dalton v. MacDonald Estate, [1938] 1 W.W.R. 758, (*sub nom. Re Testator's Family Maintenance Act and MacDonald Estate*) 52 B.C.L.R. 473 (C.A.).

Consider also the following example:

Reference Re Legislative Authority of Parliament of Canada, [1980] 1 S.C.R. 54 (*sub nom. Reference Re Legislative Authority of Parliament to Alter or Replace Senate*) 102 D.L.R. (3d) 1, (*sub nom. Re British North America Act and Federal Senate*) 30 N.R. 271.

"*Sub nom.*" is also used to show a difference in the parties' names at a lower court level, as shown below:

Giffels Associates Ltd. v. Eastern Construction Co. (1978), 84 D.L.R. (3d) 344 (S.C.C.); aff'g (1976), 68 D.L.R. (3d) 385 (Ont. C.A.); aff'g in part (*sub nom. Dominion Chain Co. v. Eastern Construction Co.*) (1974), 46 D.L.R. (3d) 28 (Ont. H.C.J.).

Where a case which has been heard at more than one level of court, has been reported in parallel series, and has appeared under different names, the complete citation may be written as follows:

Horsley v. MacLaren, [1972] S.C.R. 441, 22 D.L.R. (3d) 545; aff'g (1970), 2 O.R. 487, 11 D.L.R. (3d) 277 (C.A.); rev'g (*sub nom. Matthews v. MacLaren; Horsley v. MacLaren*) (1969), 2 O.R. 137, 4 D.L.R. (3d) 557 (H.C.).

2. Corporate Status

The style of cause should be reproduced with some modifications from a law reporter. You should always include 'Ltd.', 'Limited', 'ltee', 's.r.l' or 'LLP', and always include 'Inc.' if it is part of the company name. A reference to a definite article, such as "the" which precedes a party name is usually omitted.

Example:
Toys "R" Us (Canada) Ltd. v. Manjel Inc. (1993), 51 C.P.R. (3d) 27 (F.C.T.D.).

3. References to the Crown

With some exceptions, the Crown is referred to as "R." instead of "Regina", "The Queen", "La Reine", "Rex", "The King", or "Le Roi". This practice was standardized beginning in 1986.

Examples:
Deom v. R. (1981), 64 C.C.C. (2d) 222 (B.C.S.C.).
R. v. Inkster (1988), 69 Sask. R. 1 (Q.B.).

NOTE: The former case appears as *Re Deom et al. and The Queen* in the report series. If the style of cause in the citation adopts a reference to "v.", the "Re" is dropped; if not, the reference to "Re" is included, as in the following example:

Re Rosenbaum and Law Society of Manitoba (1983), 8 C.C.C. (3d) 255 (C.A.).

4. The Use of the Phrase "Reference Re"

The phrase "Reference Re" is used to introduce the title of a constitutional matter which has been considered under the reference jurisdiction of a court.

Examples:
Reference Re Roman Catholic Separate High Schools Funding (1987), 22 O.A.C. 321 (S.C.C.).
Reference Re Language Rights Under Section 23 of the Manitoba Act, 1870, and Section 133 of the Constitution Act, 1867, [1985] 1 S.C.R. 721.

C. RULE 3: USE OF SQUARE OR ROUND BRACKETS

Each volume of a case report must be identified to facilitate retrieval. To achieve this, publishers employ two methods:

1. Consecutive numbering

Each new volume is issued a number in a consecutive sequence and a date is indicated. The date in round brackets is the date of the decision rather than the date on the spine of the volume in a report series. It is followed by a comma. For an explanation of the citation of years and examples see (ii) below.

Examples:
Re Laidlaw Foundation (1984), 13 D.L.R. (4th) 491 (Ont. H.C.J., Div. Ct.).
Ottawa Mortgage Investment Corp. v. Edwards (1991), 5 O.R. (3d) 465 (Gen. Div.).

If there is more than one reference to the decision, then the other reporters are identified only by volume number (round bracket dates are dropped).

Example:
Cormier v. Butler (1992), 129 N.B.R. (2d) 81, 325 A.P.R. 81 (Q.B., T.D.).

2. Year

Each new volume is identified by the year it was issued. The year will appear in either round or square brackets, depending on the citation method used for the particular report series.

Example:
Re McVey, [1992] 3 S.C.R. 475.

In the example *Re McVey*, the volume is identified by the reference to 1992 of the *Supreme Court Reports*. Without the date it would be impossible to learn from the citation in which of the many volumes, numbered 3, of the *Supreme Court Reports* the case is reported. The date is placed in square brackets and is preceded by a comma.[4]

NOTE: Some volumes are identified by a volume number in addition to the year the volume was issued.

Example:
Keddie v. Currie, [1992] 1 W.W.R. 340 (B.C.C.A.).

NOTE: When the year of the decision and the year of a reporter indexed by year are different, you must include both the year of the decision and the year of the publication in the citation. In the example the year of the decision is 2002, and the publication is in 2003.

Example:
Martin v. American International Assurance Life Co. (2002), [2003] S.C.J. No. 14 (S.C.C.).

---

[4]   If there are too many cases to be reported in one volume, the report is divided into two or more volumes for the year. Thus, in 1985, the *Western Weekly Reports* were published in six volumes, each volume number following the square-bracketed date; thus, [1985] 3 W.W.R. 385.

D. RULE 4: DROPPING ROUND BRACKETS

When indicated in a previous citation, a date in round brackets need not be repeated; although the practice varies. Always include a source-bracketed date in a parallel citation, never dispense with square brackets.

Examples:

Taylor v. Co-operative Fire & Casualty Co. (1984), 35 Alta. L.R. (2d) 77, 10 C.C.L.I. 284, 57 A.R. 328 (Q.B.).

Lizotte v. Traders General Ins. Co. [B.C.], [1985] 1 W.W.R. 595, 10 C.C.L.I. 222, [1985] I.L.R. 1-1874 (B.C.S.C.).

Marwin v. Canada (Minister of Employment & Immigration) (1989), 93 N.S.R. (2d) 120, 242 A.P.R. 120, 38 Admin. L.R. 298, 9 Imm. L.R. (2d) 122 (S.C. (T.D.)).

E. RULE 5: PUNCTUATION IN THE CITATION

A comma always precedes the date when square brackets are used, and follows the date when round brackets are used.

Examples:

McLellan v. Parent, [1992] N.W.T.R. 226 (S.C.).

Canadian Indemnity Co. v. Canadian Johns-Manville Co. (1990), 50 C.C.L.I. 95 (S.C.C.).

F. RULE 6: PUNCTUATION BETWEEN CITATIONS

When more than one parallel citation is given for a case they may be separated with a comma. When giving the history of a case, a comma is used between parallel citations within each court level and a semi-colon is used to separate citations for different court levels.

Examples:

Gershman Produce Co. v. Motor Transport Bd. (1984), 14 D.L.R. (4th) 722, [1985] 2 W.W.R. 63, 32 Man. R. (2d) 308, 10 Admin. L.R. 253, 31 M.V.R. 67 (Q.B.).

First City Development Corp. v. Nogler (1991), 102 N.S.R. (2d) 444, 279 A.P.R. 444 (S.C. (T.D.)).

Gateway Construction Co. v. Provincial Drywall Supply, [1988] 3 W.W.R. 547, 51 Man. R. (2d) 275, 50 D.L.R. (4th) 154 (C.A.); aff'g (1987), 51 Man. R. (2d) 277, 28 C.L.R. 302 (Q.B.).

G. RULE 7: SERIES OR EDITIONS

Many reporters have been published in more than one series. If so, it is necessary to indicate the series in the citation. This information ("N.S." for "New Series", or 2d, 3d, 4th, etc.) is given in round brackets after the abbreviation for the report series.

> Example:
> *Comairco Equipment v. Breault* (1985), 52 O.R. (2d) 695 (Dist. Ct.).

NOTE: The "(2d)" tells the reader that the case is found in the Second Series of the *Ontario Reports*.

H. RULE 8: INDICATION OF THE JURISDICTION

Generally, the abbreviation of the court jurisdiction is given in parenthesis following the page reference to the case reported.

> Example:
> *Grand Centre (Town) v. Dalbar Feeders Ltd.* (1984), 31 L.C.R. 255 (Alta. L.C.B.).

The jurisdiction need not be indicated when it is evident from either the name of the series or the name of the court where the case was decided.

> Example:
> *R. v. Petro-Canada* (2003), 63 O.R. (3d) 219 (C.A.).

I. RULE 9: INDICATION OF THE COURT

Generally, the abbreviated name of the court is added in brackets after the jurisdiction and both follow the page reference to the reported case.

> Examples:
> *Banbury v. Tahir* (1993), 13 O.R. (3d) 609 (Gen. Div.).
> *Coderre (R.) v. M.N.R.*, [1992] 1 C.T.C. 2596 (T.C.C.).

NOTE: If the name of the court is obvious from the name of the report series, the court may be excluded.

> *Joy Oil Co. v. R.*, [1951] S.C.R. 624, [1951] 3 D.L.R. 582.

J. RULE 10: PAGE REFERENCE

The first page of a reported case is included in a case citation and follows the abbreviation of the law report or, where applicable, the series number.

Example:
Clarkson, Gordon Inc. v. United States Fire Insurance Co. (1990), 67 D.L.R. (4th) 436 (N.S.S.C. (T.D.)).

A reference to a specific page number is prefaced with the word "at" as in *Carter v. Brooks* (1990), 77 D.L.R. (4th) 45 at 50 (Ont. C.A.); although usage varies. A specific reference to more than one page is abbreviated "ff" as in *R. v. Andrews* (1990), 77 D.L.R. (4th) 128 at 135ff (S.C.C.).

K. RULE 11: ORDER OF ALTERNATIVE OR PARALLEL CITATIONS

Where more than one report is cited in reference to a case the following is recommended.

1. General Priority

First, official reports.

Examples:
Supreme Court Reports and Federal Court Reports.

Second, semi-official reports.

Examples:
Ontario Reports, Northwest Territories Reports, New Brunswick Reports (2d) and *Newfoundland and Prince Edward Island Reports.*

Third, unofficial reports.

Examples:
Dominion Law Reports, National Reporter, Western Weekly Reports, Manitoba Reports (2d), Saskatchewan Reports and Ontario Appeal Cases.

2. Priority Amongst Unofficial Reports

There is no unanimity on the correct order if all the reports referred to are unofficial.

(a) Reports with larger geographical coverage have priority over reports covering smaller areas.

Example:
The *Dominion Law Reports* are cited before the *Manitoba Reports*:
Re Bateman and Association of Professional Engineers of Manitoba (1984), 9 D.L.R. (4th) 373, 28 Man. R. (2d) 264 (Q.B.).

(b) General law reports have priority over subject reports.

Example:
New Brunswick Broadcasting Co. v. C.R.T.C. (1984), 13 D.L.R. (4th) 77, 55 N.R. 143, 2 C.P.R. (3d) 433, 12 C.R.R. 249 (F.C.A.).

NOTE: See Appendix VII for a list of official, semi-official, and unofficial reporters.

L. RULE 12: HISTORY OF A CASE

Where reference is made to more than one court which decided a case, there is no unanimity on the correct order of citation. The order recommended is the highest court followed by the lower court, or courts, in reverse chronological order.[5]

Examples:
R. v. Skinner (1985), 58 N.R. 240 (S.C.C.); ref'g leave to appeal (1984), 65 N.S.R. (2d) 313 (S.C. (A.D.)).
Xerox of Canada Ltd. v. Regional Assessment Commissioners Region No. 10, [1981] 2 S.C.R. 137; rev'g (1980), 30 O.R. (2d) 90 (C.A.); aff'g (1979), 27 O.R. (2d) 269 (Div. Ct.); aff'g (1978), 9 O.M.B.R. 330 (O.M.B.).

In the first example, leave to appeal from a decision of the Nova Scotia Supreme Court of Appeal Division was refused.

In the second example, the Supreme Court of Canada reversed a decision of the Ontario Municipal Board which had been affirmed by both the Court of Appeal and the Divisional Court.

---

[5] The form of citation may be varied so that the court level relevant to a point under discussion is cited first and previous decisions may be then given in chronological order.

M. EXCEPTIONS TO THE GENERAL RULES

1. Unreported Decisions

The form of citation for unreported decisions consists of:

(i)   the name of the parties in italics;
(ii) "*v.*" separating the names of the opposing parties, should be italicized;
(iii) the date of the decision;
(iv) the name of the judicial district;
(v)   the docket number; and
(vi) the abbreviated name of the jurisdiction and court.

Examples:
R. v. Perry (6 December 1988), Antigonish, 61457 (N.S. Prov. Ct.) [unreported].
Draney v. Yeungi (7 September 1990), Vancouver, B891310 (B.C.S.C.) [unreported].

Some authors include a reference to a digest series in a citation to an unreported decision, as in the following example:

Accord Mortgage Corp. v. Bolton (19 October 1988), Vancouver Registry, C860976 (B.C.S.C.), (1989), 8 L.W.C.D. 118 (827-004) [unreported].

Decisions which have not been reported as of the date of the student's report or memorandum are cited in the same manner as unreported decisions with the addition of the notation "as yet unreported" or "not yet reported", as in the following example:

Dawe v. Cypress Bowl Recreations (24 November 1993), Nanaimo, 01933 (B.C.S.C.) [as yet unreported].

NOTE: If the unreported case is from Quebec, and the Jurisprudence Express (JE) number is available, include it after the docket number and before the court citation.

2. Cases Viewed or Printed from Computerized Databases (Computer Cases)

The form of citation for cases retrieved from a legal database consists of:

(i) the name of the parties in italics (often the italicized words are high-lighted in bold letters);
(ii) "v." separating the names of the opposing parties;
(iii) the year of the decision in square brackets;
(iv) the database in abbreviated form;
(v) the number of the decision; and
(vi) a reference to the database provider in round brackets.

Example:
Ashdown v. Jumbo Video Inc., [1993] O.J. No. 1169.

Recommended Methods of Citation for Federal and Provincial Statutes and Regulations

A. FEDERAL

1. Statutes

A reference to a statute in the 1985 *Revised Statutes of Canada* should appear in the following form:

Postal Services Interruption Relief Act, R.S.C. 1985, c. P-16, s. 4(1).

The example citation contains:

(i)   the title, which is italicized,
(ii) a designation by the abbreviation "R.S.C." for *Revised Statutes of Canada*,
(iii) a reference to the year of the revised statutes, and
(iv) the abbreviations "c." for chapter and "s." for section.

A reference to a statute in an annual volume should appear in the following form:

Youth Criminal Justice Act, S.C. 2002, c. 1, s. 1.

The example citation contains:

(i)   the title of the act, which is italicized,
(ii) a designation by the abbreviation "S.C." for *Statutes of Canada*,
(iii) a reference to the year of the annual volume of the *Statutes of Canada*, and
(iv) the abbreviations "c." for chapter and "s." for section.

Statutes which have been amended may be cited as follows:

Diplomatic Service (Special) Superannuation Act, R.S.C. 1985, c. D-2, s. 2, as am. by S.C. 2000, c. 12, s. 99.
Criminal Records Act, R.S.C. 1985, c. C-47, s. 2, as am. by R.S.C. 1985, c. 1 (4th Supp.), s. 45.
Canadian Wheat Board Act, R.S.C. 1985, c. C-24, s. 8, as am. by R.S.C., c. 38 (4th Supp.), s. 3.
Bank of Canada Act, R.S.C. 1985, c. B-2, s. 8, as am. by S.C. 2001, c. 9, s. 189.

In these examples the volume and chapter number in which the statute was initially published is cited first. The first example citation shows that the *Diplomatic Service (Special) Superannuation Act* was amended in the 2000 volume of the *Statutes of Canada*. The reference to section 99 following the chapter reference is included because the amendment is part of an "omnibus statute"; if the amending statute had amended this Act alone, the section number would have been omitted. Generally, a reference to the amending section is omitted, unless the writer wishes to draw particular attention to the amended section.

The second example shows that section 2 of the *Criminal Records Act* was amended by chapter 1, section 45, in the 4th Supplement to the *Revised Statutes of Canada*, which in this case is an "omnibus act", referred to as the *Miscellaneous Statute Law Amendment Act, 1987*. The third example indicates that a particular section (*i.e.*, section 8) of the *Canadian Wheat Board Act* was amended by chapter 38, section 3, in the 4th Supplement to the *Revised Statutes of Canada*. The fourth example indicates that section 8 of the *Bank of Canada Act* was amended by chapter 9, section 189 of the 2001 *Statutes of Canada*.

A history of amendments to the revision, other acts included in the supplement volumes, and new acts in the annual volumes of *Statutes of Canada*, may be cited as follows:

Governor General's Act, R.S.C. 1985, c. G-9, as am. by R.S.C. 1985, c. 50 (Supp.), ss. 1-2; S.C. 1990, c. 5, ss. 1-2; 1993, c. 13, s. 9; 1994, c. 18, s. 8; 2000, c. 12, ss. 127-129.

NOTE: The abbreviations "S.C." and "R.S.C." need not be repeated if the source is evident from the description of amendments. Also, the year need not be repeated.

In both examples the order of citation is as follows:

(i)   *Revised Statutes of Canada,*
(ii)   *Revised Statutes of Canada, 1st Supplement,*
(iii)   *Revised Statutes of Canada, 2nd Supplement*, and
(iv)   *Statutes of Canada*, annual volumes.

NOTE: It is not necessary to indicate an amendment to a statute unless it is relevant to a point or a specific section under discussion, nor is it correct to simply put the reference "as am. by" in a citation. Citations are presumed to be to the statute as amended. Exception: the citation "R.S.Q. 1977" refers to the unamended statutes published in bound volumes. (The citation "R.S.Q. c. 20" refers to the updated looseleaf set.)

2. Regulations

A reference to a regulation in the 1978 *Consolidated Regulations of Canada* should appear in the following form:

Civilian Dental Treatment Regulations, C.R.C., c. 682 (1978).

A reference to a regulation published after the consolidation should appear in the following form:

Patent Cooperation Treaty Regulations, SOR/89-453.

Regulations which have been amended are cited as follows:

Potato Production and Sale (Central Saanich) Restriction Regulations, SOR/82-186, as am. by 82-612; 83-294.
Physical Security Regulations, SOR/83-77, as am. by 84-81; 85-1016; 91-585.
Steering Appliances and Equipment Regulations, SOR/83-810, as am. by 86-1027 s. 1; 2002-426, s. 1; 2003-86, s. 1.

B. ALBERTA

1. Statutes

The citation of a revised statute should be made to the *Revised Statutes of Alberta.*

Example:
Land Titles Act, R.S.A. 2000, c. L-7.

The example citation contains the title of the revised statute, the abbreviation for *Revised Statutes of Alberta,* the year of the revision and the chapter number of the act.

Citation of an amendment to the revision is made, first, to the revised statute and, second, to the bound volume of the *Statutes of Alberta.*

Example:
Seniors Advisory Council for Alberta Act, R.S.A. 2000, c. S-6, as am. by S.A. 2002, ss. 2-3.

The example citation contains the title of the revised statute, the abbreviation for *Revised Statutes of Alberta*, the year of the revision, the chapter number of the Act, the abbreviation for *Statutes of Alberta*, the year of the bound volume, and the chapter and section numbers of the amending statute. This reference to an amending statute is followed by a reference to another amending statute (where the abbreviation S.A. is optional), the year of the bound volume, the chapter number and the section number.

Citation of a new act or an amendment to a new act since the revision is made to the *Statutes of Alberta*.

Examples:
Adult Interdependent Relationhips Act, S.A. 2002, c. A-4.5.
Alberta Mortgage and Housing Corporation Act, S.A. 1984, c. A-32.5, as am. by S.A. 1984, c. P-35.1, s. 51(2); c. 43; 1985, c. 3; 1986, c. D-25.1, s. 21(2); 1987, c. 29, s. 3.

NOTE: A reference to an entry in the looseleaf consolidation of the *Statutes of Alberta* is cited in the same manner as in the above examples and includes the same chapter designation.

2. Regulations

Individual regulations are cited to their regulation number in *The Alberta Gazette, Part II*:

Adoption Regulation, Alta. Reg. 37/2002.

Amendments to regulations are cited, first, to the original regulation number, followed by a reference to the regulation number of the amending regulation(s). No other information is required.

Court Agents Regulation, Alta. Reg. 68/2001, as am. by 25/2002; 27/2002.

C. BRITISH COLUMBIA

1. Statutes

The citation of a revised statute may be made to the bound or the looseleaf edition of the *Revised Statutes of British Columbia*. In either case the citation will be the same.

Example:
Gas Utility Act, R.S.B.C. 1996, c. 170.

The example citation contains the title of the revised statute, the abbreviation for *Revised Statutes of British Columbia*, the year of the revision and the chapter number of the Act.

Citation of an amendment to the revision is made, first, to the revised statute and, second, to the sessional volume of the *Statutes of British Columbia*.

Example:
Dentists Act, R.S.B.C. 1996, c. 94, as am. by R.S. (Supp.), c. 94.1; S.B.C. 2002, c. 52, s. 37.

The example citation contains the title of the revised statute, the abbreviation for *Revised Statutes of British Columbia*, the year of the revision, the chapter number of the Act, the abbreviation for *Statutes of British Columbia*, the years of the sessional volumes, and chapter and section numbers (in the case of an "omnibus act") of the amending statutes.

Citation of a new act may be made to the *Statutes of British Columbia* with the addition of the chapter designation in the looseleaf consolidation of the *Revised Statutes of British Columbia*.

Example:
Supply Act (No.1), 1997, S.B.C. 1997, c. 1.

Citation of an amendment to a new act passed since the revision should be made to the bound volume of the *Statutes of British Columbia* with the addition of a reference to the chapter designation of the act in the consolidation.

Example:
Balanced Budget Act, S.B.C. 2001, c. 21, as am. by S.B.C. 2001, c. 28, s. 10.

2. Regulations

Individual regulations are cited with reference to their regulation number printed in *The British Columbia Gazette, Part II*:

Adult Guardianship (Abuse and Neglect) Regulation, B.C. Reg. 13/2000.
Designated Acts Regulation, B.C. Reg. 447/98, as am. by 438/99; 439/99; 440/99; 15/2000; 5/2002.

D. MANITOBA

1. Statutes

The generally accepted citation of a re-enacted statute will direct the user to the *Continuing Consolidation of the Statutes of Manitoba*, and to the bound *Re-enacted Statutes of Manitoba.*[1]

Example:
The Fatal Accidents Act, R.S.M. 1987, c. F50, C.C.S.M. c. F50.

The less commonly adopted method of citing a statute will direct the user to either the looseleaf consolidation or to the bound volume of re-enacted acts.

Examples:
The Age of Majority Act, C.C.S.M., c. A7,
or *The Age of Majority Act*, R.S.M. 1987, c. A7.

The first example citation gives the name of the re-enacted statute, the abbreviation for the *Re-enacted Statutes of Manitoba*, the year of the re-enactment and the chapter of the Act, followed by the abbreviation for the *Continuing Consolidation of the Statutes of Manitoba* and the chapter number. The second example citation contains the name of the re-enacted statute, the abbreviation for the *Consolidation* and the chapter number of the Act. The third example includes the abbreviation for the *Re-enacted Statutes of Manitoba*, the year of the re-enactment and the chapter number of the Act.

Citation of an amendment to the re-enactment is made, first, to the re-enacted statute and, second, to the bound annual volume of the *Statutes of Manitoba*, with the addition of a reference to the *Consolidation*.

Example:
The Garage Keepers Act, R.S.M. 1987, c. G10, as am. by S.M. 1989-90, c. 91, s. 6, C.C.S.M. c. G10.

The example citation contains the title of the re-enacted statute, the abbreviation for the *Re-enacted Statutes of Manitoba*, the year of the re-enactment, the chapter number of the Act, the abbreviation for *Statutes of Manitoba*, the year of the bound volume, the chapter and section numbers of the amending statute with the addition of a reference to the *Consolidation*.

Citation of a new act, an amendment to a new act since the re-enactment, an act which was passed before the re-enactment began but which was not included in the re-enactment and an amendment to such an act may be made to the bound annual volume of statutes and to the *Consolidation*.

---

[1] The *Re-enacted Statutes of Manitoba*, in bilingual versions, were published in bound and looseleaf formats, commencing in 1987.

Examples:
Holocaust Memorial Day Act, S.M. 2000, c. 2, C.C.S.M. c. H65.
The Economic Innovation and Technology Council Act, S.M. 1992, c. 7, C.C.S.M. c. E7.
The Rural Development Bonds Act, S.M. 1991-92, c. 47, as am. by S.M. 1992, c. 58, s. 31, C.C.S.M. c. R175.
Midwifery Act, S.M. 1997, c. 9, C.C.S.M. c. M125, as am. by S.M. 1998, c. 32, s. 6.

NOTE: The information tables in the bound *Statutes of Manitoba* include "Acts in the *Continuing Consolidation of the Statutes of Manitoba*", *i.e.*, re-enacted statutes and other public acts, "Public General Acts not included in the C.C.S.M." and "Acts and Parts of Acts Enacted Subject to Proclamation".

2. Regulations

Individual regulations are cited to the regulation number in *The Manitoba Gazette, Part II*:

Turkey Penalty Levies Regulation, Man. Reg. 133/2002 .
Anatomy Regulation, Man. Reg. 309/88 R.

The "R" in the second example indicates that the regulation was re-enacted in English and French.
Amendments to Manitoba regulations are cited as follows:

Designation of Wildlife Lands Regulation, Man. Reg. 171/2001, as am. by 202/2002.
Barbers Regulation, Man. Reg. 93/87 R, as am. by 8/88.

NOTE: Each re-enacted regulation is a revision and consolidation of amendments up to the date of the re-enactment of the particular regulation.

E. NEW BRUNSWICK

1. Statutes

The citation of a revised statute is made to the *Revised Statutes of New Brunswick* whether it appears in the bound volume or the continuing consolidation.

Example:
Change of Name Act, R.S.N.B. 1973, c. C-2.

The example citation contains the title of the revised statute, the abbreviation for *Revised Statutes of New Brunswick*, the year of the revision and the chapter number of the Act.

Citation of an amendment to the revision is made, first, to the revised statute and, second, to the bound sessional volume of the *Statutes of New Brunswick*.

Example:

Historic Sites Protection, R.S.N.B. 1973, c. H-6, as am. by S.N.B.   1975, c. 79; 1976, c. 30; 1977, c. 27; 1978, c. 28; 1979, c. 41; 1982, c. 3; 1983, c. 7; 1983, c. 30; 1986, c. 8; 1990, c. 6; 1990, c. 61; 1992, c. 2; 1998, c. 41; 2000, c. 26.

The example citation includes the title of the revised statute, the abbreviation for *Revised Statutes of New Brunswick*, the year of the revision, the chapter number of the Act, the abbreviation for *Statutes of New Brunswick*, the years of the bound volumes and the chapter numbers of the amending statutes.

Citation of a new act or an amendment to a new act should be made to the bound volume of the *Statutes of New Brunswick*.

Examples:

Canadian Judgements Act, S.N.B. 2000, c. C-0.1.
Higher Education Foundation Act, S.N.B. 1992, c. H-4.1, as am. by S.N.B. 1998, c. 41.

NOTE: The chapter designations of acts will be the same in the continuing consolidation and in the bound statute volumes.

2. Regulations

Individual regulations are cited with reference to a regulation number, which appears in *The Royal Gazette*:

General Regulation - Credit Unions Act, N.B. Reg. 94-5.
District Education Council Election Regulation – Regulation Act, N.B. Reg. 2001-23.
Fees Regulation - All-Terrain Vehicle Act, N.B. Reg. 85-202, as am. by 88-272; 91-72; 92-64; 95-136; 2002-84; S.N.B. 2003, c. 7, s. 39.

F. NEWFOUNDLAND

1. Statutes

The citation of a revised statute should be made to the *Revised Statutes of Newfoundland*.

Example:
Commemoration Day Act, R.S.N. 1990, c. C-24.

The example citation contains the title of the revised statute, the abbreviation for *Revised Statutes of Newfoundland*, the year of the revision and the chapter number of the Act.

Citation of an amendment to the revision is made, first, to the revised statute and, second, to the annual volume of the *Statutes of Newfoundland*.

Examples:
Human Rights Code, R.S.N. 1990, c. H-14, as am. by S.N. 1992, c. 48, s. 13.
Notaries Public Act, R.S.N. 1990, c. N-5, as am. by S.N. 1996, c. R-10.1, s. 52; 2001, c. N-3.1, s. 2.

The example citations contain the titles of the revised statutes, the abbreviation for *Revised Statutes of Newfoundland*, the year of the revision, the chapter numbers of the acts, the abbreviation for *Statutes of Newfoundland*, the years of the bound volumes, and the chapter and section numbers of the amending statutes.

Citation of a new act or an amendment to a new act since the revision is made to the bound volumes of the *Statutes of Newfoundland*.

Example:
Petroleum Products Act, S.N. 2001, c. P-11.
Prepaid Funeral Services Act, S.N. 2000, c. P-18, as am. by S.N. 2000, c. 30, s. 1; 2001, c. 3, s. 1.

2. Regulations

Individual regulations are cited with reference to a regulation number, which appears in the 1996 consolidation or to *The Newfoundland Gazette, Part II*:

Video Lottery Regulations, C.N.R. 760/96.
Liquor Licensing Regulations, C.N.R. 1162/96, as am. by N.R. 95/97; 73/99; 39/01.
Newfoundland Pony Designation Order, N.R. 114/97.
Boxing Authority Regulations, N.L.R. 46/02.[2]

---

[2] Newfoundland Regulations are noted as Nfld. Reg. Before Dec. 13, 2001 and N.L.R. after Dec. 13, 2001.

G. NORTHWEST TERRITORIES

1. Statutes

The citation of a revised statute should be made to the *Revised Statutes of Northwest Territories*.

Example:
Arbitration Act, R.S.N.W.T. 1988, c. A-5.

The example citation contains the title of the revised statute, the abbreviation for *Revised Statutes of Northwest Territories*, the year of the revision and the chapter number of the Act.

Citation of an amendment to the revision is made, first, to the revised statute and, second, to the bound volumes of the *Statutes of Northwest Territories*.

Example:
Department of Justice Act, R.S.N.W.T. 1988, c. 97 (Supp.), as am. by S.N.W.T. 1994, c. 30, s. 2; 1995, c. 11, s. 15(F).

The example citation contains the title of the revised statute, the abbreviation for *Revised Statutes of Northwest Territories*, the year of the revision, the chapter number of the Act (followed by similar citations for the three supplements to the revision), the abbreviation for *Statutes of Northwest Territories*, the years of the bound volumes, and the chapter numbers of the amending statutes.

Citation of a new act or unrevised act is made to the annual bound volumes of the *Statutes of Northwest Territories*.

Examples:
Northwest Territories Development Corporation Act, S.N.W.T. 1990, c. 12.
Architects Act, S.N.W.T. 2001, c. 10

2. Regulations

Revised regulations are cited to the 1990 bound volumes of *Revised Regulations of the Northwest Territories*:

Whale Cove Liquor Prohibition Regulations, R.R.N.W.T. 1990, c. L-48.

Amendments to revised regulations are cited as follows:

Dental Profession Regulations, R.R.N.W.T. 1990, c. 4 (Supp.), as am. by N.W.T. Reg. R-002-94, s. 2; R-064-2000, s. 2.

Amendments contained in the supplement and in the *Northwest Territories Gazette, Part II*, are cited as follows:

Electrical Protection Regulations, R.R.N.W.T. 1990, c. E-21, as am. by R.R.N.W.T. 1990, c. E-21 (Supp.); N.W.T. Reg. R-098.92.

New regulations are cited with reference to their regulation number in the *Northwest Territories Gazette, Part II*:

Hours of Service Regulations, N.W.T. Reg. R-001-92.
Amendments to new regulations are cited with reference to their regulation number in the *Northwest Territories Gazette, Part II*:
Forest Management Areas Regulations, N.W.T. Reg. R-093-95 as am. by R-037-2000, ss. 3-4.

H. NOVA SCOTIA

1. Statutes

The citation of a revised statute should be made to the *Revised Statutes of Nova Scotia* which are available in a consolidated looseleaf form.

Example:
Guardianship Act, R.S.N.S. 1989, c. 189.

The example citation contains the title of the revised statute, the abbreviation for *Revised Statutes of Nova Scotia*, the year of the revision and the chapter number of the Act.
Citation of an amendment to the revision is made, first, to the revised statute and, second, to the bound volume of the *Statutes of Nova Scotia*.

Example:
Forests Act, R.S.N.S. 1989, c. 179, as am. by S.N.S. 1992, c. 18; 1998, c. 18; 1998, c. 29.

The example citation contains the title of the revised statute, the abbreviation for *Revised Statutes of Nova Scotia*, the year of the revision, the chapter number of the Act, the abbreviation for *Statutes of Nova Scotia*, the year of the bound volume, the chapter number and section numbers of the amending statute.
Citation of a new act or an amendment to a new act since the revision is made to the bound volumes of the *Statutes of Nova Scotia*.

Example:
Kings Regional Rehabilitation Centre Act, S.N.S. 1990, c. 16, as am. by S.N.S. 1991, c. 17.

2. Regulations

Nova Scotia Regulations are all cited in the same manner, as follows:

Designation of Species-at-risk Conservation Fund Regulation, N.S. Reg. 96/2003.
Seniors' Pharmacare Program Regulations, N.S. Reg. 162/2000, as am. by 18/2002; 28/2003.

I. NUNAVUT

At the time of publication, the newly created Government of Nunavut had not yet selected an official printer. As a result, all new legislation passed in that territory has been distributed to municipalities within that jurisdiction.

Pursuant to the *Nunavut Act*, S.C. 1993, c. 28, all legislation which was in effect as of March 31, 1999 and related to the Northwest Territories was duplicated for Nunavut.

The government is planning to release a consolidation of its legislation on CD-ROM in 2000-2001.

J. ONTARIO

1. Statutes

The citation of a revised statute should be made to the *Revised Statutes of Ontario*.

Example:
Mining Tax Act, R.S.O. 1990, c. M.15.

The example citation contains the title of the revised statute, the abbreviation for *Revised Statutes of Ontario*, the year of the revision and the chapter number of the Act.

Citation of an amendment to the revision is made, first, to the revised statute and, second, to the bound volume of the *Statutes of Ontario*.

Example:
Absentees Act, R.S.O. 1990, c. A.3, as am. by S.O. 1992, c. 32, s. 1; 1996, c. 6, s. 1.

The example citation contains the title of the revised statute, the abbreviation for *Revised Statutes of Ontario*, the year of the revision, the chapter number of the Act, the abbreviation for *Statutes of Ontario*, the year of the bound volume, and the chapter and section numbers of the amending statute.

Citation of a new act or an amendment to a new act since the revision is made to the annual volumes of the *Statutes of Ontario*.

Examples:
Deaf-Blind Awareness Month Act, S.O. 2000, c. 34.
German Pioneers Day Act, S.O. 2000, c. 7.

2. Regulations

Regulations published in the latest *Revised Regulations of Ontario* are cited as follows:

First Aid Requirements Regulation, R.R.O. 1990, Reg. 1101.
General Regulations — Workers' Compensation Act, R.R.O. 1990, Reg. 1102.

Amendments to the revision are cited, first, to the revised regulations and, second, to the regulation number in *The Ontario Gazette*:

General Regulation – Change of Name Act, R.R.O. 1990, Reg. 68, as am. by O. Reg. 1326/91, 41/00.

New regulations are cited to a regulation number in *The Ontario Gazette*:

Allocation of Board of Health Expenses, O. Reg. 489/97.

K. PRINCE EDWARD ISLAND

1. Statutes

The citation of a revised statute is made to the *Revised Statutes of Prince Edward Island*. The reference may be used to locate an act in the bound volume or in the continuing consolidation which is referred to as "The Revised Statutes of Prince Edward Island 1988 ([year] up-date)".

Example:
Judicial Review Act, R.S.P.E.I. 1988, c. J-3.

The example citation contains the title of the revised statute, the abbreviation for *Revised Statutes of Prince Edward Island*, the year of the revision and the chapter number of the Act.

Citation of an amendment to the revision is made, first, to the revised statute and, second, to the bound volume of the *Statutes of Prince Edward Island*.

Example:
Planning Act, R.S.P.E.I. 1988, c. P-8, as am. by S.P.E.I. 1990, c. 44; 1991, c. 1; 1991, c. 18; 1994, c. 6; 1994, c. 46; 1995, c. 29; 1998, c. 76; 1999, c. 39; 2001, c. 47.

NOTE: Users of the consolidation would naturally look for c. G-2 which will include amendments in the latest update.

The example citation contains the title of the revised statute, the abbreviation for *Revised Statutes of Prince Edward Island,* the year of the revision, the chapter number of the Act, the abbreviation for *Statutes of Prince Edward Island,* the year of the bound volume and the chapter number of the amending statute (followed by a similar citation of another amending statute).

Citation of a new act or an amendment to a new act since the revision is made to the *Statutes of Prince Edward Island,* with further reference to the chapter number in the looseleaf consolidation, if available.

Examples:
Environment Tax Act, S.P.E.I. 1991, c. 9 (c. E-8.3).
Tourism P.E.I. Act, S.P.E.I. 1999, c. 46.
Human Tissue Donation Act, S.P.E.I. 1992, c. 34, as am. by 1995, c. 20.
Employment Standards Act, S.P.E.I. 1992, c. 18, as am. by 2000 (2nd) c. 7.

2. Regulations

Regulations that have been consolidated are cited to *The Revised Regulations of Prince Edward Island* with reference to the regulation number in the "Table of Regulations" (blue pages at the back of the revision):

Animal Protection Regulations, R.R.P.E.I. EC 1990-71.

Regulations published after the revision are cited to their regulation number in the *Royal Gazette, Part II:*

Education Negotiating Agency Regulations Amendment, P.E.I. Reg. EC 1999-86.

Amendments to revised regulations are cited:

Arterial Highways Regulations, R.R.P.E.I. EC 163/92, as am. by EC 470/92; 634/92.

L. QUÉBEC

1. Statutes

The citation of a revised statute can be made to the looseleaf edition of the *Revised Statutes of Québec* or to the bound revision of the *Statutes of Québec*.

Examples:
Lands and Forests Act, R.S.Q., c. T-9.
Lands and Forests Act, R.S.Q. 1977, c. T-9.

The first example citation contains the title of the revised statute, the abbreviation for *Revised Statutes of Québec* and the chapter number of the Act in the looseleaf consolidation. The second example includes the same information as the first, as well as a reference to the date of the bound *Revised Statutes of Québec*.

Citation of an amendment to the revision is made, first, to the revised statute and, second, to the bound volume of the *Statutes of Québec*.

Example:
Business Concerns Records Act, R.S.Q. 1977, c. D-12, as am. by S.Q. 1988, c. 21, s. 66; 1990, c. 4, s. 388; 1992, c. 61, s. 267; 1999, c. 40, s. 109.

The example citation contains the title of the revised statute, the abbreviation for *Revised Statutes of Québec*, the year of the revision, the chapter number of the Act, the abbreviation for *Statutes of Québec*, the year of the bound volume, and the chapter and section numbers of the amending statute.

Citation of a new act or an amendment to a new act since the revision is made to the annual *Statutes of Québec* or to the consolidation.[3]

Examples:
An Act respecting the Ordre National du Québec, S.Q. 1984, c. 24, as am. by S.Q. 1985, c. 11,
or
An Act respecting the Ordre National du Québec, R.S.Q., c. O-7.01.

NOTE: Acts passed after the revision have different chapter designations in the bound volumes and in the looseleaf revision.

---

[3] Reference should be made to the consolidation whenever possible.

2. Regulations

Regulations published in the revision are cited to the *Revised Regulations of Québec*, with reference to both their regulation number and to the chapter number of their enabling statute:

> *Regulation respecting the use of water for mining purposes*, R.R.Q. 1981, c. M-13, r. 13.

Amendments are cited with reference to the revised regulation number and the appropriate issue of the *Gazette officielle du Québec*:

> *Regulation Respecting the Sale of Livestock by Auction*, R.R.Q. 1981, as am. by O.C. 1262-1986, 20 August 1986, G.O.Q. 1986.II.3749; O.C. 1135-1987, 22 July 1987, G.O.Q. 1987.II.5297; O.C. 1766-1990, 19 December 1990, G.O.Q. 1990.II.1776; O.C. 337-1993, 17 March 1993, G.O.Q. 1993.II.1954; O.C. 1830-1993, 29 December 1993, G.O.Q. 1993.II.7013. O.C. 362-2000, April 12 2002, G.O.Q. 2000.II.1930.

M. SASKATCHEWAN

1. Statutes

The citation of a revised statute should be made to the *Revised Statutes of Saskatchewan*. "The" is part of all Saskatchewan titles.

Example:
The Grain and Fodder Conservation Act, R.S.S. 1978, c. G-7.

The example citation contains the title of the revised statute, the abbreviation for *Revised Statutes of Saskatchewan*, the year of the revision and the chapter number of the Act.

Citation of an amendment to the revision is made, first, to the revised statute and, second, to the bound volume of the *Statutes of Saskatchewan*.

Example:
The Grain Charges Limitation Act, R.S.S. 1978, c. G-6, as am. by S.S. 1979-80, c. M-32.01, s. 14; 1983, c. 11, s. 30; 1996, c. 32, s. 6.

The example citation contains the title of the revised statute, the abbreviation for *Revised Statutes of Saskatchewan*, the year of the revision, the chapter number of the act, the abbreviation for *Statutes of Saskatchewan*, the year of the bound volume, and the chapter and section numbers of the amending statute. A semi-colon separates a reference to a second amending statute which, like the first reference to an amending statute, contains the year of the bound volume and the chapter and section numbers of the amending statute.

Citation of a new act or an amendment to a new act since the revision is made to the *Statutes of Saskatchewan.*

Examples:
Electronic Information and Documents Act, S.S. 2000, c. E-7.22.
Education Act, S.S. 1995, c. E-0.2, as am. by S.S. 1996, c. 45; 1997, c. 35; 1998, c. 21; 1999, c. 16; 2000, c. 10; 2000, c. 42; 2000, c. 70; 2001, c. 13; 2002, c. 27; 2000, c. 29.

2. Regulations

Regulations that have been revised are cited to the *Revised Regulations of Saskatchewan*:

Ethanol Fuel (General) Regulations, R.R.S. 2002, c. E-11.1, Reg. 1, O.C. 750/2002.

Amendments to the revision and unrevised regulations are cited with reference to their regulation number in *The Saskatchewan Gazette.*

Municipal Police Equipment Regulations, R.R.S., 1991, c. P-15.01, Reg. 3, O.C. 920/1991, as am. by S.Reg. 66/93; 19/94; 81/95; 77/97; 44/2000; 101/2002.
The Housing and Special-Care Homes Care and Rates Regulations, Sask. Reg. 132/81, as am. by 147/82; 173/83; 106/84; 36/86; 23/87; 101/92.

N. YUKON TERRITORY

1. Statutes

The citation of a revised statute should be made to the *Revised Statutes of Yukon Territory.*

Example:
Age of Majority Act, R.S.Y. 2002, c. 2.

The example citation contains the title of the revised statute, the abbreviation for *Revised Statutes of Yukon Territory,* the year of the revision and the chapter number of the Act.

Citation of an amendment to the revision is made, first, to the revised statute and, second, to the bound volume of the *Statutes of Yukon Territory.*

Example:
Official Tree Act, R.S.Y. 2002, c. 161, as am. by S.Y. 2002, c. 11, s. 1.

The example citation contains the title of the revised statute, the abbreviation for *Revised Statutes of Yukon Territory*, the year of the revision, the chapter number of the Act, the abbreviation for *Statutes of Yukon Territory*, the year of the bound volume, and the chapter and section numbers of the amending statute.

Citation of a new act or an amendment to a new act is made to the *Statutes of Yukon Territory*.

Examples:
Environmental Assessment Act, S.Y. 2003, c. 2.

2. Regulations

Regulations are cited to their year of registration and Order-in-Council number:

Activities Requiring Environmental Assessment Regulation, Yukon O.I.C. 2003/67.
Equipment Regulations, Yukon O.I.C. 1987/86, as am. by 1987/191; 1988/131; 2000/50.

Abbreviations of Provinces and Territories

Jurisdiction	Statutes and Gazettes	Regulations	Courts and Journals	Law Reporter
Canada	C.	C.	C. or Can.	C. or Can.
British Columbia	B.C.	B.C.	B.C.	B.C.
Alberta	A.	Alta.	Alta.	A. or Alta.
Saskatchewan	S.	S.	Sask.	Sask.
Manitoba	M.	Man	Man.	Man.
Ontario	O.	O.	Ont.	O.
Quebec	Q.	Q.	Q. (Journals) Qc. (Courts)	Q.
New Brunswick	N.B.	N.B.	N.B.	N.B.
Nova Scotia	N.S.	N.S.	N.S.	N.S.
Prince Edward Island	P.E.I.	P.E.I.	P.E.I.	P.E.I.
Newfoundland[1]	N.	Nfld.	Nfld.	Nfld.
Newfoundland and Labrador	N.L.	N.L.	N.L.	Nfld.
Northwest Territories	N.W.T.	N.W.T.	N.W.T.	N.W.T.
Yukon	Y.	Y.	Y.	Y.
Nunavut	Nu.	Nu.	Nu.	Nu.

Taken from *McGill Guide* 5th ed.

---

[1] Regulations before Dec. 13, 2001; Gazette, before Dec. 21, 2001, Dec. 6, 2001 for Statutes and all other purposes.

Subject Reports – Publication Periods and Sample Citations

A. FAMILY LAW

Reports of Family Law, 1971 to 1978
   Rodrigue v. Dufton (1976), 30 R.F.L. 216 (Ont. H.C.J.).
Reports of Family Law (Second Series), 1978 to 1986
   Davies v. Davies (1985), 49 R.F.L. (2d) 108 (B.C.C.A.).
Reports of Family Law (Third Series), 1986 to 1994
   Lévesque v. Lapointe (1993), 44 R.F.L. (3d) 316 (B.C.C.A.).
Reports of Family Law (Fourth Series), 1994 to 2000
   Rice v. Rice (1996), 17 R.F.L. (4th) 328 (B.C.S.C.).
Reports of Family Law (Fifth Series), 2000 to date
   Miglin v. Miglin (2003), 34 R.F.L. (5th) 227 (S.C.C.).

B. CRIMINAL LAW

Canadian Criminal Cases, 1893 to 1962
   R. v. Plotsky (1962), 133 Can. C.C. 41 (Alta. S.C., A.D.)
   or
   R. v. Plotsky (1962), 133 Can. Cr. Cas. 41 (Alta. S.C., A.D.).
Canadian Criminal Cases, 1963 to 1970
   R. v. Ladelpha, [1970] 5 C.C.C. 1 (Ont. Co. Ct.).
Canadian Criminal Cases (Second Series), 1971 to 1983
   R. v. Giambalvo (1982), 70 C.C.C. (2d) 324 (Ont. C.A.).
Canadian Criminal Cases (Third Series), 1983 to date
   R. v. Crabe (1993), 79 C.C.C. (3d) 323 (B.C.C.A.).
Criminal Reports, 1946 to 1967
   Hebert v. A.G. Qué. (1966), 50 C.R. 88 (Q.B.).
Criminal Reports (New Series), 1967 to 1978
   Imrich v. R. (1977), 39 C.R.N.S. 92 (S.C.C.).
Criminal Reports (Third Series), 1978 to 1991
   R. v. Manuel (1986), 50 C.R. (3d) 47 (C.S.P.).
Criminal Reports (Fourth Series), 1991 to 1996

R. v. Brown (1993), 19 C.R. (4th) 140 (Man. C.A.).
Criminal Reports (Fifth Series), 1997 to 2002
  R. v. Domm (1997), 4 C.R. (5th) 61 (Ont. C.A.).
Criminal Reports (Sixth Series), 2002 to date
  R. v. Carpenter (2002), 4 C.R. (6th) 115 (B.C.C.A.) .
Motor Vehicle Reports, 1979 to 1988
  R. v. Killen (1985), 37 M.V.R. 190 (N.S.S.C., A.D.).
Motor Vehicle Reports (Second Series), 1988 to 1994
  R. v. Chapman (1992), 42 M.V.R. (2d) 296 (Nfld. S.C.).
Motor Vehicle Reports (Third Series), 1994 to 2000
  Villeneuve v. Scott (1998), 36 M.V.R. (3d) 147 (Ont. Gen. Div.).
Motor Vehicle Reports (Fourth Series), 2000 to date
  R. v. Mueller (2000), 18 M.V.R. (4d) 263 (B.C.P.C.).

C. TAXATION

Canada Tax Cases, 1917 to date
  Jean Lemelin Inc. v. M.N.R., [1992] 2 C.T.C. 2832 (T.C.C.).
Dominion Tax Cases, 1920 to date
  Paquin v. R., 90 D.T.C. 6663 (F.C., T.D.).
Canada GST Cases, 2003 to date
  Diep v. R. [2003], 1 G.S.T.C. 16-1 (T.C.C.).

D. LABOUR

British Columbia Labour Relations Board Decisions, 1981 to date
  Turner Distribution Systems Ltd. v. Teamsters Local Union No. 31, [1994] B.C.L.R.B. 240-01.
Canadian Labour Law Cases, 1944 to date[1]
  Gauvreau v. Banque Nationale du Canada, 92 C.L.L.C. para. 17,018 (C.H.R.T.).
Canadian Labour Relations Board Reports, 1974 to 1982
  Lester Drugs Ltd. v. U.F.C.W.U., [1982] 3 Can. L.R.B.R. 233.
Canadian Labour Relations Board Reports (New Series), 1983 to 1989
  McCance v. C.N.R. (1985), 10 C.L.R.B.R. (N.S.) 23.
Canadian Labour Relations Board Reports (Second Series), 1989 to date
  Coull v. Teamsters Local 880 (1992), 17 C.L.R.B.R. (2d) 301.
Labour Arbitration Cases, 1948 to 1972
  Re C.U.P.E. (1971), 23 L.A.C. 111 (Ont.).
Labour Arbitration Cases (Second Series), 1973 to 1981

---

[1] The current binder is titled *Canadian Labour Law Reporter*.

Re Air Canada and C.A.L.E.A. (1981), 30 L.A.C. (2d) 28 (Can.).
Labour Arbitration Cases (Third Series), 1982 to 1989
    Re City of Penticton and C.U.P.E. (1985), 21 L.A.C. (3d) 233 (B.C.).
Labour Arbitration Cases (Fourth Series), 1989 to date
    Re Fleet Industries and I.A.M., Loc 171 (1992), 30 L.A.C. (4th) 368 (Ont.).
Ontario Labour Relations Board Reports, 1944 to date
    Int'l Bros. Elect. Wks., Local 894 v. Ellis-Don Ltd., [1992] O.L.R.B. Rep.
    147.
Western Labour Arbitration Cases, 1979 to 1985
    B.C. Hydro v. Int'l Bros. Elect. Wks., [1985] 2 W.L.A.C. 1 (B.C.).

E. HUMAN RIGHTS

Canadian Human Rights Reporter, 1980 to date
    Cremona v. Wardair Canada Inc. (1991), 14 C.H.R.R. D/262.
Canadian Rights Reporter, 1982 to 1991
    MacBain v. Canadian Human Rights Comm. (1985), 18 C.R.R. 165 (F.C.A.).
Canadian Rights Reporter (Second Series), 1991 to date
    R. v. Simpson (1993), 14 C.R.R. (2d) 388 (Ont. C.A.).
Charter of Rights Decisions, 1982 to date
    R. v. Hill, [1993] C.R.D. 725.1:20-02. (Alta. Q.B.).

F. OTHER

Administrative Law Reports, 1983 to 1991
    Gershman Produce Ltd. v. Motor Trans. Bd. (1985), 16 Admin. L.R. 1 (Man.
    C.A.).
Administrative Law Reports (Second Series), 1992 to 1998
    A.T.A. v. Edmonton School Dist. No. 7 (1992), 9 Admin. L.R. (2d) 240 (Alta.
    C.A.).
Administrative Law Reports (Third Series), 1998 to date
    Khan v. University of Ottawa (1998), 2 Admin. L.R. (3d) 298 (Ont. C.A.).
Business Law Reports, 1977 to 1991
    Lake Mechanical Systems Co. v. Crandell Mechanical Systems Inc. (1985),
    31 B.L.R. 113 (B.C.S.C.).
Business Law Reports (Second Series), 1991 to 2000
    Flandro v. Mitha (1992), 7 B.L.R. (2d) 280 (B.C.S.C.).
Business Law Reports (Third Series), 2000 to date
    Cooper v. Deggan (2003), 34 B.L.R. (3d) 278 (B.C.C.A.).
Canadian Bankruptcy Reports, 1920 to 1960
    Re Letovsky (1958), 37 C.B.R. 83 (Man. S.C.).
Canadian Bankruptcy Reports (New Series), 1960 to 1990

Waverly Management Ltd. v. Sobie (1985), 58 C.B.R. (N.S.) 97 (Alta. Q.B.).
Canadian Bankruptcy Reports (Third Series), 1991 to 1998
　Royal Bank v. Zutphen Brothers Construction Ltd. (1993), 17 C.B.R. (3d)
　314 (N.S.S.C.).
Canadian Bankruptcy Reports (Fourth Series), 1998 to date
　Tildesley v. Weaver (1998), 7 C.B.R. (4d) 313 (B.C.S.C.).
Canadian Cases on Employment Law, 1983 to 1994
　Niwranski v. H.N. Helicopter Parts Int'l Corp. (1992), 45 C.C.E.L. 303
　(B.C.S.C.).
Canadian Cases on Employment Law (Second Series), 1994 to 2000
　Crary v. Royal Bank (1997), 35 C.C.E.L. (2d) 289 (Ont. Gen. Div.).
Canadian Cases on Employment Law (Third Series), 2000 to date
　Sirois v. Gustafson (2002), 23 C.C.E.L. (3d) 136 (S.Q.B.).
Canadian Cases on the Law of Insurance, 1983 to 1991
　Matchett v. London Life Insurance Co. (1985), 14 C.C.L.I. 89 (Sask. C.A.).
Canadian Cases on the Law of Insurance (Second Series), 1991 to date
　Kuan v. Insurance Corp. of British Columbia (1992), 12 C.C.L.I. (2d) 155
　(B.C.S.C.).
Canadian Cases on the Law of Torts, 1976 to 1990
　R. v. The Ship Sun Diamond (1983), 25 C.C.L.T. 19 (F.C., T.D.).
Canadian Cases on the Law of Torts (Second Series), 1990 to date
　Weber v. Ontario Hydro (1992), 13 C.C.L.T. (2d) 241 (Ont. C.A.).
Canadian Customs and Excise Reports, 1980 to 1989
　Apt Art Ltd. v. Deputy M.N.R. (1984), 8 C.E.R. 53 (Tar. Bd.).
Canadian Environmental Law News, 1972-1977
　R. v. Lake Ontario Cement Ltd., [1973] 2 C.E.L.N. 23 (Ont. S.C.).
Canadian Environmental Law Reports, 1978 to 1986
　R. v. Vandervoet (1986), 14 C.E.L.R. 140 (Ont. Prov. Offences Ct.).
Canadian Environmental Law Reports (New Series), 1987 to date
　R. v. Varnicolor Chemical Ltd. (1992), 9 C.E.L.R. (N.S.) 176 (Ont. C.J.
　(Prov. Div.)).
Canadian Patent Reporter, 1942 to 1971
　Dupont of Canada Ltd. v. Nomad Trading Co. (1968), 55 C.P.R. 97 (Qué.
　S.C.).
Canadian Patent Reporter (Second Series), 1971 to 1984
　Corning Glass Works Co. v. Canada Wire & Cable Ltd. (1984), 81 C.P.R.
　(2d) 39 (F.C., T.D.).
Canadian Patent Reporter (Third Series), 1985 to date
　Business Depot Ltd. v. Canadian Office Depot Inc. (1993), 47 C.P.R. (3d)
　325 (F.C., T.D.).
Carswell's Practice Cases, 1976 to 1985
　Continental Bank v. Rizzo (1985), 50 C.P.C. 56 (Ont. Dist. Ct.).
Carswell's Practice Cases (Second Series), 1985 to 1992
　Woolford v. Lockhart (1985), 2 C.P.C. (2d) 16 (Ont. H.C.J.).
Carswell's Practice Cases (Third Series), 1992 to 1997

Abate v. Borges (1992), 12 C.P.C. (3d) 391 (Ont. C.J. (Gen. Div.)).

Carswell's Practice Cases (Fourth Series), 1997 to 2001
  Snowmount Investments Corp. v. Elliott (1998), 13 C.P.C. (4th) 305 (Ont. Gen. Div.).

Carswell's Practice Cases (Fifth Series), 2001 to date
  Ormiston v. Matrix Financial Corp. (2002), 22 C.P.C. (5th) 37 (Sask. Q.B).

Construction Law Reports, 1983 to 1992
  Meilleur v. U.N.I. Crete Canada Ltd. (1985), 15 C.L.R. 191 (Ont. H.C.J.).

Construction Law Reports (Second Series), 1993 to 2000
  Concord Construction Inc. v. Camara (1992), 4 C.L.R. (2d) 263 (Ont. C.J. (Gen. Div.)).

Construction Law Reports (Third Series), 2000 to date
  R. v. Shulz (2003), 24 C.L.R. (3d) 13 (Alta. P.C.).

Estates and Trusts Reports, 1977 to 1994
  Ginsburg v. M.N.R. (1992), 46 E.T.R. 188 (T.C.C.).

Estates and Trusts Reports (Second Series), 1994 to 2003
  Plantz v. Plantz (1995), 8 E.T.R. (2d) 235 (Sask. Q.B.).

Estates and Trusts Reports (Third Series), 2003 to date
  Stiles Estate v. Stiles (2003), 1 E.T.R. (3d) 120 (Alta. Q.B.).

Insurance Law Reporter, 1934 to date
  Dale v. Metropolitan Life Insurance Company, [1990] I.L.R. 10,436 (Ont. S.C.).

Land Compensation Reports, 1971 to date
  Metvedt v. Credit Valley Conservation Authority (1992), 48 L.C.R. 289 (O.M.Bd.).

Municipal and Planning Law Reports, 1976 to 1990
  FoodCorp Ltd. v. City of Brampton (1984), 30 M.P.L.R. 39 (Ont. Co. Ct.).

Municipal and Planning Law Reports (Second Series), 1991 to 1999
  Bell Canada v. Olympia & York Developments Ltd. (1992), 13 M.P.L.R. (2d) 161 (Ont. C.J. (Gen. Div.)).

Municipal Planning Law Reports (Third Series), 1999 to date
  United Mexican States v. Metalclad Corp. (2001), 34 M.P.L.R. (3d) 7 (B.C.S.C.).

Ontario Municipal Board Reports, 1973 to date
  Green Road Developments Ltd. v. City of Stoney Creek (1991), 270 M.B.R. 327.

Real Property Reports, 1977 to 1989
  Dominion Stores Ltd. v. Bramalea Ltd. (1985), 38 R.P.R. 12 (Ont. Dist. Ct.).

Real Property Reports (Second Series), 1989 to 1996
  Dobson v. Christoforatou (1993), 29 R.P.R. (2d) 228 (Ont. C.J. (Gen. Div.)).

Real Property Reports (Third Series), 1996 to 2002
  Frost v. Stewart (1999), 19 R.P.R. (3d) 281 (Ont. Gen. Div.).

Real Property Reports (Fourth Series), 2002 to date
  Saskatchewan Valley Potato Corp. v. Barrich Farms (2003), 9 R.P.R. (4d) 246 (Sask. Q.B.).

Common Abbreviations of Courts and Jurisdictions

A. CANADA

A.D. .... Appeal Division
App. Div. .... Appellate Division
C.A. ....Court of Appeal
Cit. App. Ct. ....Citizenship Appeal Court
Co. Ct. ....County Court
Dist. Ct. .... District Court
Div. Ct. ....Divisional Court
F.C. ....Federal Court of Canada
F.C.A. ....Federal Court of Appeal
F.C.T.D. .... Federal Court, Trial Division
Gen. Div. .... General Division
H.C. .... High Court
H.C.J. .... High Court of Justice
Prov. Div. .... Provincial Division
Q.B. (or K.B.) .... Queen's Bench (or King's Bench)
S.C. .... Supreme Court
Reg. T.M. ....Registrar of Trade Marks
S.C. *in banco* .... Supreme Court *in banco*
S.C.C. ....Supreme Court of Canada
S.C. (Reg.) .... Supreme Court Registrar
S.C. (Tax.). ....Supreme Court, Taxing Division
Sup. Ct. ....Superior Court
T.C.C. .... Tax Court of Canada
T.D. .... Trial Division

B. PROVINCIAL COURTS

Alta. C.A. ....Alberta Court of Appeal
Alta. Q.B. .... Alberta Queen's Bench
B.C.C.A. .... British Columbia Court of Appeal

B.C.S.C. ....British Columbia Supreme Court
Man. C.A. .... Manitoba Court of Appeal
Man. Q.B. ....Manitoba Queen's Bench
N.B.C.A. .... New Brunswick Court of Appeal
N.B.Q.B. ....New Brunswick Queen's Bench
Nfld. S.C., A.D. ....Newfoundland Supreme Court, Appeal Division
Nfld. S.C., T.D. ....Newfoundland Supreme Court, Trial Division
N.W.T.S.C. .... Northwest Territories Supreme Court
N.W.T. Terr. Ct. .... Northwest Territories Territorial Court
N.S.C.A. .... Nova Scotia Court of Appeal
N.S.S.C. ....Nova Scotia Supreme Court
O.C.A. ....Ontario Court of Appeal
O.C.J. .... Ontario Court of Justice
P.E.I.S.C., A.D. .... Prince Edward Island Supreme Court, Appeal Division
P.E.I.S.C., T.D. .... Prince Edward Island Supreme Court, Trial Division
Q.C. or C.Q. ....Québec Court or Cour du Québec
Q.C.A. or C.A.Q. .... Québec Court of Appeal or Cour d'appel Québec
Q.S.C. or C.S.Q. .... Québec Superior Court or Cour Supérieure Québec
Sask. C.A. .... Saskatchewan Court of Appeal
Sask. Q.B. ....Saskatchewan Queen's Bench
Sask. S.C. ....Saskatchewan Supreme Court
Y.C.A. .... Yukon Court of Appeal
Y.S.C. ....Yukon Supreme Court

C. ENGLAND

Ch.D. .... Chancery Division
C.A. ....Court of Appeal
Fam. Div. ....Family Division
H.L. ....House of Lords
P.C. .... Privy Council
Q.B.D. (or K.B.D.).............. Queen's Bench Division (or King's Bench Division)

D. CANADIAN JURISDICTIONS

Alta. .... Alberta
B.C. ....British Columbia
C. .... Canada
Man. ....Manitoba
N.B. ....New Brunswick
Nfld. ....Newfoundland
N.S. ....Nova Scotia

N.W.T. .... Northwest Territories
Ont. .... Ontario
P.E.I. .... Prince Edward Island
Qué. .... Québec
Sask. .... Saskatchewan
Y. .... Yukon

Recommended Abbreviations for Major Canadian Report Series

Administrative Law Reports, 1983-1991 .... Admin. L.R.

Administrative Law Reports (Second Series), 1991 to date .... Admin. L.R. (2d)

Alberta Law Reports, 1908-1932 .... Alta. L.R.

Alberta Law Reports (Second Series), 1976-1992 .... Alta. L.R. (2d)

Alberta Law Reports (Third Series), 1992 to 2002 .... Alta. L.R. (3d)

Alberta Law Reports (Fourth Series), 2002 to date....................Alta. L.R. (4d)

Alberta Reports, 1977 to date .... A.R.

All-Canada Weekly Summaries, 1977-1979 ....[] A.C.W.S.

All-Canada Weekly Summaries (Second Series), 1980-1986 .... A.C.W.S. (2d)

All-Canada Weekly Summaries (Third Series), 1986 to date.............. A.C.W.S. (3d)

Atlantic Provinces Reports, 1975 to date .... A.P.R.

British Columbia Labour Relations Board Decisions,
    1981 to date ....[] B.C.L.R.B.

British Columbia Law Reports, 1976-1986 .... B.C.L.R.

British Columbia Law Reports (Second Series), 1986 to 2002 .... B.C.L.R. (2d)

British Columbia Law Reports (Third Series), 2002 to date .... B.C.L.R. (3d)

British Columbia Reports, 1867-1947 .... B.C.R.

Business Law Reports, 1977-1991 ....B.L.R.

Business Law Reports (Second Series), 1991 to 2000......................B.L.R. (2d)

Business Law Reports (Third Series), 2000 to date...........................B.L.R. (3d)

Canada Tax Cases, 1917 to date ....[] C.T.C.

Canadian Bankruptcy Reports, 1920-1960 .... C.B.R.

Canadian Bankruptcy Reports (New Series), 1960-1990 .... C.B.R. (N.S.)

Canadian Bankruptcy Reports (Third Series), 1991 to 1998 ................C.B.R. (3d)

Canadian Bankruptcy Reports (Fourth Series), 1998 to date..............C.B.R. (4d)

Canadian Cases on Employment Law, 1983 to 1994 .... C.C.E.L.

Canadian Cases on Employment Law (Second Series),
    1994 to 2000...C.C.E.L. (2d)

Canadian Cases on Employment Law (Third Series),
    2000 to date...C.C.E.L. (3d)

Canadian Cases on the Law of Insurance, 1983-1991 .... C.C.L.I.

Canadian Cases on the Law of Insurance (Second Series),
    1991 to date..C.C.L.I. (2d) 225

Canadian Cases on the Law of Torts, 1976-1990 .... C.C.L.T.

Canadian Cases on the Law of Torts (Second Series),
    1990 to date ....C.C.L.T. (2d)

Canadian Criminal Cases, 1893-1962 .... Can. C.C. or Can. Cr. Cas.
Canadian Criminal Cases, 1963-1970 ....[] C.C.C.
Canadian Criminal Cases (Second Series), 1971-1983..................... C.C.C. (2d)
Canadian Criminal Cases (Third Series), 1983 to date .... C.C.C. (3d)
Canadian Current Law ....[] C.C.L.
Canadian Customs and Excise Reports, 1980-1989 ...................................C.E.R.
Canadian Environmental Law News, 1972-1977 .... [] C.E.L.N.
Canadian Environmental Law Reports, 1978-1986 .... C.E.L.R.
Canadian Environmental Law Reports (New Series),
    1987 to date... C.E.L.R. (N.S.)
Canadian Human Rights Reporter, 1980 to date ...................................C.H.R.R.
Canadian Insurance Law Reporter, 1934 to date .... C.I.L.R.
Canadian Labour Law Cases, 1944 to date .... C.L.L.C.
Canadian Labour Relations Board Reports, 1974-1982 .... Can. L.R.B.R.
Canadian Labour Relations Board Reports (New Series),
    1983-1989 ....C.L.R.B.R. (N.S.)
Canadian Labour Relations Board Reports (Second Series),
    1989 to date .... C.L.R.B.R. (2d)
Canadian Native Law Bulletin, 1977-1978.................................... [] C.N.L.B.
Canadian Native Law Cases, 1763-1975...C.N.L.C.
Canadian Native Law Reporter, 1979 to date .... [] C.N.L.R.
Canadian Patent Reporter, 1942-1971 .... C.P.R.
Canadian Patent Reporter (Second Series), 1971-1984..................... C.P.R. (2d)
Canadian Patent Reporter (Third Series), 1985 to date .... C.P.R. (3d)
Canadian Railway Cases, 1902-1939 .... C.R.C.
Canadian Railway and Transport Cases, 1940-1966............................ C.R.T.C.
Canadian Reports, Appeal Cases, 1828-1913.................................[] C.R.A.C.
Canadian Rights Reporter, 1982-1991 .... C.R.R.
Canadian Rights Reporter (Second Series), 1991 to date ...................C.R.R. (2d)
Canadian Weekly Law Sheet ....C.W.L.S.
Carswell's Practice Cases, 1976-1985 .... C.P.C.
Carswell's Practice Cases (Second Series), 1985-1992.....................C.P.C. (2d)
Carswell's Practice Cases (Third Series), 1992 to 1997 ...................C.P.C. (3d)
Carswell's Practice Cases (Fourth Series), 1997 to 2001..................C.P.C. (4d)
Carswell's Practice Cases (Fifth Series), 2001 to date .....................C.P.C. (5d)
Charter of Rights Decisions, 1982 to date .... C.R.D.
Construction Law Reports, 1983-1992 ....C.L.R.
Construction Law Reports (Second Series), 1993 to 2000...................C.L.R. (2d)
Construction Law Reports (Third Series), 2000 to date.....................C.L.R. (3d)
Criminal Reports (Canada), 1946-1967 .... C.R.
Criminal Reports (New Series), 1967-1978.......................................C.R.N.S.
Criminal Reports (Third Series), 1978-1991 .... C.R. (3d)
Criminal Reports (Fourth Series), 1991 to 1996............................... C.R. (4d)
Criminal Reports (Fifth Series), 1997 to 2002................................... C.R. (5d)
Criminal Reports (Sixth Series), 2002 to date.................................... C.R. (6d)

Dominion Law Reports, 1912-1922 .... D.L.R.

Dominion Law Reports, 1923-1955 ....[] D.L.R.

Dominion Law Reports (Second Series), 1956-1968 .... D.L.R. (2d)

Dominion Law Reports (Third Series), 1969-1984 .... D.L.R. (3d)

Dominion Law Reports (Fourth Series), 1984 to date........................ D.L.R.(4th)

Dominion Tax Cases, 1920 to date ....D.T.C.

Eastern Law Reporter, 1906-1914 ....E.L.R.

Estates and Trusts Reports, 1977 to 1994 .... E.T.R.

Estates and Trusts Reports (Second Series), 1994 to 2003 .... E.T.R. (2d)

Estates and Trusts Reports (Third Series), 2003 to date .... E.T.R. (3d)

Exchequer Court Reports, 1875-1922 ....Ex.C.R.

Exchequer Court Reports (Canada), 1923-1971 ....[] Ex.C.R.

Federal Court Reports (Canada), 1971 to date .... [] F.C.

Fox's Patent, Trade Mark, Design and Copyright Cases,

    1940-1970 ....Fox Pat. C.

Insurance Law Reporter, 1934 to date .... [] I.L.R.

Labour Arbitration Cases, 1948-1972 .... L.A.C.

Labour Arbitration Cases (Second Series), 1973-1981 .... L.A.C. (2d)

Labour Arbitration Cases (Third Series), 1982-1989 .... L.A.C. (3d)

Labour Arbitration Cases (Fourth Series), 1989 to date................... L.A.C. (4th)

Land Compensation Reports, 1971 to date .... L.C.R.

Lower Canada Reports, 1851-1867 ....L.C.R.

Manitoba Law Reports, 1884-1890 .... Man. L.R.

Manitoba Reports, 1891-1962 .... Man. R.

Manitoba Reports (Second Series), 1979 to date .... Man. R. (2d)

Maritime Provinces Reports, 1930-1968 .... M.P.R.

Montreal Law Reports (Queen's Bench), 1884-1891 .... M.L.R. (Q.B.)

Montreal Law Reports (Superior Court), 1885-1891 .... M.L.R. (S.C.)

Motor Vehicle Reports, 1979-1988 .... M.V.R.

Motor Vehicle Reports (Second Series), 1988 to 1994 .... M.V.R. (2d)

Motor Vehicle Reports (Third Series), 1994 to 2000 .... M.V.R. (3d)

Motor Vehicle Reports (Fourth Series), 2000 to date .... M.V.R. (4d)

Municipal and Planning Law Reports, 1976-1990 .................................M.P.L.R.

Municipal and Planning Law Reports (Second Series),

    1991 to 1999 .... M.P.L.R. (2d)

Municipal and Planning Law Reports (Third Series),

    1999 to date .... M.P.L.R. (3d)

National Reporter, 1973 to date ....N.R.

New Brunswick Reports, 1825-1929 .... N.B.R.

New Brunswick Reports (Second Series), 1969 to date .... N.B.R. (2d)

Newfoundland and Prince Edward Island Reports,

    1971 to date .... Nfld. & P.E.I.R.

Newfoundland Reports, 1817-1949 .... Nfld. R.

Northwest Territories Reports, 1983 to date ....[] N.W.T.R.

Nova Scotia Reports, 1834-1929.. N.S.R.
Nova Scotia Reports, 1965-1969... N.S.R. 1965-1969
Nova Scotia Reports (Second Series), 1970 to date ...........................N.S.R. (2d)
Ontario Appeal Cases, 1984 to date..O.A.C.
Ontario Appeal Reports, 1876-1900 ....O.A.R.
Ontario Labour Relations Board Reports, 1944 to date ....[] O.L.R.B. Rep.
Ontario Law Reports, 1901-1930 .... O.L.R.
Ontario Municipal Board Reports, 1973 to date....................................O.M.B.R.
Ontario Reports, 1882-1900 ....O.R.
Ontario Reports, 1931-1973 .... [] O.R.
Ontario Reports (Second Series), 1973-1991 .... O.R. (2d)
Ontario Reports (Third Series), 1991 to date....................................... O.R. (3d)
Ontario Weekly Notes, 1909-1932.. O.W.N.
Ontario Weekly Notes, 1933-1962...[] O.W.N.
Ontario Weekly Reporter, 1902-1916... O.W.R.
Practice Reports (Ont.), 1848-1900... P.R.
Québec Law Reports, 1875-1891... Q.L.R.
Québec Official Reports (Court of Appeal), 1970-1985....................[] Que. C.A.
Québec Official Reports (Queen's Bench or King's Bench),
     1892-1941 ....Que. Q.B. or Que. K.B.
Québec Official Reports (King's Bench or Queen's Bench),
     1942-1969 ....[] Que. K.B. or [] Que. Q.B.
Québec Official Law Reports (Superior Court), 1892-1941 ....Que. S.C.
Québec Official Law Reports (Superior Court), 1942-1985 ....[] Que. S.C.
Québec Practice Reports, 1898-1944 .... Q.P.R.
Québec Practice Reports, 1945-1982 .... [] Q.P.R.
Real Property Reports, 1977-1989.. R.P.R.
Real Property Reports (Second Series), 1989 to 1996 .... R.P.R. (2d)
Real Property Reports (Third Series), 1996 to 2002............................R.P.R. (3d)
Real Property Reports (Fourth Series), 2002 to date ...........................R.P.R. (4d)
Recueils de jurisprudence du Québec, 1986 to date ....[] R.J.Q.
Reports of Family Law, 1971-1978 .... R.F.L.
Reports of Family Law (Second Series), 1978-1986 ..........................R.F.L. (2d)
Reports of Family Law (Third Series), 1986 to 1994 .........................R.F.L. (3d)
Reports of Family Law (Fourth Series), 1994 to 2000 ........................R.F.L (4d)
Reports of Family Law (Fifth Series), 2000 to date..............................R.F.L. (5d)
Saskatchewan Law Reports, 1908-1932 ....Sask. L.R.
Saskatchewan Reports, 1979 to date.. Sask. R.
Supreme Court Reports (Canada), 1876-1922...S.C.R.
Supreme Court Reports (Canada), 1923 to date .... [] S.C.R.
Tax Appeal Board Cases, 1949-1971 ....Tax A.B.C.
Taylor's King's Bench Reports, Queen's Bench, 1823-1827.........................Tay.
Territories Law Reports, 1885-1907 ....Terr.L.R.
Trade and Tariff Reports, 1990 to date.. T.T.R.
Upper Canada Chambers Reports, 1846-1852............................... U.C. Chamb.

Upper Canada Chancery Chambers Reports, 1877-1890 .... Chy. Chr.

Upper Canada Chancery Reports (Grant), 1849-1882.................................... Gr.

Upper Canada Common Pleas, 1850-1882 .... U.C.C.P.

Upper Canada Error & Appeal Reports by Grant, 1846-1866.......... U.C.E. & A.

Upper Canada, Queen's Bench Reports, 1823-1831 .... U.C.Q.B.

Upper Canada, Queen's Bench (or King's Bench) Old Series,
 1831-1844 ....U.C.Q.B. (O.S.) or U.C.K.B. (O.S.)

Upper Canada Reports, Queen's Bench, 1844-1881 .... U.C.Q.B.

Weekly Criminal Bulletin, 1976-1987 ....W.C.B.

Weekly Criminal Bulletin, Second Series, 1987 to date.................... W.C.B. (2d),

Western Labour Arbitration Cases, 1979 to 1985............................... [] W.L.A.C

Western Law Reporter, 1905-1916.. W.L.R.

Western Law Times and Reports, 1889-1896 .... W.L.T.

Western Weekly Digests, 1975-1976..W.W.D.

Western Weekly Reports, 1911-1916 and 1955-1970 .... W.W.R.

Western Weekly Reports, 1917-1950 and 1971 to date....................... [] W.W.R.

Western Weekly Reports (New Series), 1951-1954 .... W.W.R. (N.S.)

Yukon Reports, 1987-1989 .... Y.R.

Recommended Abbreviations for Major English Report Series

A. REPORT SERIES COMMENCING BEFORE 1865

Cox's Criminal Cases, 1843-1945 .... Cox C.C.
English Reports (Reprint) .... E.R.
Law Journal New Series Common Pleas, 1831-1975 .... L.J.C.P.
Law Journal New Series Exchequer, 1831-1975 .... L.J.Ex.
Law Journal New Series House of Lords .... L.J.H.L.
Law Journal New Series Privy Council, 1865-1946 .... L.J.P.C.
Law Journal New Series Queen's Bench (or King's Bench),
    1831-1946 .... L.J.Q.B. (or L.J.K.B.)
Law Journal Old Series, 1822-1830 .... L.J.O.S.
Law Times, 1859-1947 .... L.T.
Revised Reports (Reprint), 1785-1866 .... R.R.
Weekly Reporter, 1853-1906 .... W.R.

B. REPORT SERIES COMMENCING AFTER 1865

Law Reports First Series, 1865-1875

Law Reports Admiralty and Ecclesiastical Cases .... L.R.A. & E.
Law Reports Chancery Appeal Cases .... L.R.Ch. App.
Law Reports Common Pleas .... L.R.C.P.
Law Reports Crown Cases Reserved .... L.R.C.C.R[1]
Law Reports Equity .... L.R.Eq.
Law Reports Exchequer .... L.R.Ex.
Law Reports House of Lords (English & Irish Appeals) 1866-1875 ...... L.R.H.L.[2]
Law Reports Privy Council Appeals .... L.R.P.C.
Law Reports Probate and Divorce .... L.R.P. & D.
Law Reports Queen's Bench .... L.R.Q.B.

---

[1]   Also cited L.R.C.C.
[2]   Also cited L.R.E. & I.

Law Reports Scotch and Divorce, 1866-1875 ...............................L.R. Sc. & Div.

Law Reports Second Series, 1875-1890

Appeal Cases.. App. Cas.
Chancery Division ....Ch. D.
Common Pleas Division to 1880... C.P.D.
Exchequer Division to 1880... Ex. D.
Probate, Divorce & Admiralty Division, 1876-1890...............................P.D.
Queen's Bench Division ....Q.B.D.

Law Reports Third Series, 1891 to date

Appeal Cases..A.C.
Chancery Division ....Ch.
Family Division, 1972 to date .... Fam.
Industrial Cases Reports, 1975 to date ....I.C.R.
Industrial Court Reports, 1972-1974..I.C.R.
Probate, Divorce & Admiralty Division...P.
Queen's Bench (or King's Bench)................................. Q.B. (or K.B.)
Reports of Restrictive Practices Cases, 1957-1972 .....................L.R. (vol.) R.P.
Weekly Law Reports, 1953 to date ....W.L.R.

C. OTHER

All England Law Reports, 1936 to date .... All E.R.
All England Law Reports Reprint, 1558-1935 ....[ ] All E.R. Rep.
Criminal Appeal Reports, 1909-1992 .... Cr. App. R.
Justice of the Peace, 1837 to date.. J.P.
Lloyd's List Law Reports, 1919-1950 .... Lloyd's Rep.
Lloyd's List Law Reports, 1951-1967 ....[ ] Lloyd's Rep.
Lloyd's Law Reports, 1968 to date..[ ] Lloyd's Rep.
The Times Law Reports, 1884-1950.. T.L.R.
The Times Law Reports, 1951 and 1952 ....[ ] T.L.R.
Weekly Notes, 1866-1952...[ ] W.N.

Status of Reporters

In many instances, more than one citation is included when a reference is made to a case authority. If a parallel citation is given, refer first to the official reporter, next to a semi-official reporter, and last to an unofficial reporter.

A. NATIONAL

Supreme Court of Canada

Official   *Canada Supreme Court Reports* [1975 to date].

Official   *Canada Law Reports, Supreme Court of Canada* [1923-1975].

Official   *Canada Supreme Court Reports* (1876-1922), vols. 1-64.

Federal Court of Canada

Official   *Canada Federal Court Reports* [1971 to date].

Official   *Canada Law Reports (Exchequer Court)* [1923-1971].

Official   *Exchequer Court Reports of Canada* (1875-1922), vols. 1-21.

Unofficial   *Federal Trial Reports* (1986 to date), vols. 1 to date.

Other

Unofficial   *National Reporter* (1974 to date), vols. 1 to date.

Unofficial   *Dominion Law Reports* (4th) (1984 to date), vols. 1 to date.

Unofficial   *Dominion Law Reports* (3d) (1969-1984), vols. 1-150.

Unofficial   *Dominion Law Reports* (2d) (1956-1968), vols. 1-70.

Unofficial   *Dominion Law Reports* [1923-1955].

Unofficial   *Dominion Law Reports* (1912-1922), vols. 1-69.

B. REGIONAL

Unofficial	*Western Weekly Reports* [1971 to date].
Unofficial	*Western Weekly Reports* (1955-1970), vols. 14-75.
Unofficial	*Western Weekly Reports (N.S.)* (1951-1954), vols. 1-13.
Unofficial	*Western Weekly Reports* [1917-1950].
Unofficial	*Western Weekly Reports* (1911-1916), vols. 1-10.
Unofficial	*Atlantic Provinces Reports* (1975 to date), vols. 1 to date.
Unofficial	*Western Appeal Cases* (1992 to date), vols. 1 to date.

C. PROVINCIAL

Semi-official (until 1986)	*Alberta Reports* (1977 to date), vols. 1 to date.
Unofficial	*Alberta Law Reports* (3d) (1992 to date), vols. 1 to date.
Unofficial	*Alberta Law Reports* (2d) (1976-1992), vols. 1-85.
Semi-official	*Alberta Law Reports* (1908-1932), vols. 1-26.
Unofficial	*British Columbia Law Reports* (2d) (1986 to date), vols. 1 to date.
Unofficial	*British Columbia Law Reports* (1977-1986), vols. 1-70.
Semi-official	*British Columbia Reports* (1867-1947), vols. 1-63.
Unofficial	*Manitoba Reports* (2d) (1979 to date), vols. 1 to date.
Semi-official	*Manitoba Reports* (1890-1967), vols. 7-67.
Unofficial	*Manitoba Law Reports* (1884-1890), vols. 1-6.
Unofficial	*Manitoba Law Reports* [1875-1883].
Semi-official	*New Brunswick Reports* (2d) (1969 to date), vols. 1 to date.

Unofficial	*New Brunswick Reports* (1825-1929), vols. 1-54.
Semi-official	*Newfoundland & Prince Edward Island Reports* (1970 to date), vols. 1 to date.
Unofficial	*Newfoundland Law Reports* (1817-1946), vols. 1-15.
Semi-official	*Northwest Territories Reports*, [1983 to date].
Semi-official	*Territories Law Reports* (1885-1907), vols. 1-7.
Semi-official	*Nova Scotia Reports* (2d) (1969 to date), vols. 1 to date.
Semi-official	*Nova Scotia Reports* (1965-1969), vols. 1-5.
Unofficial	*Nova Scotia Reports* (1834-1929), vols. 1-60.
Unofficial	*Ontario Appeal Cases* (1984 to date), vols. 1 to date.
Semi-official	*Ontario Reports* (3d) (1991 to date), vols. 1 to date.
Semi-official	*Ontario Reports* (2d) (1974-1991), vols. 1-75.
Semi-official	*Ontario Reports* [1931-1973].
Semi-official	*Ontario Law Reports* (1900-1931), vols. 1-66.
Unofficial	*Ontario Reports* (1882-1900), vols. 1-32.
Unofficial	*Ontario Appeal Reports* (1876-1900), vols. 1-27.
Semi-official	*Ontario Weekly Notes* [1933-1962].
Semi-official	*Ontario Weekly Notes* (1909-1932), vols. 1-41.
Semi-official	*Recueils de jurisprudence du Québec* [1986 to date].
Semi-official	*Recueils de jurisprudence du Québec, Cour d'appel* [1970-1985].
Semi-official	*Recueils de jurisprudence du Québec, Cour du Banc de la Reine/du Roi* [1942-1969].

Semi-official   *Les Rapports judiciares officiels de Québec, Cour du Banc de la Reine/du Roi* (1892-1941), vols. 1-71.

Semi-official   *Les Recueils de jurisprudence du Québec, Cour superiéure* [1967-1985].

Semi-official   *Les Rapports judiciares officiels de Québec, Cour superiéure* [1942-1966].

Semi-official   *Les Rapports judiciares officiels de Québec, Cour superiéure* (1892-1941), vols. 1-79.

Semi-official   *Recueils de jurisprudence du Québec, Cour provinciale, Cour des Session de la paix, Cour du bien-être social* [1975-1985].

Unofficial   *Québec Appeal Cases* (1987 to date), vols. 1 to date.

Unofficial   *Saskatchewan Reports* (1979 to date), vols. 1 to date.

Semi-official   *Saskatchewan Law Reports* (1907-1931), vols. 1-25.

Semi-official   *Yukon Reports* (1987 to 1989), vols. 1-3.

Index